Erskine Caldwell : Selected Letters

ERSKINE CALDWELL

Selected Letters, 1929–1955

Edited by
Robert L. McDonald

McFarland & Company, Inc., Publishers
Je›erson, North Carolina, and London

ALSO EDITED BY
ROBERT L. MCDONALD
Reading Erskine Caldwell: New Essays (McFarland, 2006)

Frontispiece: Erskine Caldwell, ca. 1932 (Erskine Caldwell Collection [#7971], Clifton Waller Barrett Library, Special Collections Department, University of Virginia Library)

The present work is a reprint of the library bound edition of Erskine Caldwell: Selected Letters, 1929–1955, *first published in 1999 by McFarland.*

LIBRARY OF CONGRESS CATALOGUING-IN-PUBLICATION DATA

Caldwell, Erskine, 1903–1987
 [Correspondence. Selections]
 Selected letters, 1929–1955 / Erskine Caldwell ; edited by Robert L. McDonald.
  p. cm.
 Includes index.

 ISBN 978-0-7864-7398-4
 softcover : acid free paper ∞

 1. Caldwell, Erskine, 1903–1987—Correspondence.
 2. Novelists, American—20th century—Correspondence.
 I. McDonald, Robert L., 1964– . II. Title.
 PS3505.A322Z48   2013
 813'.52—dc21   98-46975
 [b]

BRITISH LIBRARY CATALOGUING DATA ARE AVAILABLE

Letters © 1999 Virginia Caldwell Hibbs. All other text © 1999 Robert L. McDonald. All rights reserved

No part of this book may be reproduced or transmitted in any form or by any means, electronic or mechanical, including photocopying or recording, or by any information storage and retrieval system, without permission in writing from the publisher.

On the cover: Photograph of Erskine Caldwell in 1938 by Carl Van Vechten (Library of Congress)

Manufactured in the United States of America

McFarland & Company, Inc., Publishers
 Box 611, Jefferson, North Carolina 28640
 www.mcfarlandpub.com

For Christina

EDITOR'S ACKNOWLEDGMENTS

Work on this collection has been enabled by a host of friends, colleagues, and correspondents who deserve gratitude beyond what I express here. From the moment I approached her with the idea, in the fall of 1992, Virginia Caldwell Hibbs has been a steady source of encouragement, support, and insight. I am deeply indebted to her. For their diligence in helping find a home for the manuscript, I also thank Eugene Winick, agent for the Caldwell Estate, and his assistants at McIntosh and Otis, Inc., particularly Jakki Spicer.

While these letters come from collections at seventeen institutions, I consulted, either in person or in correspondence, nearly fifty different archives during my research. Without the efficient and generous assistance of countless reference personnel, my work would have been impossible. Especially helpful were Daniel Meyer at Chicago; Patience-Anne Lenk at Colby; Jean Ashton and Bernard Crystal at Columbia; Philip Cronenwett at Dartmouth; L. Rebecca Johnson Melvin at Delaware; Beverly B. Allen and Linda M. Matthews at Emory; Mary Ellen Brooks and Melissa Bush at Georgia; G. Thomas Tanselle at the Guggenheim Foundation; Leslie A. Morris and Emily C. Walhout at Harvard; Charles J. Kelly at the Library of Congress; Dallas R. Lindgren at the Minnesota Historical Society; Nancy M. Shawcross at Pennsylvania; Margaret M. Sherry at Princeton; Cathy Henderson, Cliff Farrington, and Rachel Howarth at the Harry Ransom Humanities Research Center, Texas; Carolyn A. Davis and Sharon Hitchcock at Syracuse; Michael Plunkett at Virginia; Alfred Mueller and Patricia C. Willis at Yale. At the Virginia Military Institute, I have been fortunate to have the assistance of two of the finest reference librarians anywhere, Janet Holly and Elizabeth Hostetter. The word "no" does not seem to be in either one's vocabulary, a remarkable fact for which I am deeply grateful.

Several people were kind enough to respond to queries as I worked to locate, arrange, and annotate the letters: Daniel Aaron, Matthew Bruccoli, Tim Campbell, Eileen Fawcett, Andre Freeman, Margaret Hedrich, Eugene Joffe, Harvey Klevar,

Editor's Acknowledgments

Michael Millman, Wayne Mixon, Richard Shrader, Nadine Siegel, and William Stott. While this collection was well under way before any of the recent biographical studies of Caldwell were published, I benefited from having had these works to double-check and occasionally supplement my own research: Harvey Klevar's *Erskine Caldwell: A Biography* (1993), Dan Miller's *Erskine Caldwell: The Journey from Tobacco Road* (1995), and Wayne Mixon's *The People's Writer: Erskine Caldwell and the South* (1995). And although I have not corresponded with them, I want to acknowledge the abiding influence of three particular Caldwell scholars—Edwin T. Arnold, Sylvia J. Cook, and Scott MacDonald—whose work paved the way for a book like this one.

I am thankful to the VMI Faculty Research Committee for two generous summer grants-in-aid which permitted me to travel to various archives and to purchase literally hundreds of photocopies of Caldwell's letters. And my department head, Emily Miller, has always acknowledged my research in ways that matter. I appreciate the time that she and two other colleagues, Bill Badgett and Gordon Ball, took to offer thoughtful, useful suggestions for improving my introductory essay.

Over the past six years, Christina Russell McDonald has read every word here more times than she should have had to—but always with care and perception. She is the best teacher I know.

R.L.M.
Lexington, Virginia
May 1998

CONTENTS

Editor's Acknowledgments vii
Preface 1
Introduction 5
Chronology 13

The Letters 21

Index 243

PREFACE

In order to retain the flavor of their composition, Caldwell's letters are published herein without corrections of either his poor typing or his occasionally unsure spelling, punctuation, grammar, or usage. For the record, brackets or notes are used to indicate correction spellings of misspelled personal names. An individual's full name is provided the first time he or she is mentioned; the last name is added in brackets whenever Caldwell used a first name alone. Identifying notes are limited to those figures who were most important to Caldwell and those of most potential interest to literary critics or historians. Unless required for clarity, notes are not provided for figures mentioned in passing.

In the interest of space, I have omitted portions of some letters that repeat basic information given in other places or seem beside Caldwell's immediate purpose for writing—e.g., his frequent detailed invitations for his friends and associates to visit, including times of available trains and viable dates. All omissions were judiciously considered so as not to distort either substance or tone. Ellipses indicate omissions; those after Caldwell's signature indicate an omitted postscript. The only exceptions are the letters dated 11-15-32, 10-23-44, 7-21-52, and 9-13-52, where the ellipses all appear in the originals. Given Caldwell's admittedly difficult handwriting and the damage that some letters have suffered over time, a very few passages are indecipherable; these are indicated with a question mark in brackets.

Each item of correspondence is introduced with the full name of the recipient and the place and date of composition, with the latter supplied in brackets when not indicated on the original. Archival information is provided directly beneath the recipient's full name. Source abbreviations used are as follows:

    CBY   Colby College Library Special Collections, Erskine Caldwell Papers

    CHI   University of Chicago Library Special Collections, Ronald Latimer Papers of the Modern Poetry Collections

    CU1   Columbia University Rare Book and Manuscript Library, James Oliver Brown Papers

CU2   Columbia University Rare Book and Manuscript Library, J. Freeman Papers
CU3   Columbia University Rare Book and Manuscript Library, Manuel Komroff Papers
DAR   Dartmouth College Library Special Collections, Erskine Caldwell Collection
DEL   University of Delaware Library Special Collections, *Pagany* Collection
EMO   Emory University Library Special Collections, Frank Daniel Papers
GU1   University of Georgia Library Special Collections, Erskine Caldwell Papers
GU2   University of Georgia Library Special Collections, I. S. Caldwell Papers
HAR   Harvard University, Houghton Library Manuscript Department, Erskine Caldwell Papers (bMS Am 1638)
HRC   Harry Ransom Humanities Research Center, University of Texas at Austin, *Contempo* Archives
JSG   John Simon Guggenheim Memorial Foundation Archives, Erskine Caldwell File
LOC   Library of Congress Manuscript Division, Erskine Caldwell Papers
MHS   Minnesota Historical Society, James Gray Papers
PEN   University of Pennsylvania, Van Pelt Library Special Collections, Lewis Mumford Papers
PRI   Princeton University Library Special Collections, Archives of Charles Scribner's Sons
PR2   Princeton University Library Special Collections, Carl Van Doren Papers
PR3   Princeton University Library Special Collections, Archives of *Story* and Story Press
SU1   Syracuse University Library Special Collections, Erskine Caldwell Papers
SU2   Syracuse University Library Special Collections, Granville Hicks Papers
VIR   University of Virginia Library Special Collections, Clifton Waller Barrett Library, Erskine Caldwell Collection (#7971)
VR2   University of Virginia Library Special Collections, Erskine Caldwell Papers (#4076)
YUL   Yale University Collection of American Literature, Beinecke Rare Book and Manuscript Library, Charles Henri Ford Papers.

The archival source is followed by a description of the item, using standard abbreviations: tls=typed letter signed; als=autograph letter signed; tl(cc)=typed letter carbon copy; tl=typed letter. Postcards, telegrams, and miscellaneous documents are identified. In 1936, for most correspondence Caldwell began using personalized stationery, usually bearing just his name in a simple typeface; this fact is not noted on individual letters. All material is reprinted or quoted by permission.

Unfortunately, letters to some significant correspondents are largely absent from this collection—namely, those to Caldwell's first and longtime agent, Maxim Lieber, and those to his editors at both the Viking Press and Duell, Sloan and Pearce (DS&P). Though I have uncovered a few copies, this material is not archived, and despite repeated efforts, I have been unable to locate it. Several people speculate that Lieber took all his files to Mexico with him when he fled the country to escape the heat of early 1950s anti-communism. A current editor at Viking "supposes" that Caldwell's letters to Marshall Best and Harold Guinzburg might be deposited in uncatalogued boxes, perhaps in a Tennessee warehouse, but he is uncertain. Finally, all records of DS&P seem to have been lost (or destroyed) after that firm was absorbed by the Meredith Publishing Group in 1961. I am not the first to search for these papers; I hope I will not be the last.

In addition, I should note that Caldwell's correspondence was generally sparse during some extended periods, particularly from the late 1930s onward. During these years, he traveled extensively, especially while he was married to Margaret Bourke-White, and as a consequence wrote fewer letters that have much to say beyond reporting the basic details of his itinerary. (For example, this is true of letters written during war years, when Caldwell knew that international mails were going to be scrutinized for breaches of security.) Furthermore, when he was away from home, or out of the country, or had sequestered himself in order to write, much of Caldwell's occasional correspondence was handled by personal secretaries and, during the years of their marriage, by his third wife, June. At one point, in fact, June routinely announced that she was handling her husband's mail since he wanted to spend as much concentrated time as possible at the typewriter. I have included the most interesting and revealing pieces from these "dry spells" and have composed notes to bridge gaps in the chronology.

INTRODUCTION

I've always wanted to be a story writer, a story teller. The only thing that interests me is the story itself. I have no message, I'm not trying to prove anything. I'm not trying to change anything—I'm trying to tell a story. I try to tell it as interesting as I can, but it has to interest me. I don't care whether it interests you or not. If I were trying to tell a story that would interest you, I would be so baffled that I wouldn't know how to do it. I have to tell it so that I like it, and if I like it, I'm willing for you to try to see if you like it. If you don't like it—well, that's okay.... But as long as I like it, I'm satisfied. —Erskine Caldwell[1]

Long before Erskine Caldwell became America's bestselling author, he was one of the country's most controversial writers—indeed, perhaps America's most banned writer in the first half of this century.[2] With the publication of such novels as *Tobacco Road* (1932) and *God's Little Acre* (1933) and stories collected in volumes like *Kneel to the Rising Sun* (1935), Caldwell quickly developed a reputation as the nation's foremost purveyor, if not exploiter, of the spiritual and physical grotesques who populated the backwoods communities of his native South. The tropes became familiar by their repetition: the slack-jawed, pellagra-ridden sharecroppers, the repressed farmwives, the oversexed nymphets, the moronic and impulsive adolescents—all those men and women looking vaguely for *something* or, more seriously, those so dulled by the circumstances of their hard lives that they seem to feel no need beyond the basics of food, shelter, and sex. Both his

---

[1] Donald Lewis and Richard Wertman, "The Art of Fiction: An Interview with Erskine Caldwell" [1968], Conversations with Erskine Caldwell, ed. Edwin T. Arnold (Jackson: UP of Mississippi, 1988), p. 110.

[2] In 1949, Publisher's Weekly featured Caldwell in an interview which labeled him "America's Most Censored Author." At that point, Caldwell estimated that he had been the target of ten full-scale attempts to ban his works during the sixteen years since the landmark 1933 censorship trial in which the New York Society for the Suppression of Vice unsuccessfully tried to ban God's Little Acre on charges that it was pornographic (Publisher's Weekly [14 May 1949], pp. 1960–1961).

critics and his general readers have always found it difficult to understand how Caldwell intends us to take his stories of such lives. There has never been much agreement about his sense of the line between caricature and satire, between comedy and tragedy—between pulp and literature. By 1939, just as Uncle Remus and Babbitt had come to represent certain "American types," Jeeter Lester, perhaps Caldwell's supreme creation, had been established as "a name for his class." But, we continue to ask, a name signaling *what*?[3]

From the outset of his career, when editors were rejecting his stories for their overemphasis of what one called "sawdust and blood," Caldwell spent a good deal of emotional energy considering the consequences of having "a reputation built entirely on negatives."[4] Of course, writers know that any notice is better than no notice at all, but Caldwell could not abide what he considered willful misreadings of his books by those who wished to deny the essential truths that they contained. For every T. K. Whipple, who in reviewing the young writer's first nationally promoted book, *American Earth* (1931), spoke of his "unmistakable ability, his out-of-the-ordinary and interesting talent," there was a Harry Hartwick, who in examining the state of contemporary fiction in 1934 invoked the name of Caldwell only to caution William Faulkner against letting his "naturalism ... become a parody of itself, and like parts of ... *Tobacco Road* step over into the ridiculous." It seems that for every letter Caldwell received from an admiring reader he received one either questioning his competence ("I wonder if you wrote [these novels] while drunk"), condemning his loyalties ("We can't understand what you have against the South!"), or deploring his politics. A letter written in February 1938 by an anonymous correspondent who had attended a performance of the stage adaptation of Caldwell's novel *Journeyman* reveals the intense reaction that his work could inspire:

> To every thinking adult who has seen your play "Journeyman" they will wonder what kind of person you be, they will either curse you, or pity you, in my case I condemn you, as being a man of base intention. ... In case you do not know it—we have no class-conscious in these (U,S,A) we have only the lazzy and the willing worker—and the chissler such as you are, but too yellow to admit it. When you write about the character of a people, such as you have, why have you wrote about only one side-of the people. I'll tell you it is because you wanted to get you dirty (PROPAGRAND befor an uninterested suppressed individual person such as the (REDS) which you are a member ... you scum. ... Understand this, "YOU-SON-OF-A-BITCH" (Autocratic Rule) in this country will endure as long as their is a white man on this earth. If you cannot explain this, have one of your enemies explain it to you, as I know they would love. ... In our own silent, but sure way we will get you in a spot, that for you their will be no way out, only when they

---

[3]*Shields McIlwaine*, The Southern Poor-White from Lubberland to Tobacco Road *(Norman: U of Oklahoma P, 1939), p. 240. For a representative chronology of critical debates about Caldwell, see Robert L. McDonald, ed.,* The Critical Response to Erskine Caldwell *(Westport, CT: Greenwood, 1997).*

[4]Caldwell to Richard Johns, DEL 7-12-30; Caldwell to Maxwell Perkins, PRI 8-22-30.

carry you out. So write and talks fast, for when the time comes only the one you doubt will be able to save you.[5]

In response to such distortions of his work, Caldwell developed a public persona whose toughness matched that of his detractors. Rather than address specific objections, or for that matter dwell on any compliments, he began to cast himself in the role of the autonomous artist whose sole obligation in the end was to his own sense of creative integrity. In published interviews and autobiographical writings, Caldwell spent much of his career explaining that his books were always written for the sake of the "story," never to promote causes, whether political, social, or aesthetic. Insisting from the start that he possessed "no philosophical truths to dispense, no evangelical urge to change the course of human destiny," he asserted that he was interested only in recording, uncensored, "the inner spirit of men and women as they responded to the joys of life and reacted to the sorrows of existence."[6] The austerity of this posture appears designed in part to counter critics' claims that his books seemed increasingly to pander to popular tastes for the quasi-pornographic.[7] But it may also be self-protective, for it appears to cloak Caldwell's creative process in mystery—some might say, in arrogance—rather than laying it open for critical examination and debate.

Although he claimed that he "like[d] adverse criticism [because] … it keeps you on your toes, keeps you sharp,"[8] and frequently asked friends to comment on what they *didn't* like about his books, Caldwell clearly worked hard at cultivating the image of the writer who is compelled to craft fiction out of what he knows, what he has seen in his life, because doing so satisfies some inner need. Without irony, as the epigraph to this introduction suggests, he assumed the pose of the storyteller telling stories primarily to himself, but with the expectation that because he wrote without pretense, "simple-minded" people like him—common folk—would be able to appreciate the kinds of stories he wanted to tell.[9] "I'm just a common ordinary writer," he said. "I'm not trying to sell anything; I'm not trying to buy anything. I'm just trying to present my vision of life." Caldwell invited

---

[5] *T. K. Whipple (and Malcolm Cowley), "Two Judgments of 'American Earth,'"* New Republic *(17 June 1931), p. 131; Harry Hartwick,* The Foreground of American Fiction *(New York: American Book Co., 1934), p. 166. The quotations from Caldwell's readers are from the rich trove of unpublished "Fan" and "Pan" letters preserved in the Erskine Caldwell Collection at Dartmouth College.*

[6] *Erskine Caldwell,* Call It Experience: The Years of Learning How to Write *(New York: Duell, Sloan and Pearce, 1951), p. 132;* With All My Might *(Atlanta: Peachtree, 1988), p. 330.*

[7] *Granville Hicks, for example, concluded his review of a 1951 omnibus of previously published short fiction and novel excerpts with this veiled admonishment: "Twenty-five million purchasers of paper-covered books can't be wrong, at least about what they like. What they like, one surmises, is raw sex and raw violence. These Mr. Caldwell gives them. If 'The Humorous Side [of Erskine Caldwell]' is intended to prove that there is more to Mr. Caldwell than the rawness, it is not a success" ("One Side of Caldwell," New York* Times Book Review *[10 June 1951], p. 30).*

[8] *Jack McClintock, "Erskine Caldwell: Down South Storyteller" [1968], Arnold,* Conversations, *p. 108.*

[9] *Carvel Collins, "Erskine Caldwell at Work" [1958], Arnold,* Conversations, *p. 51.*

readers to find whatever meaning they could in his work,[10] though he was quick to insist that not *all* of them were fit to "pass judgment" on it. Too often, he complained, reviewers were "contemptuous or sadistic in their appraisals," and he regarded critics as mere "dilettantes" and "egotists"; if for anyone other than himself, he declared, "I write for the ordinary man in the street, the golden mean."[11] These are the maverick sentiments that Erskine Caldwell packaged for the public, whose eagerness for his stories made him a celebrity of popular culture; but perhaps especially to reject the disapproval of those professional readers, the reviewers and literary critics, who had, by the mid-1950s, relegated him to "the mansions of subliterature."[12]

As Edwin T. Arnold observes in the introduction to *Conversations with Erskine Caldwell* (1988), although Caldwell could be forthcoming about particular personal experiences or aspects of his writing, he "was usually unwilling to discuss what he considered private or personal matters about his life or his art, deflecting these inquiries with 'Oh, I'll leave that up to you' or 'Well, I've discussed that in my book' or sometimes a smiling silence."[13] Indeed, Caldwell was an intensely private person who, despite all his public displays of self-assurance, harbored deep uncertainties about his work. He was infinitely more comfortable seated behind the keyboard of his typewriter than while greeting fans, giving lectures, or managing business affairs. As his widow Virginia said in an interview held soon after his death in 1987, "His writing was his life. He and his writing were inseparable in my mind." He was also, she said, "a sensitive person,"[14] and as such, it was safer for Erskine Caldwell to give terse, conventional answers to questions about his fiction than it was for him to participate in conversations in which he might be misread, mis-taken. Reading through his interviews and autobiographical writings, one gets the distinct impression that he worked hard in advance to package his thoughts in careful terms which in the end merely reasserted his creative autonomy. Such

---

[10] *Lewis and Wertman, p. 118–119; D. G. Kehl, "Portrait of an American Primitive: A Conversation with Erskine Caldwell" [1984], Arnold, Conversations, p. 234. Declaring "no esthetic bias," Caldwell rejected what he perceived as a critical commonplace that "you can get away with anything if you will be smart and write in double meanings" ("Autobiographical Sketch," Wilson Bulletin 7 [1933], p. 300; "Mr. Caldwell Protests," New Republic [27 June 1934], p. 32).*

[11] *Caldwell, Experience, p. 107; Richard B. Sale, "An Interview in Florida with Erskine Caldwell" [1970], Arnold, Conversations, p. 129; Elizabeth Pell Broadwell and Ronald Wesley Hoag, "The Art of Fiction LXII: Erskine Caldwell" [1980], Arnold, Conversations, p. 196.*

[12] *Edward Wagenknecht, Cavalcade of the American Novel (New York: Holt, 1952), p. 415. A reviewer of his 1946 novel A House in the Uplands already sneered that Caldwell's greatest contribution to literature had been the creation of "stereotyped human beings who have become the familiar subjects for cartoonists and the advertisers of Cream of Wheat" (Harrison Smith, "Well-Controlled Anger," Saturday Review of Literature 29 [29 May 1946], p. 8).*

[13] *p. xi.*

[14] *Edwin T. Arnold, "Interview with Virginia Caldwell," Erskine Caldwell Reconsidered, ed. Edwin T. Arnold (Jackson: UP of Mississippi, 1990), pp. 100–101. The first quotation here practically echoes Caldwell's comment in a 1951 letter to his agent, "I live to write, and writing is my living" (Caldwell to Max Lieber, DAR 3-26-51).*

statements provide only limited glimpses into the creative process which has, over the years, excited so much controversy. Storytelling was not as simple for Caldwell as he liked to suggest, and too seldom are we permitted a substantial revelation of the man who would admit that fiction must be "creative," that the writer must work consciously to render "reality" in ways that "concentrate, eliminate, add to life."[15]

An image—and opinion—of Erskine Caldwell assembled from the public evidence alone is therefore bound to be incomplete and unreflective of the complexity of his life and his art. Missing from the polished documents are examples of the writer's mind struggling with itself in ways that reveal motivation, concentration, a sense of achievement, and the effects of frequent bouts with insecurity and self-doubt. For a more complete portrait of Caldwell—for a record of the man's spontaneous responses to the challenges of writing and of life and a means of detecting the ways, both unspoken and acknowledged, in which the art and the life intersect—we must turn to his letters.

As a letter writer Caldwell was not in the same league with, say, Thomas Wolfe or William Faulkner, whose richly textured correspondence can be studied almost as a gloss on their fiction, or F. Scott Fitzgerald, whose letters, although more casual than Wolfe's or Faulkner's, likewise reveal a remarkable capacity for critical self-reflection. Indeed, given their quality, one occasionally suspects that such letters were composed with an eye to publication. Caldwell, by contrast, corresponded out of necessity, writing to communicate his responses to the everyday events of his life rather than to publish his ruminations about aesthetics or philosophy. His letters have a spontaneous, visceral quality, and convey an unmoderated response to life as it is happening. In a variety of voices, Caldwell addresses correspondents both personal and professional—friends, wives, relatives, editors and agents, people from whom he solicits support and encouragement and to whom he dispenses the same. His letters provide rich primary documentation of a man's life and work, of his artistic intentions as well as the distractions that frequently kept him from fulfilling them.

Although Caldwell's career spanned six decades and produced some sixty books of both fiction and nonfiction, in assembling this first collection of his letters I have chosen to focus on the first twenty-five years. In order to contribute materials that might help to fuel the ongoing scholarly reconsideration of his aims and achievement, I have selected those letters which most clearly illuminate the period when, as most agree, Caldwell was at his best and most influential—indeed, his most promising.[16] Taken individually, they can seem quite commonplace, even

---

[15] Roy Newquist, "Erskine Caldwell" [1963], Arnold, *Conversations*, p. 59.

[16] *The bulk of the recent scholarship on Caldwell has focused on his writing from the 1930s and 1940s, particularly that before* Georgia Boy *(1943); this is the body of work Malcolm Cowley once said he was "angry with recent critics for neglecting" ("Erskine Caldwell's Magic," Pembroke Magazine 11 [1979], p. 7). In response to bursts of scholarly activity—which has included the publication of the first comprehensive study of his corpus, Sylvia Jenkins Cook's* Erskine Caldwell and the Fiction of Poverty: The Flesh and the Spirit *(1991)—the university presses of both Louisiana State and Georgia are currently reissuing selected Caldwell titles, all of which had gone out of print in the past decade.*

mundane. Soon after I had completed the first draft of this manuscript, one reader suggested that they might be too "boring" to warrant publication. But I maintained then, and still believe, that *as a composite* the letters are our best unmediated means of understanding the particulars of Caldwell's professional and private lives.

The letters tell a story little different from the familiar story of Caldwell's life, but they both humanize the protagonist—the stalwart independent author whose work perhaps indeed "gradually grew towards trash"[17]—and add moving, even tragic, dimensions to his life. Here is the young writer, at age twenty-six, telling his parents how difficult it is to "have hopes" without the "encouragement" that comes with having just "one piece accepted by an important magazine or publisher." Here is the same young writer fumbling before a powerful editor at one of the country's most prestigious publishing houses: "I evidently do not know how to explain my stories. I admit it." Here, upon finishing a little novel that he will call *Tobacco Road*, is the more confident author telling an editor-friend, "It's not sensational, experimental, nor important; it's just human." Here is the sensitive author bristling at his publisher's expression of concern that the "unpleasant" story won't sell and, again, at the news that reviewers are beginning to label it "obscene." Here is the experienced author, sagely advising friends in their own efforts to write—don't be "too obvious," he urges one—and warning them, as he always did, against "listening seriously to haphazard and other stray advice." ("Don't let anyone tell you how to write or what to write about," he goes on to say. "A serious writer can never be anything more than an echo if he once begins listening to someone else.") Here is the busy, distracted author trying his hand at screenwriting in order to earn "picture money," while pleading for his wife to help him revise a new novel: "I wish to God I knew it was good." Finally, here is the wealthy and famous writer complaining of the distractions of wealth and fame: "[H]ow can a guy go into business when he thinks he is a writer?" Here, ultimately, is the very American story of a man who is virtually consumed by his own success.[18]

The letters written during the first twenty-five years of Erskine Caldwell's professional life do not, of course, tell the whole story. Eventually, he would grow beyond the frustration and discomfort we hear in the correspondence written in the mid-1950s when his reputation as a "serious" author was in serious decline. Virginia Caldwell Hibbs recalls that soon after their marriage in 1957, despite the distress caused by both his diminishing reputation and the extraordinary financial difficulties attending his recent divorce, Caldwell eventually regained his bearings

---

[17] *The phrase is William Faulkner's (William Faulkner,* Faulkner at Nagano *[Tokyo: Kenkyusha, 1956], p. 58). Still, Faulkner would soon issue his famous appraisal of Caldwell as one of the top five writers of his generation—in rank order: Thomas Wolfe, himself, John Dos Passos, Caldwell, and Ernest Hemingway (Frederick L. Gwynn and Joseph L. Blotner,* Faulkner in the University *[Charlottesville: U of Virginia P, 1959], p. 143).*

[18] *Caldwell to Ira S. Caldwell, GU2 3-13-29; Caldwell to John Hall Wheelock, PRI 1-19-31; Caldwell to Richard Johns, DEL 4-12- 31; Caldwell to Richard Johns, DEL 6-15-31; Caldwell to Alfred Morang, HAR 3-1-32; Caldwell to I. L. Salomon, LOC 3-26-33; Caldwell to Alfred Morang, HAR 7-17-33; Caldwell to Helen Caldwell, DAR 11-18-33; Caldwell to Alfred Morang, HAR 10-17-34.*

and began writing with a new vitality.[19] Although there is little agreement about the quality of this later work, by the 1970s intermittent efforts to reappraise his entire corpus had begun to appear in scholarly journals. Caldwell received a number of prestigious awards, both at home and abroad, including a citation for Poland's Order of Cultural Merit (1981); distinguished rank as France's Commander of the Order of Arts and Letters (1983); and Bulgaria's Medal of Merit (1984). Most significantly, perhaps, he was elected to the American Academy of Arts and Letters in 1984. In 1987, the year of his death at age eighty-three, one respected scholar predicted that "a full-scale revival [of interest in Caldwell] seems imminent."[20] While there have been some real indications that a reconsideration is both warranted and possible, the revival has been something less than "full-scale." The omission of Caldwell from *The Literature of the American South*, the 1998 anthology that is certain to establish a "canon" for the study of Southern literature for years to come, indicates a remarkably persistent tendency to overlook his achievement.[21]

By providing a more intimate portrait of the artist than has been previously available, this collection of letters will, I hope, prove useful to readers interested in revisiting Caldwell's best work, particularly the novels and stories of the 1930s and early 1940s. I have attempted to establish a selective and descriptive, rather than comprehensive and evaluative, record of the most important years of Caldwell's writing life: from 1929, when he published his first story, to 1955, when his career had effectively reached a standstill. With very few exceptions, I have excluded letters that Caldwell wrote expressly for publication—e.g., his numerous letters to newspapers and editors of magazines like the *New Republic* defending his work—or those offering obviously "canned" responses to the questions of fans or critics. This collection therefore contains only those letters—to family, friends, editors, and others—which in some way document the currents of Caldwell's life and art.

The letters appear in strict chronological order. After considering the possibility of presenting them according to theme or topic, or of grouping them by correspondent, I decided that such an arrangement would prove needlessly distracting, and that the most vital story emerged through the accumulative method. Read in conjunction with the interviews he granted, his two primary autobiographies, and the very good (if very different) biographical studies of him that have appeared in the past few years,[22] Caldwell's letters reveal the unsettling effects

---

[19] *This description emerges from the several conversations in which Virginia Caldwell generously discussed her husband's later years with me.*

[20] Ronald Wesley Hoag, "Erskine Caldwell," Fifty Southern Writers after 1900: A Bio-Bibliographical Sourcebook, ed. Joseph M. Flora and Robert Bain (Westport, CT: Greenwood, 1987), p. 94.

[21] *Caldwell's only mention occurs in an introductory essay, where he is noted in passing as a writer who "built a critical reputation as a realist and satirist" during the 1930s (William L. Andrews, et al., eds.,* The Literature of the American South: A Norton Anthology *[New York: Norton, 1998], p. 251).*

[22] *Full citations for Arnold's collection of interviews and Caldwell's autobiographies,* Call It Experience *and* With All My Might, *appear above. The biographies are Harvey L.*

of the tension between a man's stubborn desire to tell stories his way and his perfectly clear understanding of the business of publishing—including, ultimately, the business of being Erskine Caldwell.

Klevar's Erskine Caldwell: A Biography *(Knoxville: U of Tennessee P, 1993); Dan B. Miller's* Erskine Caldwell: The Journey from Tobacco Road *(New York: Knopf, 1995); and Wayne Mixon's* The People's Writer: Erskine Caldwell and the South *(Charlottesville: U of Virginia P, 1995).*

CHRONOLOGY

This chronology emphasizes major books published by Caldwell during the years highlighted in this collection of letters, 1929 to 1955. The following abbreviations are used: (n) = novel; (s) = short stories; (nf) = non-fiction. To my knowledge, the most complete listing of Caldwell's books appears in Edwin T. Arnold's Conversations with Erskine Caldwell *(Jackson: UP of Mississippi, 1988), pp. v–vi. For an exhaustive bibliography of short-story publications, including books, see Scott MacDonald's "An Evaluative Check-List of Erskine Caldwell's Short Fiction,"* Studies in Short Fiction *11 (1978), pp. 81–97.*

1903
Erskine Preston Caldwell is born to Caroline Preston Bell Caldwell, a teacher, and Ira Sylvester Caldwell, an itinerant minister in the Associate Reformed Presbyterian Church, in White Oak, Georgia, on December 17.

1918
The Caldwells settle in Wrens, Georgia.

1920
Caldwell enrolls in Erskine College, in South Carolina, his father's alma mater.

1923
Enrolls in the University of Virginia.

1924
Enrolls in summer courses at the University of Pennsylvania's Wharton School.

1925
Marries Helen Lannigan, daughter of a famous track coach at the University of Virginia; leaves the university for newspaper work at the Atlanta *Journal*.

1926
First child, Erskine Preston, Jr. ("Pix"), is born.

1927
Moves to Mount Vernon, Maine, in order to concentrate on his writing; supports family by writing book reviews and running the Longfellow Bookshop in Portland; a second son, Dabney Withers ("Dee"), is born; meets and befriends artist Alfred Morang.

1929
"Midsummer Passion," his first published story, appears in *The New American Caravan* after first appearing, retitled as "July," in the French little magazine *transition*; *The Bastard* (n) is published and quickly banned in Portland; Caldwell responds by issuing a broadside, "In Defense of Myself."

1930
Poor Fool (n) is published; Caldwell begins correspondence with Maxwell Perkins, who accepts two stories for publication in *Scribner's Magazine* and, with John Hall Wheelock, offers to publish a book of Caldwell's short stories; Caldwell's story "The Strawberry Season" is named to the Roll of Honor in O'Brien's annual *Yearbook of the American Short Story*, the first of thirty-six such citations Caldwell will win during the next eleven years.

1931
Scribners publishes *American Earth* (s); Caldwell travels to New York City and drafts a new novel, about sharecroppers in the South, which he calls *Tobacco Road*; lives for a time in a hotel run by Nathanael West, and the two become friends; drafts a second novel about life in rural New England, titled *Autumn Hill*; begins association with Maxim Lieber; applies for but does not win a Guggenheim Fellowship to support the writing of his next book.

1932
Tobacco Road (n) is published; Perkins rejects *Autumn Hill*, and Caldwell moves to Viking Press; drafts a new novel about "the masses in the South," which Viking accepts immediately.

1933
God's Little Acre (n) and *We are the Living* (s) are published; obscenity charges are filed against *God's Little Acre* by the New York Society for the Suppression of Vice, but dismissed in a landmark court decision; for "Country Full of Swedes" Caldwell wins the *Yale Review*'s annual prize for fiction; Caldwell is recruited to replace William Faulkner as a screenwriter for MGM; begins drafting a new novel,

Journeyman; his daughter, Janet, is born; Jack Kirkland's stage adaptation of *Tobacco Road* opens and, surprising everyone, begins a record-breaking run in New York at the Masque Theatre.

1934

Works to revise *Journeyman*, about which Viking expresses considerable reservations; begins assembling a new collection of stories; accepts invitation to write series exposing deplorable working conditions in the Detroit auto industry for *the Daily Worker;* returns for more contract writing for MGM in Hollywood.

1935

Journeyman (n) and *Kneel to the Rising Sun* (s) are published; Caldwell tours the South gathering material for a series of *New York Post* articles which verify conditions of poverty represented in his fiction; the series is reprinted as a pamphlet entitled *Tenant Farmer* (nf); gathers material for his first full-length documentary work, *Some American People* (nf); travels to Chicago when Mayor Edward J. Kelly shuts down a road-company production of *Tobacco Road*; is featured on the cover of the *Saturday Review of Literature*.

1936

Caldwell and Margaret Bourke-White travel the Southern states gathering material for *You Have Seen Their Faces* (nf); Caldwell and Bourke-White begin an affair.

1937

You Have Seen Their Faces (nf) is published; Caldwell begins assembling a new collection of short stories.

1938

Short-lived dramatization of *Journeyman* opens at New York's Fulton Theatre; Caldwell lectures at New York's New School for Social Research; *Southways* (s) is published; Helen files for divorce; Caldwell and Bourke-White travel to Czechoslovakia, gathering material for their second collaborative book, *North of the Danube;* Caldwell and Bourke-White purchase a house together, called "Horseplay Hill," in Darien, Connecticut.

1939

North of the Danube (nf) is published; Caldwell and Bourke-White marry in Reno, Nevada, and embark on a celebrity honeymoon in Hawaii; Caldwell moves to a new publisher, Duell, Sloan & Pearce, and begins editing a series of books on "American Folkways"; drafts a new novel, *Trouble in July*; Bourke-White volunteers for an assignment in England for *Life* magazine, leaving Caldwell at their home in Darien.

1940
Jackpot (s) and *Trouble in July* (n) are published; Caldwell and Bourke-White travel to gather material for a new documentary book on American life; Caldwell accepts an invitation from Friends of the Dartmouth College Library to establish a primary repository for his books, manuscripts, and memorabilia.

1941
Say! Is This the U.S.A.? (nf), Caldwell's third collaborative work with Bourke-White, is published; Caldwell and Bourke-White travel to China and then to Russia, where the two cover the Russian-German war from Moscow; John Ford's film version of *Tobacco Road* premiers.

1942
Back at home, Caldwell is celebrated for his intimate knowledge of Russian life; writes three books based on his experiences, *All Night Long* (n), *All Out on the Road to Smolensk* (nf), and, with Bourke-White, *Russia at War* (nf); returns to contract writing in Hollywood while Bourke-White continues foreign assignments for *Life*; Caldwell and Bourke-White divorce, and he marries June Johnson, a student in his old friend Harry Behn's radio-writing class at the University of Arizona; Caldwell is elected to the American Academy of Arts and Letters.

1943
Georgia Boy (s) is published; Caldwell and his new wife settle in Tucson.

1944
Tragic Ground (n) and *Stories by Erskine Caldwell*, with an introduction by Henry Seidel Canby, are published; his fourth child, Jay Erskine, is born; Caldwell's father dies.

1945
The Caldwells are featured in *Life*.

1946
A House in the Uplands (n) is published; Caldwell is elected to honorary membership in the International Mark Twain Society.

1947
The Sure Hand of God (n) is published; the Caldwells travel to Europe.

1948
This Very Earth (n) is published.

1949
Place Called Estherville (n) is published.

1950
Episode in Palmetto (n) is published.

1951
Call It Experience: The Years of Learning How to Write (nf) and *The Humorous Side of Erskine Caldwell* (s and n excerpts), with an introduction by Robert Cantwell, are published; Max Lieber moves to Mexico, and Caldwell hires James Oliver Brown as his new agent.

1952
In association with DS&P, Little, Brown & Company assumes primary responsibility as Caldwell's publishers; old manuscript of *Autumn Hill* is resurrected and published as *A Lamp for Nightfall* (n).

1953
The Complete Stories of Erskine Caldwell (s) is published; Caldwell is invited to address the Congress of Soviet Writers in Moscow but does not accept after his application to renew his passport is rejected.

1954
Love and Money (n) is published.

1955
Gretta (n) is published.

1956
Divorce from June Johnson; *Gulf Coast Stories* (s) is published.

1957
Marriage to Virginia Moffett Fletcher, his administrative assistant, also a talented painter and sketch artist.

1958
Anthony Mann's film version of *God's Little Acre* premiers.

1965
In Search of Bisco (nf), a memoir of childhood, is published, signaling Caldwell's renewed interest in race relations.

1966
In the Shadow of the Steeple (nf), an examination of Southern religion, is published in England; published in America in 1968 as *Deep South: Memory and Observation*.

1967
Caldwell's mother dies; he is diagnosed with emphysema and moves with his wife to Florida.

1968
Serves as writer-in-residence at Dartmouth College.

1973
Annette, Caldwell's final novel, is published.

1974
Diagnosed with lung cancer.

1975
The Caldwells work on collaborative book documenting their impressions of the American Midwest.

1976
Afternoons in Mid-America (nf), with illustrations by Virginia Caldwell, is published.

1977
Moves to Scottsdale, Arizona; honored by the University of Georgia.

1978
University of Virginia celebrates Caldwell's seventy-fifth birthday and elects him to the university's elite Raven Society.

1981
Recieves the Republic of Poland's Order of Cultural Merit.

1982
Addresses inaugural meeting of Japan's Erskine Caldwell Literary Society.

1983
Receives the Republic of France's Commander of the Order of Arts and Letters.

1984
Is elected to the American Academy of Arts and Letters.

1986
Lung cancer recurs and is treated with chemotherapy as Caldwell works on his last book, an autobiography.

1987
With All My Might (nf) published; Caldwell dies at home on April 11.

THE LETTERS

In the spring of 1927 Erskine Caldwell and his young wife Helen moved from Atlanta to Mount Vernon, Maine, where Helen's family maintained a summer house called Greentrees. Caldwell wanted a place where he could concentrate on his writing and thought Maine would be ideal, since it was such a "faraway place on the map." "I intended to write about Southern life as I knew it," he explained in his 1951 autobiography *Call It Experience*, "and it seemed to me that I could best view it from a distance."

The idea that he could make a career out of writing had become fixed in Caldwell's mind during the year he worked as a cub reporter for the Atlanta *Journal*. From the start he was committed to the effort, at least: "All wisdom and human experience aside, I was going to quit my job and devote full and exclusive time to the writing of short stories and novels.... I put aside the next five years in which to accomplish my ambition, with the reservation that I would take an additional five years if necessary. I had no idea how I would support myself and fulfill personal obligations until I could learn to write fiction that editors would pay for, but that did not seem important at the time."[1] He and Helen opened the Longfellow Square Bookshop in nearby Portland to help pay the bills.

Caldwell kept his parents, who still lived in Wrens, Georgia, posted on his progress.

---

[1] Call It Experience: The Years of Learning How to Write *(New York: Duell, Sloan and Pearce, 1951), pp. 47–48. Hereafter cited as* Experience. *Also see Erik Bledsoe, "Erskine Caldwell and the Atlanta* Journal: *One Year of Learning How to Write,"* Profils Americains: Erskine Caldwell, *Ed. Michel Bandry (Montpellier: Université Paul-Valéry, 1995), pp. 27–41.*

Opposite: Erskine Caldwell, ca. 1950. Photo by Tony Archer. (Dartmouth College Library.)

THE LETTERS, 1929

To the Rev. Ira S. Caldwell:

[GU2.tls] [Longfellow Square Bookshop stationery]
[Portland, Maine]
3/13/29

Dear Father:

... You must have had a flood in Georgia. I hope the damage wasnt as great as the papers said it was. I have been reading a Miami paper and consequently I have been taking all news with much salt. The Miami papers run sensational headlines about some great and injurious storms that seem to hibitually live in the North. According to them everyone here is freezing to death, all trains have stopt running, and snow is everywhere from three to eleven feet deep. Nothing could be more rediculous of course. The Miami papers want the tourists to stay there as long as possible and that is their means of propaganda. It's pleasant here and has been except for possibly five or six sub-zero days the past winter. There is no snow left on the ground and the temperature has been around 50 and 60 for the past week. I hope the rains didnt ruin the crops, or havent none been planted yet?

I havent heard anything else about my writing yet. Two or three pieces are in New York now, but I dont suppose anything will be done with them in spite of what Alfred Kreymborg said about my work.[2] If I could only get one piece accepted by an important magazine or publisher possibly it would be easier to hape hopes. Just now the one thing I do need is that kind of encouragement. I have been trying to write for a long time and it is becoming discourageing. Did you try the Macmillan Company (60 Fifth Avenue, New York)? They publish just about every kind of book there is and if your work will

[2] *With Lewis Mumford and Paul Rosenfeld, Kreymborg edited* The New American Caravan, *a yearly anthology featuring some of the most distinguished voices in American literature. He would print two pieces by Caldwell in the October 1929 issue, which also included the work of e.e. cummings, Yvor Winters, Jean Toomer, and Paul Green, among others. For an account of the response to Caldwell's appearance in the* Caravan, *see Dan B. Miller, Erskine Caldwell: The Journey from Tobacco Road (New York: Knopf, 1995), pp. 100–102. Hereafter cited as Miller.*

[3] *Caldwell's father had aspirations of his own for writing, and his son did all that he could to encourage him. In 1930, the Rev. Caldwell contributed a five-part piece to* Eugenics: A Journal of Race Betterment, *detailing a case for radical solutions to problems associated with the nation's poor, such as sterilization to curb what he saw as an exploding birth rate (see Miller, pp. 122–127). Also, it seems, he was planning a book based on the life of "one of the strangest men with whom I have ever come in contact"—the son of German immigrant parents who had become a doctor, "married a South Carolina landowner who was the daughter of a wealthy member of the old South Carolina aristocracy," abandoned her for a child bride, and was at present "building an unusual tourist village on the highway that leads from Augusta [Georgia] to Florida" (Ira S. Caldwell to John Hall Wheelock, PRI 3-15-31).*

fit in it should stand a very good chance.³ They are publishers primarily of books of non-fiction on every conceivable subject. And once a book is issued by them it will be kept in print just about as long as people live. The Oxford University Press, for eaxample, keeps every book published forever in print. They began publishing in the early part of the Sixteenth Century, and everything is kept in print. The reason for that is because the press is endowed for the purpose. I wouldnt suppose a book of the nature of yous would be acceptable to them however. They publish very few books of American origin. Other publishers who would be possible are Henry Holt & Co, 1 Park Avenue, New York; Harcourt Brace & Co, 383 Madison Ave, New York; and The Century Company, 353 Fourth Avenue, New York. It wouldnt hurt to try them, anyway.

Did Mother get the letter I sent from the U of Maine? It would be best for her to write and tell them her case, as perhaps there are special rulings for advanced students.⁴ We are counting on both of you coming up this summer. Dont disapoint us at the last minute.

We have hit a soft spot in the road and its a hard pull to get out. There is a seasonal depression now and that of course hits us hard. Babson⁵ says it comes in February, donent he? Or does it come to different sections at different times. For instance the book trade in general faces a depression in February, yet our last months business as fairly good; and now it comes to us in March. I suppose it will last from everywhere from three weeks to six weeks or longer. We will know from experience next year. This year we have to take what comes.

As soon as Marj [Morse] (our new assistant) comes down, which well be next week I think, I am going out after some business. I havent got Bowdoin College yet and that is my first goal. After that there are about a dozen libraries I'm going to work for. If possible I am going to try to buy some kind of a car. Train fare eats up everything in sight. If I can get a car I will be able to see more librarians and see them often ebough to bring them around to buying from us. I hope so anyway. I have found that New Englands are hard as the dickens to changing their habits of buying, but once they change they are loyal. That naturall is much better than having them desert you as fast as you can win them.

⁴*His mother, Caroline Preston Bell Caldwell, was a graduate of Augusta Seminary in Staunton, Virginia, and was a teacher.*
⁵*Probably Roger Ward Babson, whose new book,* Storing Up Triple Reserves *(Macmillan, 1929)—a forerunner of New Age self-help guides, containing lessons on creating "reserves" of money, health, and spiritual power—would have interested Caldwell's father.*
⁶*Caldwell had hired Marjory Morse to help Helen manage the bookshop. According to Helen, Erskine and Marjory eventually had an affair—"Not romantic, but bed-partners,*

Marj Morse is a friend of Ann Morrow's (of Lindburgh fame).[6] They went to Smith together. Marj is quite nice, typically Bostonian. Bostonian means absolutely correct in everything one does. In speech, dress, actions, habits, and thought. Your true New Englander (outside of Boston) is also precise in what he does. Close living has made him shrewd and conservative. He takes a chance but he dosent wait to see what the outcome will be; he makes the outcome as he wants it. That of course is as it should be. Mere chance is nearly always folly. . . .

                                Erskine

One of Caldwell's first publications was the brief story "Joe Craddock's Old Woman," which appeared in the fall 1929 issue of *Blues: A Magazine of New Rhythms*, a short-lived literary magazine based in Columbus, Mississippi. Caldwell's contribution earned not only the admiration of the editor, Charles Henri Ford, but also of associate editor Kathleen Tankersley Young and contributing editor William Carlos Williams.

To Charles Henri Ford:
[YUL.tls]   [Longfellow Square Bookshop stationery]
                                              [Portland, Maine]
                                                       9/10/29

Dear Ford:

I'm afraid I have nothing you'd like to see just now. Everything I have is the kind of thing you saw before, and the evolution of it is more or less a perfection of the old. If there is any change in me it is coming slowly, so slow in fact that I don't believe you could see an dif between what I sent you now and what you saw several months ago. I am more intent on the emotional content than on form, hence you can hardly find anything on the surface you didn't see before. I should like the honor, though, very much.

My first novel is coming next month: The Bastard. I hope you like it. I am getting another one ready for the Spring.[7]

I should like very much to sell Blues but the trouble is this: we take pride in advertising that our's is the only bookshop in Northern New England devoted exclusively to the sale of books. We made an exception when we took Transition for this section -- why I don't know.[8] However we keep it under the counter even now. I should like

---

shall we say." See Harvey Klevar, "Interview with Helen Caldwell Cushman," Erskine Caldwell Reconsidered, ed. Edwin T. Arnold (Jackson: UP of Mississippi, 1990), p. 93. Hereafter cited as Klevar, "Interview."

[7] Caldwell had begun work on The Bogus Ones.

[8] The Paris-based little magazine transition, edited by Eugene Jolas and Elliot Paul, had published Caldwell's story "July," a slightly reworked and retitled version of "Midsummer

to subscribe to the new quarterly Blues though. You may send me a bill for one year's subscription when it's ready to start. I hope you'll have lots of luck with it.

(Hell, send us the two copies of the Fall No on Consig anyway. I'm going to Northern Ontario next week for ten days and one hell of a big time doing everything but hunt and fish. I wouldn't give a dime for all the game and fish in No. America.)

((Where is Columbus anyway? It seems to me I was pulled off a freight there one night. What R[ailwa]y is it on?))

(((What are you in need of? fiction? If you really want to see something of mine I'll try to find something. But fiction is all I have))).

Best wishes,
Erskine Caldwell

Caldwell wrote the following playful but self-reflective letter in a spiral on a single sheet of paper.

To Charles Henri Ford:

[YUL.als] [Mount Vernon, Maine]
[Fall 1929]

Dear Ford -- You are going to keep after me until you do get something that is worth publishing -- The four best stories I have are with an agent who is holding them till the market rises, which I hope will be in this decade or the next. I'm sending you a piece I've just done I don't know if its any good or not. I wish I had something damn good to send you -- maybe this one is -- I don't know. I'm also sending you some phases of an industrious life. Can you read this whirlwind? I can't keep up with it myself. I'm coming South in January & I would like to see you if I have an opportunity: Atlanta & Augusta & maybe more. It depends on how my money holds out -- if I have any at all. Be sure and enter my sub to the new Blues & send me a bill for it. I haven't read a magazine in 3 years -- none of them are worth a damn -- I think <u>Blues</u> will be the exception. Can you still read this scrawl? If you really want to see my stuff I'll send it -- but between you & me I don't think so much of it -- I want to get something really good out of myself and it may be coming -- we'll see

---

Passion," which Kreymborg had solicited for inclusion in The New American Caravan. *Elated to have* anything *accepted for publication, there was nevertheless much confusion as Caldwell had to sort out which place had first rights to the story. For details, see Miller, pp. 100–101.*

about that. This is getting crazy as hell -- I don't know what made me start it. Best wishes anyway if you are still reading. Sincerely Erskine Caldwell . . .

When he decided to begin *Pagany: A Native Quarterly*, Richard Johns envisioned a publication devoted to "the best and most exciting writing being done, primarily from the experience of American writers, regardless of their affiliation with constrictive literary camps."[9] Johns soon became one of Caldwell's steadiest champions and advisors.

To Richard Johns:
[DEL.tls]   Portland Maine
October fourth Twenty Nine
    Dear Mr. Johns: Charles Henri Ford has told me about the work you are doing with a new magazine to be called PAGANY and that you may use contributions in it. The two pieces I'm enclosing are for you to consider. You don't know me and neither does anybody else. I've been working for seven or eight years unsuccessfully, though several of my pieces are comibg out this fall. Short stories in TRANSITION, BLUES, and THE NEW AMERICAN CARAVAN.[10] And a novel called THE BASTARD, which I hope doesn't shock you. In case you should want to see anything else by me I'll be glad to send what I have that you would consider. That's about all I have to say.
                                                     Sincerely,
                                                     Erskine Caldwell

---

To Richard Johns:
[DEL.tls]   Portland, Maine
December 4, 1929
Dear Mr. Johns:
    I hope the writing of this note will not cause you to become impatient with me and refuse to have anything to do with me. Let me

---

[9] *Stephen Halpert, ed., with Richard Johns,* A Return to Pagany: The History, Correspondence, and Selections from a Little Magazine, 1929-1932 *(Boston: Beacon, 1969), p. 9. Hereafter cited as Halpert.*

[10] *For complete bibliographical citations of Caldwell's short fiction, see Scott MacDonald, "An Evaluative Check-List of Erskine Caldwell's Short Fiction,"* Studies in Short Fiction, *11 (1978), pp. 81-97. Hereafter cited as MacDonald, "Check-List."*

explain why I am writing it: I am anxious to submit some pieces to the editors of the Fourth American Caravan,[11] but I have so very few stories that I am having a hard time finding anything to send them. Even after six years work I have only eight or ten pieces worth mentioning. As you know I sent three of these to you -- which you kept for consideration. Since then The Hound & Horn wrote for a story for consideration and they now have three over which they are evidently holding a clinic. That makes six stories. Now I have only two more in my hands and I don't believe one of these will suit the Caravan. So my position is: I haven't any work to send the Caravan. But I want my position made clear: if you believe you will be able to use one of my pieces I want you to keep them until a decision is made. On the other hand if you have decided not to use any of them I should like to have the opportunity of sending them to The Caravan. (I hope I have made myself clear -- this seems to be a paragraph without an end.)

A strange situation has developed: with the exception of Blues[12] I have not had a story in a magazine published in this country, yet one was printed in <u>transition</u> (Paris)[13] and now another one is being translated into German by Hermynia Zur Mühlen for publication in a Berlin magazine.[14] And still they say: Vanity Fair -- too rough; Mercury -- uninteresting; Scribner's -- send them back in six months; Century -- you are too young to write, wait till you grow up; Forum -- our short stories must be clean.

Finally, for God's sake don't return the stories if you think there is a chance for them to be used -- probably The Caravan wouldn't take them after all.

Will you enter my subscription to PAGANY for a year, and bill me for it? I do not know the price. But I want to be certain to have the issues from the beginning.

Sincerely,
Erskine Caldwell

Would you care to see any thing else of mine? I'd be glad to send you what I have -- EC

---

[11] *Alfred Kreymborg, Lewis Mumford, and Paul Rosenfeld, eds.*, The New American Caravan *(Macaulay, 1929).*

[12] *"Joe Craddock's Old Woman."*

[13] *"Midsummer Passion," retitled as "July."*

[14] *"Tracing Life with a Finger," published in* Frankfurter Zeitung *in 1931, translated and reprinted from Kreymborg, Mumford, and Rosenfeld's 1929* The New American Caravan.

The inaugural issue of *Pagany* appeared in January 1930, featuring contributions by William Carlos Williams, Gertrude Stein, Norman Macleod, and Manuel Komroff, among others. It also included Caldwell's "The Strawberry Season," the first of his stories to be named to the "Roll of Honor" in Edward J. O'Brien's annual *Yearbook of the American Short Story*.[15]

To Richard Johns:

[DEL.tls]
Portland Maine
January 7th 1930

Dear Johns: You probably have already had and will continue to have for the next several weeks so many letters telling you how damn good PAGANY is that you will soon be a little sick of so much praise. And too much praise is like too many roasted sweet potatoes. But you mustn't think that because I'm not saying how damn good it is it's not good. It stands at the head of the list by all methods of count and recount.

I hope (this is a personal prejudice I have had for a long time) you never go in for names. To hell with "names". If I were king and could run a magazine and, let's say for instance, [Theodore] Dreiser, [Sherwood] Anderson and [James] Joyce sent me some pieces I didn't like and I thought were rotten I'd stick a one-cent stamp on each piece and shoot them back like a bad check. Let Harpers and the L[adies] H[ome] J[ournal] and the P[artisan] R[eview] buy the names and let PAGANY print the stories. From the point of view of business management that is pretty rotten as policies go but from the eye-view of the reader who has tastes like mine it is the only possible way to make a quarterly worth paying for a year in advance. And paying a year's subscription in advance is a pretty good test of value, don't you think?

And you have partially exploded the folkway that women can't write. Janet Lewis can and Margery Latimer can. Ninety % of the stuff written by women is junk, but when you find the ten % you have work well worth reading. Janet and Margery so-and-so can write as well as a man. But don't try to find many others -- they are not to be found. You shouldn't stop looking for them just because they are scarce, however.

And the contributions are intelligible. Experiment is sometimes necessarily unintelligible, in a shell like a green walnut; but any man who consciously covers up his work in difficult technicalities is robbing himself and his readers. The easiest way the reader's emotions

---

[15]*In* The Best Short Stories of 1930 *(Dodd, Mead, 1930). The* Yearbook, *including stories O'Brien named to his "Roll of Honor," appeared annually as the appendix to each* Best Short Stories *edition. MacDonald's "Check-List" indicates the three dozen stories by Caldwell selected for the "Roll" between 1930 and 1941.*

can be reached (the hardest way to write however) is the perfect way. The work leaves a deeper and more sincere impression on the mind.

A quarterly like PAGANY shouldn't be a mouthpiece of a group or a collection of groups. It shouldn't be Catholic or Methodist, Surrealist, Republican, Single-Tax, New England, or dogmatic. As it turns out to be PAGANY is exactly what it should and never what it should not be. It will become the target of every new magazine beginning hereafter. Most of them will miss, a few will hit, and possibly one or two will score. None however will surpass what PAGANY NO 1 VOL 1 is. I'm sure of that. And I hope PAGANY will never slip within reach of any of them. PAGANY should never become a sort of national privy where every body with dissentary makes a dash for. There are too many toilet-paper magazines already.

You see I have talked about the stories only. I leave the poetry and essays for others who work with poetry and essays. The fiction ranks, I believe, one hundred %. I am not counting the story by [Edwin] Seaver and the one by myself. I have not yet read Seaver's story because I did not care for the title,[16] for some unknown reason. That is merely foolishness on my part because it may be the finest in the entire issue. Honestly, you have passed, as far as fiction goes, every magazine printed in the english language. There are no exceptions whatever. I believe those fellows who work with poetry and essays will say the same thing when you hear from them.

Erskine Caldwell

I would like to hear from you when you have time. Best wishes, sincerely.

Note Well: After re-reading what I have written I am not sure that I have said exactly what I had intended saying -- I'll try again some time and perhaps it will read differently -- E.C.

Although he would later express a strong distaste for "critics," a young and humble Caldwell necessarily appreciated any attention to his work. Hearing that Lewis Mumford, one of the most distinguished arbiters of contemporary American letters, had commented on his appearance in the *Caravan*, Caldwell was moved to thank him with this note and a copy of his first novel, *The Bastard* (1929).[17] It

[16] *"The Boss."*
[17] *The following year Mumford would write a letter supporting Caldwell's application for a Guggenheim fellowship, citing the "strong, masculine appetite for life" apparent in Caldwell's fiction and predicting, "If a picture of proletarian life, without sentimentality, without false idealization or simplification is to come out of American letters, it will come, as like as not, through Caldwell himself" (qtd. in Miller, p. 102).*

was a curious choice, for that book had recently come under fire in Portland when the District Attorney banned it as "obscene, lewd, and immoral" and ordered all copies removed from the city. Enraged, Caldwell responded by writing and distributing a broadside entitled "In Defense of Myself"—his first in a career-long series of battle with censorship.[18]

To Lewis Mumford:

[PEN.als] [Portland, Maine]
2/13/30

Dear Lewis Mumford:

I am sending you a copy of this novel in deepest appreciation of your encouragement. Unfortunately I have yet not met you, but some of the things you have said about my work were repeated to me. This first novel I am sorry to say has very little in it of any importance, yet some day I hope to write one that will have a certain quality of worthiness -- one that I should like to dedicate to you.

Faithfully
Erskine Caldwell

Caldwell's association with Charles Scribner's Sons began in February 1930 when the legendary Maxwell Perkins, after noticing Caldwell's work in *The New American Caravan*, invited him to submit some stories for consideration by *Scribner's Magazine*—an outlet that paid well and promised exposure to a national readership. "The Mating of Marjory" and "A Very Late Spring" both appeared in the June 1930 issue of *Scribner's*.[19]

---

[18]*The Bastard features a hard-boiled cast, including assorted physical grotesques and a protagonist who coldly commits two violent murders. In the broadside, Caldwell defended the book as an honest depiction of life among people who are "realistically uninhibited," insisting that it was "conceived and written as an important and untouched phase of American mores." Though it perhaps has "grave faults" as a novel, Caldwell said, his motives were pure: "I did not write this novel with obscenity, lewdness and immorality in mind. I wrote it ... because I have a deep sympathy for the people in it. ... I know them and I like them. I have slept with them in jails, I have eaten with them in freight cars, I have sung with them in convict camps, I have helped the women give birth to the living, I have helped the men cover up the dead -- but I have said enough. I have said that I know these people, that I love them. That is why I could not stand silent while the story of their lives was branded obscene, lewd and immoral; because this story belongs to them even more than it belongs to me. It is of no concern to me that I, too, have had this same brand placed upon me by Cumberland County. But these friends of mine—I shall defend them until the last word is choked from me. I cannot disown them"* ("In Defense of Myself," DAR undated [1930]).

[19]*F. Scott Fitzgerald claimed credit for having noticed Caldwell in the* New American Caravan *and for having brought him to Perkins's attention—though "he interested me less*

To Maxwell Perkins:

[PRI.tls]

Portland, Maine
March -- 1930

Dear Mr Perkins:

I found your letter waiting me when I came home yesterday. Your attitude about the censorship of a writer's work strikes me as being far more intelligent than one usually finds.[20] As for myself, as I told you, I do not write for the sake of obscenity any more than I write for a cause like Communism, -- or propaganda for Single-Tax, the Pope, more sewers, bigger Buicks, and fewer babies. You understand that, I know.

I am enclosing a short piece, which you asked me to send. It happens that MEMORANDUM is told in the first person, and for that reason may strike you as the other first-person stories did. My reason for writing partly in the first-person is that I have a belief that an idea can sometimes be more richly expressed from the personal point of view. Naturally, I am not to be confused with the "I"; it is merely a method. As a matter of fact if there is any autobiographical experience in my work it will be found to a greater extent in those stories which are written objectively. I hope this explains why I seem to run to so many "I" stories. It is merely my method -- and I hope to make it a better one -- of telling a story. MEMORANDUM is the only piece of work left just now. Later if I have something that may interest you I should like to submit it.

I want to thank you for calling me Saturday to say that you accepted the story. The truth was I was so certain you would not that I did not have the courage to call you myself. I hope there will be a possibility of seeing more of my things under the name of Scribner: in Magazine and book!

Best wishes,
Erskine Caldwell

---

than the others [Robert Cantwell and Gerald Sykes] because of the usual derivations from Hemmingway [sic] and even [Morley] Callaghan—still read him," Fitzgerald wrote in January 1930 (F. Scott Fitzgerald: A Life in Letters, ed. Matthew J. Bruccoli [New York: Scribner's, 1994], p. 175). When Perkins printed Caldwell's two stories, a header announced: "Presenting for the first time in a general magazine the work of one of the most talented of the new American writers. His milieu is the New England of to-day" (Scribner's [June 1930], p. 636).

[20] Perkins had written Caldwell concerning the censorship troubles with The Bastard: "The trouble is very few people, even in the least provincial communities, seem to understand that the motive for fiction, or the impulse from which it arises, is a serious one. They think of fiction as having no value excepting that of amusing and passing the time; and so it is impossible for them to understand why it could not just as well be pleasant and pretty. They think a writer can write one thing just as well as another, and so he is perverse if he writes about things they do not like to think about" (Perkins to EC, PRI 2-26-30).

Buoyed by his recent successes, Caldwell shared greater aspirations with his parents.

To the Reverend and Mrs. Ira S. Caldwell:

[GU2.tls]   [Portland, Maine]
                                        Monday [March 24, 1930][21]

Dear Mother & Father:

I am sending you a clipping from a paper that is the strangest thing I ever heard of. I don't see how it could happen unless the truck that passed them had a sword hanging over the side.

I am also sending notice of this year's Guggenheim Fellowship awards. I've made up my mind to win one if it possible. If I get my novel published this fall by Harcourt Brace I will apply then.[22] I don't know yet if that will be too late for the 1930 awards or not. Anyway, I'll be in time for the 1931 awards. They amount to a year's residence abroad with all living and traveling expenses: about two or three thousand dollars. I will have to have a number of prominent people endorse me, and when I get ready to apply I'll ask you to help me if you can. My ambition is to write a novel that will win the Pulitzer Prize, and if I could win one of these awards it would give me a lot of help on account of the weighty name. I may be disappointed and win neither of these because it may not be in me to amount to much, but I'm going to try. I was determined to get in the Caravan, and after that Scribner's. I've got this far, and I've got to go further. (The stories will not appear, by the way, before the June Scribners) If I can get my book published this fall I'll have enough work to submit to the committee. Some of this year's winners have only written one or two books so far. I will perhaps be handicapped because the committee is a bunch of professors, and I'm not in that kind of a boat, but if my work is good enough it should carry me over. I'm going to do my best anyway. And after that I-m working for the Pulitzer Prize, so help me God!

Helen is going after Pixie and Dabney about the fifteenth of next month.[23] We don't know yet where we will live. We are leaving Maine next October I think. It's not decided yet, but we'll know later. We want you both to come up this summer because it may be the last time we have a house for you. . . .

                                                Erskine

---

[21] *The place and date of this letter are in Caldwell's handwriting, apparently added much later. The clipping he mentions in the opening paragraph does not survive.*

[22] *Caldwell had nearly completed* The Bogus Ones, *a novel that would remain unpublished.*

[23] *The Caldwells' two sons, Pix (Erskine, Jr.) and Dabney (also called Dee), had been staying with Helen's parents in Charlottesville, Virginia.*

To Maxwell Perkins:

[PRI.tls]   Mount Vernon, Maine
                                                  April 18th 1930

Dear Mr Perkins:

    I was very glad to receive your answer to my telegram about the two manuscripts. One is a short novel, the other a selection of short stories. I hope you will be no less interested after reading them than your message indicated.

    THE BOGUS ONES is the novel I was working on when I talked with you. I have not yet arrived at a title for the short stories, but this will not be at all difficult to find if your decision is favorable. Some of the stories have or will appear shortly in the following magazine, including SCRIBNER'S -- TRANSITION, AMERICAN CARAVAN, BLUES, PAGANY, and THE HOUND & HORN.

    After receiving your answer I want to work just a little more on the manuscripts: I believe I can get them off to you on Monday.

    I have just moved, by the way, to Mount Vernon, Maine, which is my address hereafter. I expect to be here in the woods until October.

    And after many long years of disappointment I'll still have enough enthusiasm left in me to await with eagerness your final decision. But some of these days -- at the present pace -- none at all will be left to offer any sort of encouragement.

                                       Sincerely,
                                       Erskine Caldwell

To Richard Johns:

[DEL.tls]   Mount Vernon, Maine
                                                  May 12th 1930

    Dear Johns: You must agree that twelve bucks is cheap for a swell looking girl -- this is not intended humor, merely my way of acknowledging your letter and enclosure.[24]

    And as for the kicking of the fairy crowd I would consider them as I do the season of black-flies; they are stingingly mean while they last but when they go there is a damn fine feeling to be had in knowing they couldn't last. If you keep Pagany on the principle you wrote me at the beginning I know it will be a finer magazine. That is, print what you like and believe is good and let the back-biters try to get

---

[24] *Caldwell's story "A Swell-Looking Girl" appeared in the Spring* Pagany.

one out as good as yours. If you don't object to the comparison, the first two numbers beat The Hound & Horn by any measure. The H & H is not creative, Pagany is. And that's what it should be. Anybody can write a book about a book, but the original book is the only one of any value in the end. Are you making any plans for Pagany 1931, by the way? I would be greatly interested to know. And if I can help you in any way I wish you would let me. I don't know what I could do, but I should like to try.

I'm working like hell here in the country. I've always been able to do better work here than in New York or Phila, and I hope to finish some pieces this summer that I can be proud of. There will be two stories, by the way, in June Scribner's. One is rotten, (Mating of Marjory), the other possibly passable.[25] The strangeness is that the editor selected these two from several other stories which I think are better. But I may be no critic myself. . . .

          Best wishes,
          Erskine Caldwell

To Maxwell Perkins:

[PRI.tls]   Mount Vernon, Maine
                May 12th 1930

Mr Maxwell Perkins:

Dear Mr Perkins: I am sending you two short stories but before you condemn the intrusion I wish you would let me explain why I am sending them.

To begin with they were not finished at the time I sent the other manuscripts. I am sending them now with the wish that whatever weight they may have might help the finding of a decision in my favor. In the case that they would not make a material difference, then of course I should much rather try to find magazine publication for them before book publication. Naturally, in any case I would far rather have a book in print at any sacrifice, however.

Incidentally, you will discover that the story called "Inspiration for Greatness" begins where "Tracing Life With A Finger" ended last year in The American Caravan, although like its paragraphs it is complete in itself. However, it is my ambition to some day finish the novel of which these two are the beginning. It has taken me three years to write the first two episodes in this imaginary life. I am working now

---

[25] *"A Very Late Spring."*

on the third under the title (temporary perhaps) of "Falling Leaves".[26] Nobody knows to what it will lead, and especially through what it will lead me to reach the end.

I hope to God the time-element involved in making a decision on my other manuscripts has no ratio to disappointment!

Best wishes,
Erskine Caldwell

A week later, Perkins informed Caldwell that Scribner's would be interested in publishing a volume of his stories, but they had found his short novel, *The Bogus Ones*, unacceptable: "Publishers always prefer to bring out a novel first, but while it seems to us that almost every part of your novel taken alone, is very striking, the whole does not seem to us to be successful."[27]

To Maxwell Perkins:

[PRI.tls]   Mount Vernon, Maine
May 23rd 1930

Dear Mr Perkins: When I saw you last winter I believe I told you how little faith in publishers I had, but now I know there is one that I shall always respect. The glib promises, the unkept promises, the deceiving lies -- these must be confined to a class different from you. You see, I love the truth with all the passion that makes me hate a lie.

Your offer to publish a book of short stories in February 1931 is herewith accepted. The additional 30,000 words (more or less) will be done, I believe, within the next six months. I can't promise the maximum because the things I will try to do may not satisfy me, and in that case I would much rather have the privilege of doing a few good stories than writing a lot of rotten stuff that I myself would be ashamed of. And yet there may be more stories than the required amount.

About the novel: there is only one thing I should like to know -- whether in your opinion it should be shelved as a curiosity, or if correctly directed work could make it of any value. Perhaps one of the handicaps I have is that no one has the opportunity to criticize my

---

[26] *The title became "Hours Before Eternity" when the three parts were published, initially comprising the last section of* American Earth, *then as a separate volume entitled* The Sacrilege of Alan Kent *(Portland: Falmouth Book House, 1936; with wood engravings by Ralph Frizzell).*

[27] *Perkins to EC, PRI 5-20-30.*

work until it is finished and out of my hands. And, for all I know, that may not be a handicap.

And about the short stories, I should like to know which you think more successful -- the stories about Maine, or those about the South. I can't make up my mind over the problem of which place I should dig in, and concentrate.

I have probably overlooked several things in this letter, and if I have I am ready for the next move.

Sincerely,
Erskine Caldwell

To Richard Johns:

[DEL.tls] Mount Vernon, Maine
June 10th 1930

Dear Johns:

I wish I had never written that line about the cheapness of the story: I was afraid when I said it that you might mistake my meaning. I intended it in fun, probably a pun. Please forget it. I'm not writing stories for money primarily. -- I want to ask you if you want to read another manuscript, possibly for your first issue in 1931. My reason is this: I have about ten or twelve stories that are unpublished and I would like to find a place for them before February 1st 1931. Charles Scribner's Sons are publishing a book of mine called AMERICAN EARTH next Spring, and all my stories will be included in it. Naturally, if they appear in magazines they will have to be published before the book comes out. The story I would like to send you, if you want to see it, is called <u>Falling Leaves</u>: it is the third part of a trilogy (unnamed, so far); the first of which was published in <u>The Caravan</u> under the title of <u>Tracing Life With A Finger</u>; <u>the Hound & Horn</u> is publishing in the Fall number the second part, called <u>Inspiration for Greatness</u>; do you want to see the third and concluding story? It will be ready to send some time in July, I think. -- And as I said, there are ten or more others unprinted that you can read if you should want to. But I wouldn't want you to consider more than you can use before the book is published. -- I hope you haven't gone completely Humanist: <u>The Bookman</u> wrote me a rejection letter saying, "The truth is we like the way you write and hate the way you see. We have no weakness for sweetness and light, but we have a distaste for sawdust and blood". Have you ever seen any great creative literature written by a Humanist? <u>The Bookman</u> will probably begin voting on it shortly. My nomination is Kathleen Norris. Or Fannie Hurst.[28] -- Best wishes.

        Sincerely,
        Erskine Caldwell

      To Richard Johns:
[DEL.tls]   Mount Vernon, Maine
                July 12th 1930

 Dear Johns: [William Carlos] Williams gives me an inelegant puke with his White Mule but he's got <u>something</u> (God knows I don't know what it is) that nobody else has ever had.[29] He's as creative as a bull jumping a fence but I don't like the windward smell. It's a hell of a sight better though than the "sweetness and light" that the monthlies turn out. -- No 3 has some fine stuff -- very fine. The stories are better than ever, one or two or more. Personally, I like anything that has the utmost in vitality, no matter what the style, subject or point of view. -- God, as long as you don't grind any axes or let some scented paper drive you off your wheels, I'm with you. -- I hope you don't change your mind about having done with pieces-about-pieces. Criticism wears out the best of creative work, after a time. -- I still have fifty pages more to read yet, and I might have something else to say afterward. -- I'm sending the final draft of Hours Before Eternity. I think it is better than the other one and I'm ready to let it stand. It will go in the book as it is now. The end is worked up to a finer point, I believe, and should be more effective.

        Hastily,
        Erskine Caldwell

      To Maxwell Perkins:
[PRI.tls]   Mount Vernon, Maine
                July 18th 1930

Dear Mr Perkins:
 I'm certainly sorry now that I ever asked you in the first place to let me send the story you had to the Mercury, because they didn't like its short length and consequently sent it back. I've not fully con-

---

[28] *Norris and Hurst were popular sentimental writers; Hurst was particularly famous for her depictions of society's downtrodden.*
[29] *Johns published chapters of* White Mule *as Williams completed them, the first appearing with Caldwell's "John the Indian and George Hopkins" in the Summer 1930* Pagany.

vinced myself that I should attempt at this time a story of the length they want. I may be doing wrong, but I have never been able to undertake anything at all without complete confidence in my ability to make a good job of it. So in the meanwhile, may I send The Corduroy Pants to you again? hoping that it will meet your requirements? and promising to do nothing like that again? I'm enclosing another story that I've finished. It is called Dorothy. . . .
           Sincerely,
           Erskine Caldwell

Two days later Caldwell revealed that there was more on his mind than sending off new stories.
 Erich Posselt, whose Heron Press published *The Bastard*, had offered Caldwell a contract for *The Bogus Ones* and his next two books; at the same time, Harcourt Brace had expressed an interest in optioning his next full-length novel. Caldwell thus presented Perkins with his dilemma.

         To Maxwell Perkins:
[PRI.tls]   Mount Vernon, Maine
                        July 20th 1930

Dear Mr Perkins:
 I'm writing you in regard to the novel of mine called THE BOGUS ONES and my future work: I'm in a position where it is necessary for me to live and support my family with the money I can make by writing. --- if possible!
 One of the new publishing houses has offered to publish THE BOGUS ONES provided I make certain revisions in the manuscript, and to also publish my next two books. Another house, larger and older, has offered me a sum of money for an option on my next novel. This is naturally a good offer, in fact both of them are; but I want to go with Scribner's if it is humanly possible to do so. In one sense, it is immaterial who publishes a book in so long as it reaches the public for which it is intended; but in another way there is a certain security and confidence in a publisher that one admires and respects -- and that is why I don't want to turn my work over to another house, or even two of them, if it would be possible to settle down with you. Considering the fact that the publication of THE BOGUS ONES would enable me to exist, I am forced to look upon it is a source of income. I know it is not a great book, but I know that I could make it into one that I would not be ashamed of. Naturally, it is not the best

novel I will write. Just now it is the one I have written, and I want to publish it. Now it boils down to this: do you believe it could be revised (with your suggestions and criticism, perhaps) into a novel that you would want to publish? You see, I am trying to say that I am willing to do for you what I have been asked to do by another publisher because I would rather stick with you than go elsewhere. I don't know what you will think of this suggestion of mine. In fact you may think I have a lot of nerve to make it; but I believe you will understand why I made it. When one has a very difficult economic life to live he has to do some very disagreeable tasks. Just now my job is trying to live and write, but in order to write I've got to live. The Bogus Ones is the only thing I have to offer at this time.

    I have finished the third part of THE SACRILEGE and put an end to it for the present. As you know, the first part was published last year in the Caravan. Part two will be published this fall in The Hound & Horn, and Part Three will be published in Pagany this fall also. I would like to take it out of the book of short stories, finish the other three parts, and publish it seperately. Naturally however, it is entirely up to you to decide upon it. If you would like it in a book of itself, well and good; other wise I shan't finish it. When fully completed it would be about 25,000 words I suppose. I have about 10,000 done now. The Hound & Horn, by the way, said it was the best short story they ever had! In its finished form it would be a novel.

    I've received several letters about the stories in the magazine: they were from Nathan Asch, Alfred Kreymborg, Eugene Jolas, Edward J O'Brien, etc. What pleased me was that most of the letters were from people I do not know.

                                        Sincerely,
                                        Erskine Caldwell

To Maxwell Perkins:

[PRI.tls]   Mount Vernon, Maine
                                                                        July 31st 1930

Dear Mr Perkins:
    Evidently there has been a misunderstanding all around the circle: you are perhaps wondering why I have apparently been two-faced -- offering the novel to another publisher etc; and I did not know until your letter came today that you were intending to publish

my future works.[30] That being the case, the wisest thing I can do is state my understanding of the situation.

When you rejected the novel (and accepted the stories) nothing was said to me (that I can recall) about the things I would write in the future, and that being the case I naturally thought that you were not interested in me beyond the stories. Consequently, I set out at once to find a publisher. I found one, two to select from, and the offers were made to publish the novel and my next two books. And that is where the matter stands today. I have not accepted the offer, because I was waiting to hear from you in reply to the letter I wrote. Needless to say, I thought from the beginning that it was strange on your part to take one book and turn me loose with my others!

As I said in my other letter, I want to stay with you -- if you want me -- if I can possibly do so. And as I stated further, the economic phase looms quite high with me just now. Therefore, what I am about to suggest is a sacrifice in the most exact meaning of the word. The suggestion is this: If you will assure me that you are interested in me as an author, that you had every intention of publishing my books, and that you want to publish them, then I will exercise my privilege to refuse the offers made and call in the manuscript (and destroy it if necessary). Incidently, I have been greatly tempted by the offer because it was accompanied with several hundred dollars in advance royalty, and this has been difficult to resist in my present state of broke-ness. But away with that now. I am far more interested in my future with Scribner's than I am in the present with someone else I don't especially care for. And if The Bogus Ones isn't a good novel, after all, I certainly don't want it published.

The above statement should take care of the book of short stories, too, and I only hope you are as enthusiastic about them now as you were at the beginning.

The only question now in my mind is concerning the future: Will you accept my next book, and the next? I believe the answer to that rests in your reply concerning the desirability of having me for one of your authors. If you still like my work, and if you want to publish me whole-heartedly, then everything from now on rests in me.

---

[30] *Granting that his professional "judgment [of the novel] may have been wrong," Perkins had urged Caldwell to decide for himself whether he would like to move to another publisher. However, he cautioned,"a publisher wishes to publish all that is to be published of the work of an author he takes up,—particularly as he begins more upon the author's promise for the future, as he sees it, than upon prospect of immediate returns." Should Caldwell decide to place the novel elsewhere, "therefore, we should relinquish the right to publish the stories, and you might rightly agree to this since the other publisher by taking up the novel would have undertaken much more, in your interest, than should we" (Perkins to EC, PRI 7-26-30).*

In consideration of the fact that I am throwing away the present and the ultimate income the novel would have brought, would it be possible for you to give me an advance against royalty on the book of short stories, either on or before publication? preferably before? I hesitate making this request, but cold weather is coming, and recent history reminds me that there are some damn mean winters down here in Maine and I want to get out this year before another comes.

By the way, have you thought about the suggestion I made in my last letter about the separate publication of THE SACRILEGE? I'll have the complete manuscript of the first three parts ready to send to you very shortly, at which time I'm also sending about fifty more pages of manuscript.

I'm sorry I've made such a mess of things generally, and it would never have happened if I had only known that you were intending to publish me in the future.

I've sent you in care of the magazine four of my new stories. No doubt you have seen them by this time.

With best wishes, I am
Sincerely,
Erskine Caldwell

Note Well:
Please don't write saying that you advise me to accept the offer of one of the other two publishers! I believe I have studied the question as deeply as a human could possibly go! EC

To Maxwell Perkins:

[PRI.tls] Mount Vernon, Maine
August 7th 1930

Dear Mr Perkins:
Your very clear and understanding letter has been received and read.[31] I appreciated the things you said, and now forty-eight hours

[31] *In a friendly letter, Perkins had restated the Scribner's position: "We did not think the novel a success. We did think that your stories—and in fact the novel too—showed great promise. We thought the likelihood of their having a sale which would be profitable to us was not great;— but in view of the promise your writing seemed to have, we were willing to incur a loss for the sake of becoming your publishers. Whether we should be able to take the next book you wrote, would have to depend upon our opinion of it, but we should have every desire in the world to do so because of the talent it seemed to us that you had, and would develop.... I should have explained to you that a publisher of the sort we are, publishes not isolated books, but publishes for an author, and works toward his development and the development of his public...." (Perkins to EC, PRI 8-5-30).*

later I am fully convinced that my wisest course is down your stream. For my own part, the matter is closed, and I hope you will continue your plans for the present book of short stories and the work I shall do in the future.

I am sending some additional manuscript for the book. First, there is a plan for the arrangement of contents. (I have included three titles for which the manuscript is yet to be sent; and the story titled Tracing Life With A Finger is now a part of The Sacrilege, so I wish you would extract it from the manuscripts you already have). Second, there will be several new stories later to bring the length nearer the required number of words, and these can be inserted without injury to the enclosed plan of arrangement. I thought it was possible that you would like to have a plan at hand when you begin to prepare the book. At the present time, I believe there are, roughly, 60,000 words, including the three stories I'll have in shape to send later.

Needless to say, I am very pleased with the magazine's acceptance of the two stories![32]

Sincerely, Erskine Caldwell

N B: I presume that you will look after the matter of securing permission to reprint those stories which appear in magazines, if such permits are necessary. I must confess I am ignorant of those things. EC

Also: The Heron Press is publishing this fall, in a limited edition, that second novel of mine, Poor Fool, which I mentioned earlier in the year. EC

To Richard Johns:

[DEL.tls]   Mount Vernon, Maine
August 22nd 1930

Dear Johns:

I'm sending this to East Gloucester, and I hope I'm not too late to catch you there. -- [Lincoln] Kirstein (Hound & Horn) wrote me this week that [Bernard] Bandler cabled him from Europe, "Under no cir-

---

[32] *"Dorothy" and "The Corduroy Pants." Edward J. O'Brien would later select "Dorothy" to reprint in* The Best Short Stories of 1931 *(Dodd, Mead, 1931), the first of six of Caldwell's stories chosen for that honor over the next several years. Caldwell was in good company in the 1931 volume; also reprinted were stories by Kay Boyle, Louis Bromfield, Whit Burnett, Martha Foley, Josephine Herbst, Dorothy Parker, among others, and two modern classics: William Faulkner's "That Evening Sun Go Down," reprinted from the* American Mercury, *and F. Scott Fitzgerald's "Babylon Revisited," from the* Saturday Evening Post.

cumstances print Caldwell", and the story called Inspiration for Greatness was sent back.[33] I had an idea that you might want it. If it could be done it would be great to print them together, that is, Inspiration for Greatness, and Hours Before Eternity, and in that order.[34] I know it's pretty late, but I'm sending it to you the same day I got it back from Kirstein. If you should decide to do this you could use the general title, The Sacrilege. And if this does fit in with your own plans, please see that the correct order is not disaranged; because after reading them both you can easily see why Hours Before Eternity should be last. Truthfully, I believe this is the best thing I've done so far, an I want to give you this opportunity before they are put into the book. I wish I could have sent it sooner, but you know how it is with the Hound & Horn. They, by the way, still have one other story of mine, which Kirstein says he will either print in the Fall no., or resign! Inspiration for Greatness was set-up, proofs sent me, and everything! That happened once before to me with transition, too! ---

Hastily,
Erskine Caldwell

P.S. I've read Williams over again, and I'm beginning to like his novel more & more -- perhaps I was a little hasty in my initial opinion. It's great stuff! EC

To Maxwell Perkins:

[PRI.tls]   Mount Vernon, Maine
August 22nd 1930

Dear Mr Perkins:

I am sending you a rough draft of that second novel of mine which the Heron Press contracted last year to publish in a limited edition.[35] It has been postponed until this fall. I don't like the present title so very much. I don't know if it's worth the trouble, but I

---

[33] *Kirsten and Bandler were then co-editors of the* Hound & Horn, *which Kirstein and his fellow Harvard undergraduate Varian Fry had founded three years earlier, in 1927. Bandler brought to the little magazine a deep commitment to Humanism, and he was particularly influenced by Harvard's Irving Babbitt. Kirstein recalled that Bandler "had a mind that was so fluent, so much the master of intellectual and philosophical abstractions, so deeply involved with the real business of the spirit, that when he first talked to me at any length I was exhausted for two days" (Mitzi Berger Hamovitch, ed., "Introduction,"* The Hound & Horn Letters *[Athens: U of Georgia P, 1982], p. 8).*

[34] *Johns printed "Inspiration for Greatness" immediately but held "Hours Before Eternity" for the Winter 1931 issue.*

[35] Poor Fool.

thought possibly you might like to see it in view of the general edition. No other publisher has read it.

You might be interested to hear about the hot water I'm in! Evidently the impression has got around that I'm NOT a Humanist -- whatever that is. The editor of The Bookman wrote me that they would not care to read anything of mine after seeing the first story I submitted there. They wrote: "We are not bathed in sweetness and light, but we positively hate the way you see". And now today The Hound & Horn writes that I may not get in there. Kirstein, one of the editors, accepted a story of mine last December. This spring two of the other editors said they wouldn't print it. One of them, in Europe, cabled Kirstein, "Under no circumstances print Caldwell". And there you are! My very small reputation seems to be built entirely on negatives. Kirstein, however, swears he will print a story of mine in the Fall number of Hound & Horn even if he has to resign the next day. The Humanists are dead! Long live the humansists!

By the way, about a month ago you said in a note that the magazine was accepting a story, two stories, and that I would be notified. Has any trouble developed since then? I haven't heard from the magazine, and from the note I presumed that I would hear from them shortyl after. And I have wondered too, if the story called The Visitor, which I submitted in June, became lost somewhere? You wrote that you wre holding it until the first of August but since you have not mentioned it I have thought of the possibility of it going astray in the mail returning.

The advance of the book sounds good to me. You did not say when you could send it, so I am asking if it can be sent now? Three hundred dollars from that source, and three-fifty from the short stories, if you really did take them, will let me make my plans for the next six to eight months. During that time I hope to go from Maine to the West Coast, to Georgia and back to New England again.
      Sincerely,
      Erskine Caldwell

To Maxwell Perkins:

[PRI.tls]   Mount Vernon, Maine
                  September 11th 1930

Dear Mr Perkins:

This is a note to let you know that both checks have reached me safely. They make a lot of difference!

I'm anxious to hear your criticism of the stories and to know what suggestions you have to offer. After what has been said by The Hound & Horn and The Bookman and one or two smaller magazines I certainly do want to make this book TNT. The Hound & Horn is publishing a story in Oct. issue,[36] but it is not, sadly, as good as the one the words were passed about.

                Sincerely,
                Erskine Caldwell

To Richard Johns:
[DEL.tls]   Mount Vernon, Maine
                                                                        October 6th 1930

Dear Johns:
    I was sorry to hear of the troubles you had with the puritan printer, because as you know I came into contact with something of the same thing myself last winter[37]; and yet, perhaps, it was fortunate, because it means that you will be more critical of material and in the end-result print proof of good writing. At least that is the way I see it, and if the experiment didn't waste too much of your patience and money it's possible you'll get some such benefit from it. Just now I'm hoping there won't be a great delay in Pagany #4 because I'm anxious to see it.
    I'm glad you like both pieces (from The Sacrilege) and are going to use them. I can't understand the attitude of the H[ound]&H[orn] at all. Unquestionably the story they had was far better than the one they are printing -- and if that's true then you can chalk up 1 point in your favor. To hear you say that Williams liked it did me a lot of good. I respect him highly, both as critic and as creator.
    Did I tell you that Scribner's Magazine accepted two more stories? They will probably be printed in Dec, Jan, or Feb issue. They haven't told me the exact date yet. I'm counting on the book they are doing for me to give me a much needed boost. With the Bookman and the H&H sitting so hard on my neck Emerson's law of compensation should begin working for me![38]

---

[36] *"The Automobile That Wouldn't Run."*

[37] *Likely Caldwell is referring here to Portland's suppression of* The Bastard, *but Johns's "problem" is unknown.*

[38] *In* "Compensation" *(1841), Ralph Waldo Emerson argued a natural relationship, "a perfect equity" (159), between adversity and success. "As no man thoroughly understands a truth until he has contended against it," Emerson wrote in a passage Caldwell might have recalled here, "so no man has a thorough acquaintance with the hindrances or talents of men until he has suffered from the one and seen the triumph of the other over his own want of the same" (Donald McQuade, ed.,* Selected Writings of Emerson *[New York: Modern Library, 1981], pp. 154–173).*

Do you remember one of the first letters I wrote you last January when Pagany first appeared? when I predicted that you had started a magazine that would be imitated, and later recognized as an origional contribution to American writing? The starting of the magazine in Ohio called Nativity: An American Quarterly wins the first point for me.[39] And I'm confident that by this time next year you'll find that the second point has been won also. The very title is, of course, a juggling of the same title you evolved. And I can imagine that the material it prints will show your influence. I can honestly believe that your transfer to N Y is the second major step -- if you can manage to keep your originality intact in a nest of bogus bohemians. Myself, I'm afraid to go there for that very reason. Instead I'm going West this winter for six months. I'll be through N Y about the first of next month and I hope I can see you for a few minutes. . . . .[40]

Sincerely
Erskine Caldwell

John Hall Wheelock, Perkins's colleague at Scribner's, worked as Caldwell's editor on *American Earth*. On November 12, he posted a six-page letter commenting on each story and detailing "the changes which seem desirable to me upon a careful rereading of your manuscript, and which we suggest be made by you at your convenience prior to the placing of 'American Earth' in the hands of our printers." In that same letter, Wheelock noted Caldwell's "natural talent for understanding people and the inner relation of events coupled with a talent for writing ... which ought, if you are willing to keep at it and discipline yourself rigorously, to make you one of the really outstanding writers of our time. At the moment you have, it seems to me, only one serious artistic failing and that is the quite natural and rather hopeful one of over-emphasis."[41] Caldwell received the letter during his first trip to California, where he had gone alone to concentrate on his writing—finalizing the contents of *American Earth* and developing his ideas for the novel that would become *Tobacco Road*.[42]

---

[39] *Founded by Boris J. Israel "to counteract the failure of respectable letters" to illuminate the circumstances of contemporary America,* Nativity *existed just over a year, from Winter 1930 to Spring 1931. The first issue included one of Caldwell's most admired stories, "Saturday Afternoon." For information on this and other little magazines of the 1920s and 1930s, I am indebted to an old but rich and reliable source, Frederick J. Hoffman, Charles Allen, and Carolyn F. Ulrich, eds.,* The Little Magazines: A History and a Bibliography *(Princeton: Princeton UP, 1946), p. 297. Hereafter cited as Hoffman, et al.*

[40] *In late 1930, Johns moved* Pagany's *administrative operations from Boston to New York City.*

[41] *Wheelock to EC, PRI 11-12-30.*

[42] *Caldwell wrote to his friend, the artist Alfred Morang, back in Portland: "Just a hasty note to let you know that I actually did get out here according to schedule -- don't think much of this ungodly country -- mostly desert, no trees no grass -- nothing but Sand & Sage Brush.*

To John Hall Wheelock:

[PRI.tls] Hollywood, California
November 22nd 1930

Dear Mr Wheelock:
    Just received your letter, which was forwarded to me here. I am very glad you saw fit to take some interest in my work, and I appreciate your suggestions.
    First of all, I should like to comment on the two stories you ask to be taken out of the book. Frankly, I myself do not care for The Artists (others did), and I am willing to have it removed entirely. But the one called Var-monters has me guessing.[43] It seems to me that if there is objection to only one point in the story it could be remedied in the same way you suggested for the others. Perhaps your objection was to the entire story: in that case it is a different matter. But from your letter I read into it the one point concerning the rather unusual marriage ceremony. Naturally, I was not present and I cannot verify it, but it seems to me that the incident, or rather the perversity of it, is entirely in keeping with the tale. I may be wrong, often I am. If I did not understand your letter at this point, and the objection is to the story itself, then I will bow in your favor, though I must say in fairness to myself that I still think it is a good story. (We are not the first two men to pull straws over such a matter!). If, then, you believe it is to the best interest of the book I agree to the withdrawal. My sole object is to have a book to be proud of, and I have confidence in your editorial ability. Unfortunately, I do not have at present anything to submit in substitution.
    Which do you suggest -- sending me the manuscripts of the stories to be revised, or sending you the revisions to be made on the manuscripts? It would perhaps be safest for me to do the latter (if you want it that way), and in that case there would be no danger of loss and delay. It will take me about a week to make the revisions required and I can get them off to you during the first week in December. If the manuscripts are to be sent to me we will have to allow an additional ten days or two weeks for transit time, making it late December before the final manuscript could reach you. I suggest that the revisions be made in your office from my notes and

---

Am coming back East early next year -- will probably go to Georgia first. Let me know how your work is coming. Dont spend all your time away from painting -- you are too good to let anything else ruin your work" (EC to Alfred Morang, HAR 11-18-30).
    [43]*In submitting it, Caldwell had called this story "the one I like best of anything I've written in six months" (EC to Perkins, PRI 8-26-30). It was never published.*

if my notes are not complete at the time I can finish the work in the proofs. . . .
    With many thanks for your suggestions, and best wishes, I am
Sincerely,
Erskine Caldwell

Note:

Please send me the two stories (Artists & Var-monters) that are to be taken from the book.

To Richard Johns:

[DEL.tls]   Hollywood, California
                                          December 2nd 1930

Dear Johns:
    I'm submitting a story for you to read, but I want to make it clear that it is NOT an anecdote, in case the form in which it is written seems to make me a liar at first glance. I believe you'll understand what I've tried to do with a story that could not successfully be done with any other form. It is true I could have written it with the historical tense, but it would not have been the same. It happens that this is the biggest lie I ever told in print, because the story never took place, nor could it have under the conditions used. But the base of it is factually correct and if is any good as a piece of writing it is because it is a lie and not a re-telling of an oft-told tale.
    I've just heard from [Edward W.] Titus that he's using a story of mine in This Quarter for March.[44] It is a passable tale, but not as good as some of mine you've published.
    The enclosed story -- An Old Man's Tale: The Handsome Filly of Bangor -- will not be included in the book, and you can hold it if you wish. I've finished the stories for the book, and the work I'm doing now is revision before they go do the printer.
    I'm looking with much interest for Pagany No 5. Hope you don't have to delay getting it out on time, because I wont be able to do any work from Jan 1st until after it has arrived. -- I'm leaving here -- thank God -- in about ten days, so note that my address hereafter,

---

[44] *"An Autumn Courtship."*

until further notice, is Wrens, Georgia. -- Hope to see you this Spring when I have longer to stay. -- Best wishes.

> Sincerely,
> Erskine Caldwell

To John Hall Wheelock:
[PRI.tls] Hollywood, California]
12/15/30

Dear Mr Wheelock: I am returning the manuscripts (six) with my changes. All of your suggestions have been included, and I have made a few of my own which seemed necessary. I hope we can get 100% on these. The trouble is, though, a story is never perfect. . . .

I believe these, with the stories I have revised, include everything you have told me about.[45] If there are others that I do not know of I wish you would let me know. I am very anxious to have this become a <u>good</u> book. So many books are not.

My address hereafter (until further notice at least) will be Wrens, Georgia.[46]

I am working on a novel[47] which I hope will be better than the book of stories. At least in my mind it is better, and, if that is any indication of a successful story, it shall be better. In other words, it will be better.

You may count on the two additional stories -- at least I have sketched two -- and they will probably be finished by the first of the year. That would make a full 25 for the book.

Best wishes,

> Sincerely,
> Erskine Caldwell

To John Hall Wheelock:
[PRI.tls] Wrens, Georgia
December 30, 1930

Dear Mr Wheelock:
I would have answered your letter earlier but for a death in Helen's family,[48] and I returned here only last night. I am returning

---

[45] Caldwell provided brief notes for changes to four stories—"It Happened Like This," "Molly Cotton Tail," "An Autumn Courtship," and "The Corduroy Pants"—most indicating minor deletions for clarity.
[46] Caldwell left California that day, headed for Georgia to visit his parents.
[47] *Probably* Tobacco Road.
[48] Her father had died in Charlottesville just after Christmas.

revised proof of the two stories to the magazine today under separate cover. With the final manuscript version of "Dorothy", they should be in shape for publication.

About the story "John the Indian & George Hopkins"; I do not know what to do. Your suggestion that the story be rewritten from the point of view of the Indian seems justifiable; and yet I do not feel capable of doing it. Principally because I do not feel that the story would have even the slight value it may now possess. I do not know the Penobscot Indian, or any other, well enough to use subjectively in a piece of fiction. I could try it of course, but I do not believe the resulting story would be as good as the present one; in fact I am sure it would definitely be less good. And furthermore, personally, and incidently, I do not believe there would be a story, told by the Indian; because in that case we would not have the subjective feelings and reactions of the daughters -- the Indian being of another world could not possibly understand the curious, and sometimes perverse behavior of these typical Northern New England women. The daughters would have to tell (i.e. act) the story to make it plausible. But perhaps that is beside the point, and in that case my only suggestion now is that the version of the story as originally published in "Pagany" last spring be used (which is substantially the same as the manuscript), and then allow me to make my revisions in that version. But if you still insist, and have confidence in your first suggestion, I will try to do something about it. In the meantime I am holding the story here until I hear from you, at which time I will take definite steps in one or the other direction. I hope you can answer at your earliest convenience, as there will not be much more time for me to work on the story.

I hope you will not think that I am hard-headed about this matter: my desire, as well as yours, is to have the best possible tale. . . .[49]

Sincerely,
Erskine Caldwell

Wheelock liked both "Ten Thousand Blueberry Crates" and "The Dream," the replacement stories Caldwell sent to complete *American Earth*. He found them confusing on a couple of points, however, and suggested that Caldwell consider "possible revisions."[50]

[49] *Wheelock replied: "I think the objections against our suggestion for the rewriting of this story are good ones and probably it would be best to leave the story as it is, trusting to the somewhat fantastic mood of the tale to carry it off" (Wheelock to EC, PRI 1-2-31).*
[50] *Wheelock to EC, PRI 1-8-31.*

To John Hall Wheelock:

[PRI.tls] [Augusta *Chronicle* stationery]
Wrens, Georgia
January 11th 1931

Dear Mr Wheelock:
The reference to the existing difference between the two types of crates was made purposely vague for the reader's amusement and mental agility. A statement of fact in the story would, I feared, give away a treasured secret: that there is a difference; that there is not a difference. Actually there is nothing to distinguish one from the other; put together and nailed, knocked down, or in parts; and yet each of the buyers was correct in his designation, because of a custom among makers, buyers and users of changing the name to suit their purposes, and their business deals. Yet in this case each of the buyers called the crates by their correct name; the maker was the only one of the three not on to the secret. My purpose was for the reader to stumble upon this discovery himself, thereby in his sympathy for Brown to acquire the same acuteness the two buyers had. I am afraid, however, there is a great danger of explaining the story away. If you think best, you may insert the mere statement of fact (that there is no actual difference) in a sentence.

About "The Dream": Harry's vision of the girl as he had seen her gave him the distinguishing features of her face and appearance; this would be enough identification to find her. He would perhaps ask for a girl with black hair, brown eyes, oval face, small mouth, etc. He would have enough information about her as a police officer needed in his search for a criminal -- every needed point except finger prints and gallery portrait. That is how I look at it. If you think it should be noted in the story that he had a complete description of her, derived from his dream, it could be stated in a few words. I did not write that because I believed the reader would immediately identify the person in this dream with one from his own. I myself can describe every person I have seen in a dream. You can write a sentence with that idea for the story: I am sure it would be much better than I could do, because I honestly do not see where it would fit in. As you have already thought this question out, you can put your finger on it immediately.

Please do not think, because I offer an arguement each time, that I do not appreciate your suggestions. I understand exactly what you mean, and I for the greater part concur. I know that the suggestions you made for the other stories made them much better than they were at the beginning. And I believe, in the end, that your suggestions for these two stories will help them reach an end.

At this time I am sending you (enclosed) a dedication sheet.[51] I should like to have this inserted in its proper place. I am sorry I left this to the last minute, and that I am apparently a source of everlasting trouble.

With best wishes, I am

                Sincerely,
                Erskine Caldwell

Wheelock replied that production of the book was underway. He deferred to Caldwell's defense of "The Dream," but persisted, "I don't quite get your point, perhaps, in regard to the other story."[52]

To John Hall Wheelock:

[PRI.tls]   Wrens, Georgia
                                                        January 19th 1931

Dear Mr Wheelock:

I'm afraid you have me cornered; no way I turn can I find a way to keep from trying to answer your question about the crates. You see, it is almost impossible for me to explain anything I have written, and when I do try it I always make a fool of myself, because no one else has ever been able to follow my evasions. The truth, therefore, is that I evidently do not know how to explain my stories. I admit it.

I do not believe the buyers were fooling Brown. That does away with that possibility.

Since there was no noticable difference between the two kinds of crates, except that one was put together while the other was in parts -- the point we want to make is, as I said in my other letter, that the crates were called one name under certain conditions, and by the other name under other conditions. In this case the raspberry crate buyer wanted raspberry crates: he called them raspberry crates. The reason that he could use them for <u>raspberry</u> crates was, on the contrary, that it was customary in the crate industry to ship <u>blueberry</u> crates a distance, say three hundred miles, and to save expense they had to be in bundles, or parts. Raspberries on the other hand grew adjacent to the crate mills, and raspberry crates could be hauled more cheaply a few miles, after being nailed together at the mills, than they could be by hauling them in parts, and thereby causing delay at the

---

[51]*American Earth was dedicated to Erskine and Helen Caldwell's planned but yet unborn daughter, "Janet."*
[52]*Wheelock to EC, PRI 1-15-31.*

fields while they were being put together. -- If that explains it satisfactory, let us put in this new, separate paragraph in the space following the buyers' offer to buy them for raspberry crates:

> Walt could not understand why the man called them raspberry crates. If he had learned the business of making crates before he jumped into it, he would have known that blueberry crates had to be made up in bundles because most of them were shipped several hundred miles down east on the coast, while raspberry crates were usually nailed together at the time they were made because they were used in this section of the State and it was cheaper and a saving of time to truck them to the fields directly from the mills. A distance of fifty miles was all that was necessary at times to change the name of a crate.

If you believe the above paragraph explains everything that was clouded, I should think nothing more needs to be said.[53] The buyer says he is ready to haul them away in his trucks, therefore the idea expressed above is carried out to its full length in the story.

If this does not clear up the point, though, do not hesitate writing me about it. My own wish now, since I have seen how the question could be raised by a reader, is to make the story perfectly clear in all its details. I'm sorry I could not see this in the first place.

Thanks for writing me about these stories. And best wishes.
Sincerely,
Erskine Caldwell

To Maxwell Perkins:

[PRI.tls]　　　　　　　　　　　　　　　　　　　　Wrens, Georgia
January 27th 1931

Dear Mr Perkins:

I honestly hate to bother you and make a pest of myself, and I even tried to keep from writing anything for awhile so I wouldn't be tempted to submit it to you, but regardless of what I wanted to do this story worked into me and I just had to write it.[54] Sometimes when a story comes it wont let you read a book or go hunting or even sit in the sun and listen to crazy fools talk until you write it. -- But that's enough.
Sincerely,
Erskine Caldwell

---

[53] *The paragraph was inserted exactly as Caldwell provided it here.*
[54] *Caldwell enclosed "The Grass Fire," which Perkins soon rejected because "we are so*

To Richard Johns:

[DEL.tls] Mount Vernon, Maine
April 12th 1931

Dear Johns:

Sorry as I can be that I couldn't see you in New York. Called once when you had not got back from Boston, and was unable to raise anyone with the bell twice. Did you find the note I left?

Would it be possible (bluntly) to send me a payment for the story in Winter no.?[55] I wouldn't ask but I'm down on the bottom and can't see anything coming my way.

And will you do this, too: change Helen Caldwell's subscription address from Ga. to here? If the new issue has already been put in the mail, will you send us a copy here, subtracting the cost from that check above? I'd appreciate it; I want to see something worth reading for a change. I want to see something worth reading, written by some one who has something to say, for a change. Me, I have finished the book I've been doing these long, sometimes hungry, most of the time painful months.[56] Ten of them. I got to page The End by working for 22 days, from 12 p.m. to 12 a.m. That last month was hard, but the other 9 were unbearable. Now that it's over, except another month to revise it for the last time in manuscript, I feel confident that Scribner's will want to publish it. It's not sensational, experimental, nor important; it is just human. Maybe it's not so good; but I have a sympathy for the people in it, and I have become attached to it. Enough....

Sincerely,
Erskine Caldwell

---

crowded, and we have two stories of yours to publish right away, and because to some extent this New England characteristic that Carl exhibits is shown in 'Corduroy Pants'" (Perkins to EC, PRI 2-6-31).

[55] *"Warm River."*

[56] Tobacco Road *was drafted largely in New York City, beginning on March 9, 1931. For Caldwell's recollection of the writing, see* Experience, *pp. 104–106. For an excellent analysis of the ways in which Caldwell's father's ideas on the Southern poor white influenced this novel, see Miller, pp. 127–133.*

Perkins mailed Caldwell an advance copy of *American Earth* on April 13, praising it as "a very impressive book."[57]

To Maxwell Perkins:

[PRI.tls] Mount Vernon, Maine
April 17th 1931

Dear Mr Perkins: Many thanks for your note and your thought in sending me an advance copy of the book. I must say that in format and character it is more pleasing than I had hoped for. What pleases me especially is the binding and the jacket. A pictorial cover as this one is, provides a finer index to the book than any other means can do. I have nothing but praise for each step in making "American Earth".[58] I hope to have my new novel in shape for you to read in about a month. I'll send it to you as soon as I can pull myself away from it. There is nothing to say about it now; I should much rather wait and let you get its story in your own way. I am very sorry that I did not see you in New York. I was there about three weeks, but I was working all the time, and I did not wish to disturb you in your office when the burden of my call would have been very slight. Again may I thank you for such a good-looking book. Here's hoping there'll be many of them. Best wishes.

Sincerely,
Erskine Caldwell

To John Hall Wheelock:

[PRI.tls] Mount Vernon, Maine
May 4th 1931

Dear Wheelock:
I want to tell you that the author's copies came safely last week,

[57] Perkins to EC, PRI 4-13-31.
[58] The cover featured a simple drawing of a man and a woman seated, as if courting, in a plowed field overlooking a small house and barn. Just below them was an unattended plow hitched to a mule looking off toward distant hills. Inside the front flap of the dust jacket, Scribner's described the work of the twenty-seven-year-old writer whose biography was presented on the back cover: "In the fields and orchards and villages of New England and the South, American life is exceptionally rich in human drama of an intense and uncomplicated kind. Love is direct and immediate; hate the same. Caldwell's stories of that life in America which is close to the earth, are told in an individual way. He further simplifies these already simple pastoral scenes. Tales of surprising power are the result.... [T]he reader finds within their brevity all the flavor and mood of some American incident which, in Caldwell's hands, becomes a story—interesting, individual, authentic" (American Earth *dust jacket, DAR 1931*).

and to thank you for your note. I mailed the manuscript of Tobacco Road a few days ago, and it should have reached the office by the first of the week.

Probably one was sent, but I should like to suggest the sending of a review copy of the book to The New Masses. Our pathes do not touch frequently, but when they do come together, they form an interesting, if not an exciting, union. We have not had a scrap recently, and this may be the means of creating a harmonious friendship, or a bloody cock-fight. Mike Gold, of course, is the thunder and lightening at The New Masses, and if the book is to be sent, it should be put into his hands, if possible.[59]

With best wishes, I am

Sincerely,
Erskine Caldwell

[GU1.tls]

To the Reverend and Mrs. Ira S. Caldwell:
Mount Vernon, Maine
May 4th 1931

Dear Mother and Father:

I sent you a copy of the book last week, and it should have reached you now. Hope you can find somebody on the [Augusta, Georgia] Chronicle to say something about it. I have seen only four or five reviews so far, and they have beeng good. The country-wide rush of them will be coming in within the next two or three weeks, and I expect half of them to be favorable, the other half unfavorable. The one in The N Y Herald-Tribune was favorable, and so was the one in the N Y Evening Post. The Times is generally more conservative in its estimates, and I don't expect much from it.[60] I have finished the novel

---

[59] Wheelock replied that they would send Gold a review copy, but that, in general, "We have more or less given up sending review copies to The New Masses since their procedure in most cases has seemed to be a notice consisting chiefly of a few sarcastic references to the capitalistic nature of the work" (Wheelock to EC, PRI 5-4-31).

[60] Caldwell's 1931 scrapbook (in the Dartmouth Collection) preserves clippings of all these notices. Horace Gregory reviewed the American Earth for the Herald Tribune, calling the stories evidence "of a new and original talent that will grow far beyond the limitations imposed by the form of the short story. Mr. Caldwell seems ripe for a full length novel of unusual distinction" ("Tom Sawyer's Children," 4-26-31). The Post named the volume "among the season's best work" ("A Bookshelf," 4-28-31), while an anonymous review in the Times, just as Caldwell predicted, was favorable but more reserved: When writing so exclusively about "the inhabitants of Moronia," Caldwell's style, like that of Sherwood Anderson and Morley Callaghan, "has a freshness, and there is an innocence of feeling in him that saves him from conveying the

I was working on and it was sent to Scribner's Saturday. They are anxious to get a novel, but I do not know if this is the one they have been waiting for. I hope so. It will be about a month before I know their decision. The title is: TOBACCO ROAD. That should sound familiar to you. The story is about some people not far from Augusta. I would rather that you didn't mention the title to anyone yet; someone may jump up and pre-empt its usefullness.

The Golden Bantam corn I sent may turn out fine. It requires a good amount of moisture, I understand, and if it gets too dry there you should get a colored boy to water it with plenty of bucketsful. It is the best eating corn I know of.

It has been cool here for the past two weeks, and spring hasn't had a chance yet. The grass is starting to grow green now, though, and the apple trees are ready to blossom with the first two or three warm days. It has been too wet so far to plant the garden, but I hope we can plant a few things this week.

Can't you come up to Maine this summer? There is no reason why you shouldn't, if you can get away; because there is this whole house and two cottages to stay in, and there is no one here but us. Mrs. L[annigan][61] may come up sometime this summer, probably August, but there is still a place for you no matter how many others are here. Helen and I have the cottage at the lake that no one can use, and it is yours as long as you want to stay.

Pixy and Dabney are growing bigger all the time. Dabney says to tell you he wants you both to come right away.

Write when you have time.

Love,
Erskine

Perkins forwarded some reviews of *American Earth*, remarking, "They are not bad, either. Of course a reviewer always has to discover that a writer derives more or less from some other writer, instead of talking about the thing in hand. — But apart from that the reviewers at least realize that they are in the presence of something of importance."[62]

---

dullness that is usually inherent in stupid material to the reader." Too often, however, he becomes "falsely sentimental in his attempt to achieve the hard-boiled objective pose" ("Youths and Yokels," 5-10-31).

[61] *Helen's mother.*
[62] *Perkins to EC, PRI 5-4-31.*

To Maxwell Perkins:

[PRI.tls] Mount Vernon, Maine
May 7th 1931

Dear Perkins:

I am returning the clippings which you were good enough to send me. I was greatly interested in knowing the names of the men from whose work mine has been derived.[63] Probably the surprises are not yet over.

With best wishes, I am

Sincerely,
Erskine Caldwell

The Caldwells' friendship with the painter, musician, and aspiring writer Alfred Morang and his wife Dorothy began in 1929, soon after the move to Maine. The two men shared the common difficulties of being virtually unknown and desperately impoverished artists, and Morang was inspired by Caldwell's eventual successes. Over the years he repaid Caldwell's advice (and, eventually, his routine financial assistance) with an unflagging enthusiasm and admiration for nearly everything his old friend published.

To Alfred Morang:

[HAR.tls] Mount Vernon, Maine
June 3rd 1931

Dear Morang:

Great to hear from you again, and to know that you and Dorothy are in Portland. I should like to come down to see you, and, if you can put me up overnight, I may do it. Tell me what part of the week, or which particular night suits you better, though. Helen and I want you both to come up and spend a week end sometime this month. Can you make it? Perhaps if I came down, you would come back with me -- how's that?

We have been here a month. After I got back from Los Angeles I stayed two months in Georgia, two months in N Y, and came up here to stay until September perhaps. Want to get to Germany and Russia early next year, but will have to do some damn tall financing this fall if I am to get away. Right now the financial life isn't so hot; it's pretty

---

[63] *Early reviewers frequently compared Caldwell to Mark Twain, Bret Harte, Sherwood Anderson, and Ernest Hemingway. Representative reviews of* American Earth *and Caldwell's other major works can be found in Scott MacDonald, ed.,* Critical Essays on Erskine Caldwell *(Boston: G. K. Hall, 1981) and in Robert L. McDonald, ed.,* The Critical Response to Erskine Caldwell *(Westport, CT: Greenwood, 1997). Hereafter cited as MacDonald,* Critical Essays, *and McDonald,* Critical Response.

cold. Have finished a novel though, and hope to get it accepted and an advance out of it.

Marge [Morse] was up here to see Helen last month. She's in Europe now, to be gone until Fall. I knew you would be interested to know that!

Spent a lot of time with Mike Gold in New York. He's a damn fine [?]. He doesn't think so much of my Communism, though, and he devolved[?] most of our conversations to harangue (that isn't the way to spell it though, is it?) He had just got back from the Soviet, and he is still full of it. I tried to argue my special brand of Communism with him, but I had little success.[64]

Would have written to you before, but, for one thing, I have been working most of the time; and, too, I did not know when I might have the chance of dropping in on you sometime. Now, however, there is no reason why you should'd come up, if you can stand simple fare, simple quarters, and simple manners. Potatoes and cornbread most of the time, with cheese for dessert. Can you stand that?

Glad to hear that you liked the book. Did you get a copy? If you haven't one, I'll put one aside for you until you come up. Have wondered if they were being sold in Portland; can't imagine anyone there buying it, though.[65] Hope you are doing some sales-talk for it on the side.

Let me hear from you again soon. Want to see you soon, too. Best to you and Dot.

Sincerely,
Erskine

The manuscript of *Tobacco Road* arrived at Scribner's on May 4. Over a month later, Perkins expressed some doubts about its publication: "I'll tell you plainly that I think myself it is well-nigh perfect within its limits. The difficulties of the sales account, however, are very great, and that side of the argument has gained

[64] *Sympathetic in spirit but uninterested in politics per se, Caldwell's "special brand of Communism" was most certainly less confrontational than that of Gold, who positioned himself as the firebrand of the American working class. For an account of Caldwell's encounters with Gold and the emergence of a literary Communism, see Miller, pp. 153–159.*

[65] *Of course, Caldwell imagined that his troubles with censorship of* The Bastard *just two years earlier would affect local opinions of* American Earth. *He must have been surprised when an anonymous review in the Portland* Express *concluded: "Essentially native and essentially American—that best describes Mr. Caldwell's stories. His talent, further, is novel, different, and gives promise of greater things from his pen, perhaps, ere long, in the field of the long story" ("Collection of Stories by Erskine Caldwell: Former Portland Man Shows Original Talent," Erskine Caldwell Scrapbooks, DAR 6-27-31).*

great force on account of the depression.... The reason the sales problem is difficult is that all the people in the book are of such a nature that although they arouse your sympathy in a curious way (the humor that pervades the whole book is magnificent), they do not interest the reader in the ways usual in a novel. For instance, there is nobody any reader could possibly identify himself with, with any sort of pleasure."[66]

To Maxwell Perkins:

[PRI.tls]   Mount Vernon, Maine
June 11th 1931

Dear Perkins:

Your note has just come and I want to write a word about the novel, not that I intend it to have any influence upon your ultimate decision; as that is a matter for you alone to deal with. However, I must say that I feel a keen disappointment. You must know that is so; after having spent something more than a year on the book one can not lay a thing like that aside lightly. If you had said the book were rotten, it would be a different matter; but since I know <u>whatof</u> it was written, and the trueness of its people and story, I cannot bring myself to believe that it should be thrown away unread with the published trash of yesterday. I should hate to be disbarred from writing because I had made myself aloof to the "tricks" of hacks; the sympathy of a reader -- in my mind -- is won and held by the intense reality of a story, not by its pleasure-pain. And I do not believe the sympathy of any reader is worth the holding thereof if the winning was not at first difficult; the ease with which friends are made is the index to their short life. -- On the other hand, on the financial side, I cannot see how I could afford to lose a year's labor without something to show for it, and have another year to look forward to, with nothing in sight. You see, I am not trying to get rich with writing; I want to have some sort of a sign to stand for the labor of it. -- Please don't take this to mean anything more than what you can see. What I have written is merely a thought I have put down as it came to me.

I have one more story at this time to send you. I hope I won't have to bother you again soon with them; they come out on paper and it seems as if there is only one thing to do -- send them to you.

One more thing: Do you think it would be advisable for me to apply for a Guggenheim Fellowship in creative writing at this time? I have been thinking of doing it for some time, and it occurred to me that perhaps I might have a chance on the basis of "American Earth". I know two or three men and women to whom I can refer the committee to, but outside of those I do not know any others that would

---

[66]*Perkins to EC, PRI 6-10-31.*

be suitable as references. If you think I should apply, and if you would give me some advice and help, I should appreciate hearing from you about it. I have the application forms for next year now on hand.

Looking forward to hearing from you soon about the novel, and with best wishes, I am

Sincerely,
Erskine Caldwell

Note:

Please by all means let me see a copy of The New Republic review![67] The New Masses is reviewing it next issue, favorably!! E.C.

To Richard Johns:

[DEL.tls]
Mount Vernon, Maine
June 15th 1931

Dear Johns:

Thanks for your note; mighty glad to hear from you again, but sorry as hell to know about the loss of your stuff: the other fellow usually has copies and can make up for it. Hope you can get a trace of the thief and get it back.[68]

By all means, make the changes in the story (A Message for Genevieve) that you think are needed. I have enough confidence in your judgement to feel that you know what is needed. I sent another story last week: "Country Full of Swedes."[69] Was it one that was lost?

Helen and I are expecting you up soon. The sooner the better (June or early July); because there is no one else here now, but there will be (probably) (relatives) starting in late July. Am trying to get [Norman] Macleod to come up and bring his wife, in three or four

[67] *In a dual review, T. K. Whipple and Malcolm Cowley both praised the freshness* American Earth—*though they differed pointedly on the apparent (and eventual) effects of Caldwell's regular appearance in little magazines. Whipple worried that Caldwell would be stifled by his attempts to write like the "high-brows"; Cowley celebrated as most original the very passages which alarmed Whipple ("Two Judgments of 'American Earth,'"* New Republic *[17 June 1931], pp. 130–132).*

[68] *This situation is unknown, but is possibly related to the fact that financial exigence had already forced Johns to use "small, undistinguished print shops," with "slovenly" operations, in the production of Pagany (Halpert, p. 228).*

[69] *Perkins had rejected "Country Full of Swedes," calling the idea "grand" but finding it "one of those stories you have very much overdone, so that it has become burlesque" (Perkins to EC, PRI 6-10-31). The story finally appeared in* The Yale Review *in 1933, winning the* Review's *annual $1000 prize for fiction.*

weeks, sooner if he can.⁷⁰ It would be great to have you both here at the same time.

The novel is having a hell of a time. Scribner's can't make up their mind: editorially, they say it is a masterpiece and all that rot: sales department, they say they can't make a best seller out of it, probably not a good seller. That's what's holding up a decision. The real trouble is that it is a story of a Georgia family (10,000 persons) who are starving of malnutrition and pellagra because the absentee landlord has stopped giving them credit for food and seed. Will let you know what S's final decision is as soon as I am told.

Sincerely
Erskine

On June 12 Perkins had already written with some good news about the novel: "This is just to tell you that we are for 'Tobacco Road' and we shall plan to publish it in the spring of 1932." His letter was somehow misdirected, however, and Caldwell probably received it, along with the contract, around June 19.⁷¹

To Maxwell Perkins:

[PRI.tls]   Mount Vernon, Maine
June 21st 1931

Dear Perkins:

Everything has apparently worked out to the satisfaction of all concerned, and I am glad. There is hardly any use in saying that I am pleased to know "Tobacco Road" is to be published, but I do want to say that I am in a position to appreciate your interest and your faith in my work. I hope after this that there will be no more trouble (of which I once told you); just now it is my concern to completely wipe out all the obligations I took on. The one remaining one is with Harcourt Brace & Company, as you will remember, perhaps. One hundred dollars of the original $250. has been written off, and now there remains the balance of $150. due them. It will be necessary for me to repay this amount to them before I can be legally free of the option. (I signed the options with them for three books, and my release can only be affected by the re-payment of the money paid out by them). I find that I simply cannot raise the balance of $150. at this time, and I am in hopes that you will let me have an advance on the novel. I need not say that I should like an advance of more than

⁷⁰ *Macleod would review* American Earth *very favorably in the July* New Masses. *See Caldwell's July 23 letter to Wheelock for details.*

⁷¹ *Perkins to EC, PRI 6-12-31, 6-16-31.*

$150., because you will know I do, and I would like for you to let me have what you think is right. The advance of $300. on "American Earth" was perfectly satisfactory to me, and I hope you will think as much or more of the novel.

There is no need of going into my reasons for liking Scribner's more than I believe I would Harcourt Brace. The advantages are obvious; but more than that, I was treated rather shabbily in their hands at the beginning (something more than a year ago -- before I came into contact with you). I would not now offer them a book of mine for any consideration.

I am enclosing the contract, signed. I do not see any use in holding it until I can send the money to Harcourt Brace, because that is a matter easily adjusted.

In regard to talking with your about the novel: it is my plan to be in New York sometime this summer for a few days, and I shall certainly come to see you then. I have found your criticism and suggestions always worth taking into account, and I believe we can make "Tobacco Road" just about as good as we hope it will be.

I am going ahead with my plans for applying for a Guggenheim fellowship. I shall certainly use your name, along with three or four others.[72]

With best wishes, and with thanks, I am
                            Sincerely,
                            Erskine Caldwell

The cover letter for Caldwell's Guggenheim application was routinely destroyed, but these sections of his application survive as an extraordinarily valuable early statement of his goals as a writer—and particularly of his plans for the work that would become *God's Little Acre*. In the summary of his education, Caldwell cited his years at the University of Virginia but under the category "Special Study" indicated that he was "Mostly self-educated."

        To The John Simon Guggenheim Memorial Foundation:
[JSG.application]   [Mount Vernon, Maine]
                                                          [Received July 21, 1931]
["Concise statement of project"] My aim is to write a full-length novel of proletarian life in the South; an inclusive study, from the

---

[72]*Perkins urged Caldwell to use him as a reference so that he might "speak of 'Tobacco Road' in the highest terms" (Perkins to EC, PRI 6-13-31). His other references were Lewis Mumford, Edward J. O'Brien, and Atcheson T. Hench, his English professor and mentor at the University of Virginia.*

point of view of the worker, of the fall of agriculture and of the rise of industry. A worker, however, without the most remote tinge of propaganda: propaganda in art is furtherest from my mind. I am a creative writer, not an evangelist.

["Plans for Study"] I am afraid I cannot go much further beyond my "concise statement of project": My aim is to write a full-length novel of proletarian life in the South; the time is the present. However, whereas <u>Tobacco Road</u>, and to a lesser degree, <u>American Earth</u>, is a study of a group of people existing under an outmoded system of agriculture and economics, I want to write in the book I have in mind something of the direction which the masses must turn to in order to live under the present and forthcoming conditions of life. It is a sort of union of agrarian and industrial societies. This is a condition that exists to some extent in all sections of the Nation, but it is, I believe, affecting more peculiarly the millions in the South. The tenant farmer, the textile mill operative, and all those living somewhere between those two occupations, cannot continue living under present conditions without losing a great part of their moral, social, and economic stamina. This is no longer a debatable problem, and yet no one, with any degree of sureness has pointed out the direction the masses must take in order to keep from falling below the deplorable standard of living the Negro has already become heir to. And the problem, while acute to the masses, is of even greater significance, or should be, to the Nation at large. I do not pretend to say that my solution would be better than another man's, but I do insist that no writer has yet undertaken to go beneath the surface of the subject, and I am confident that no person who knows the South will fail to see the usefulness of an initial undertaking. I believe I have the necessary understanding of the white tenant farmer and the white textile mill operative to enable me to write the novel which would at least lay open the sore which is spreading the germs to every man, woman, and child. I am a Southerner by birth, by inheritance, and by residence, and my sympathies lie with the millions who do not know what to do. Shall they continue a precarious existence, living from hand to mouth, always in debt, uneducated, and solemnly waiting for "a better day"? Or shall they be given an opportunity to become educated, independent, and self-respecting? Ther answers to these questions lie in an inclusive novel of proletarian life, purely creative, written perhaps from the point of view of the masses. There is no use in waiting endlessly for "better times": the masses in the South have always been undernourished, uneducated, and without a spokesman. There has already been too much of "romance", of "magnolia blossoms", of "Negro dialect"; it is time someone really wrote about "life". I should like to have the leisure, the funds, and the time to try to let "the poor whites", "the white trash", and "the lint-heads" present a different picture. I am confident that I have the material, my work in the past should show my ability to undertake the writing, and my seriousness of purpose will, I believe, give to the completed task the sincerity and significance that it requires. Outstanding, as in any creative work, should be the quality of the writing. I am confident that I can bring to it the best that is in my power.

I propose to do the writing of the book in America.

[PRI.tls]

To Maxwell Perkins:

Mount Vernon, Maine
July 22nd 1931

Dear Perkins:

I have just got the Guggenheim application off, and you should be hearing from them within the next few weeks.

Now that the application has been sent, I feel that perhaps I should have left unsaid much that I wrote in my "Plans for Study". However, I was assured that an applicant should by all means outline a project, especially with reference to scope and character. I find this is silly, because I have yet to discover the medium through which I can see in advance what I am going to write about in the future. But since the project I outlined fell, more or less, within what I have already done and what I am striving to do, it may not be so very far amiss after all. I should think that a writer could be left apart from the professors and their thesises; but no, the creative life must be scientific, according to these presents. . . .

That was a fine piece by Struthers Burt in the new Scribner's. I think it is the best piece of work I have read in any magazine in over a year -- anyway, since Josephine Herbst's story last year, called, I think, "A Bad Blow".[73]

Sincerely,
Erskine Caldwell

---

[73]*Burt's essay celebrated the splendid variety of "life" in the United States, despite the ongoing economic (and spiritual) depression. Given Caldwell's aims in writing—as expressed, for example, in his Guggenheim application—he would have found Burt's conclusion particularly appealing: "It is more difficult to love a great land than a small one, and yet a man or a woman who has no love of land is but a half-creature. I do not mean patriotism as generally understood. For that I have the necessary contempt. I mean a quiet, abiding, clear-sighted passion for your own, through good or evil, with a full knowledge of faults or virtues, such as a wise, mature man has for a woman. At the beginning of such a passion is the ability to regard*

To John Hall Wheelock:
[PRI.tls]
Mount Vernon, Maine
July 23rd 1931

Dear Wheelock:

I have another suggestion to offer, and I hope you will consider its possibilities, if it has any. -- I should like a review copy of my book sent to <u>Contempo</u>. It is a review published at the University of North Carolina. At present its form is much like a small newspaper, and starting in September it will appear in magazine size. It is publishing a short story of mine then; and I am considering writing a self-review of <u>American Earth</u> for it. Its "self-reviews" are more or less unique, I think, but anyway, even if I don't write it, I believe they will run some sort of notice of the book. This is merely a suggestion for you to take at its value, such that it may have. . . .[74]

I don't know what you thought of the way the review copy turned up in <u>The New Masses</u>. Probably it wasn't so bad -- considering.[75] However, I notice in the July issue that the book is being advertised in <u>New Masses Book Service</u>, so perhaps all in all, it was not a total loss; possibly of some value after all.

America—the country—as a separate entity apart from whatever certain fools, or rascals, may, at the time, be doing to her. It is this feeling which reduces the supply and the power of fools. And when you have this feeling you would no more think of dishonoring or desecrating your country than you would think of throwing mud on the skirt of your wife. Part of this feeling consists in getting back to the naked body of the country, is compounded of a love of American sights, sounds, smells, and horizons, even if the last are nowadays too often littered with ugliness. But it is also through this feeling that this transitory ugliness will one day pass" ("The Subtle Land," Scribner's Magazine *[August 1931], pp. 119–131).* Herbst's story, *"A Bad Blow,"* had appeared in Scribner's *(July 1930), pp. 25–32.*

[74]Contempo's *"self-reviews" provided authors with the opportunity to respond to published remarks on their newest works. In an essay entitled "Dilletantism [sic] and Propaganda," Caldwell did just that: "[L]et it be shouted at the outset that* American Earth *is neither capitalist propaganda nor is it communist; it is merely some stories about people of the south—mostly in the Carolinas and Georgia—and about people Down East. It seems to be necessary to make such a statement, because the book has been accused, at different times, of fostering the ideals of each. I am sorry to have to disappoint both camps, but the truth is that I was so busy trying to tell tales that I forgot to further either cause"* (Contempo *[21 Aug. 1931], pp. 1, 4).*

[75]*In a short but influential review, Norman Macleod hailed Caldwell as one of the promising new voices for the American proletariat: "His style is staccato and sometimes 'hardboiled' but beneath the surface one often perceives a fine strain of sensitivity to human emotions. He is in reality an idealist of the finer sort who (as most of our young writers do today) hesitates to admit it. As far as his characters have led him, he has done an excellent piece of interpretive writing. What he lacks is the ability to place them in the social scheme of things.... We need writers like Caldwell. He should go left"* ("A Hardboiled Idealist," New Masses *[July 1931], p. 18). In the* Contempo *essay cited in the previous note, however, Caldwell accused Macleod of being "uninformed" about the availability of unions and organizations in the lives of typical Southern workers, and resented that Macleod had "implied that I had deliberately ignored members of the unions to focus attention on the individual" (p. 1).*

With best wishes, I am
> Sincerely,
> Erskine Caldwell

PS: Some of the contributors to <u>Contempo</u> are: John Dos Passos, Max Eastman, Paul Green, Sinclair Lewis, Lewis Mumford, Norman Thomas, Stark Young. A very good line-up, in the way of names. EC

Caldwell's most recent submission to *Pagany* was a long story entitled "A Message for Genevieve." Apparently, Johns did not care for it, and although any correspondence giving his reasons has been lost, we do have the reasons Maxwell Perkins had already rejected the story for *Scribner's*. Perkins felt it was too "largely a matter of reflecting upon an episode of the past," and so not as appropriate "for our general sort of circulation as others that you do."[76]

To Richard Johns:

[DEL.tls] Mount Vernon, Maine
November 1st 1931

Dear Johns:
I don't know what in hell to say about the story except to ask you to wait until I can see you and talk with you about it. At any rate, don't think for a moment that I resent what you said: I'm as glad as hell to have your criticism, and to know that you think enough of me and my work to write as you did.

I'm not going to try to explain anything about the story until I can talk with you; because in all sincerity I plead ignorance. For one thing, I am no critic, not even of my own stuff, and consequently I am forced to suffer for my own ignorance. Perhaps its' the title that's wrong; if so, I can readily see how you disliked it. But whatever the error is, I beg you to tell me. Perhaps it is the whole general tone of the thing; perhaps it is something I would never suspect unless I was told. The truth is I wrote the story with a sort of satanic smile, aiming the thing at myself (for writing a piece -- as the inclosure certainly is -- like that), at editors in general, and at readers in particular. Those three elements prompted the whole thing at the start. When it was done, I thought the joke was one me (as the author) as well as on others. But as for <u>what editors want</u> -- whether it is a certain kind of

---

[76] *Perkins to EC, PRI 1-20-31. This story remained unpublished until 1933 when Caldwell and Alfred Morang brought it out in a limited-edition pamphlet, with illustrations by Morang (Portland: Old Colony Press, 1933).*

short story, or a certain kind of female -- I cannot honestly say which point I was trying to make. If it matters. But the word 'editor' does not mean a thing, unless it could be synonym for 'people'.

But can't we postpone this until I can talk with you? I can't say what I want to until I know what I am talking about. The thing has upset me so much (for fear I have turned out an outright rotten piece of work) that I cannot write with any clarity. I'll try to explain it when I see you. . . .

Sincerely,
Erskine Caldwell

To Alfred Morang:

[HAR.tls]   Wrens, Georgia
                                                                 January 26th 1932

Dear Morang:

I've been wondering what you have been doing since last summer. Sold any oil or water color -- given any exhibitions since then? Write me all about it.

I have at last finished another book (I hope it is finished for good). It's another novel, about the Mount Vernon country of Maine this time, and I've been working on it since October, four months of actual writing. I shall send it off in a few days, half-way expecting it to be turned down. Anyway, I'll let you know if it is taken.[77]

"Tobacco Road" should be out next month some time. Don't know the publication date yet, but I shall send you a copy as soon as I get one. I haven't seen the completed book yet, although I did see the artist's drawing for the jacket. It looks fine to me. Hope you can speak a word for it in Portland. But Portland is the last place I should expect to see a copy sold. If everyone there believes everything that has been said about me, I would expect to be sent to prison for the rest of my life.

I have found several copies of some magazines here, and I'll send them to you with the book. You may have already seen them, and if you have you can throw them away. Haven't published much recently, although I do have stories in the current issues of CLAY, PAGANY, and STORY (Vienna). I've been so busy on this new novel

---

[77] *Originally called* Autumn Hill, *this novel was not published until 1952, when it was retitled* A Lamp for Nightfall. *Caldwell later claimed it was "undertaken in an effort to clear my mind of the experience of writing* Tobacco Road*" (*Experience, *p. 123).*

that I haven't written a short story in five months, but now that it is finished I want to do several while I am down here.

Saw Johns while I was in New York last fall. He came to see me several times, and neither time was he drunk. He's all right when he hasn't been drinking, although he never talks very much. I was there two months, and came down to Georgia the first of January. I shall probably stay here another month and then go to Virginia a while. But nothing can keep me from going to Mount Vernon in the early spring. Will get there by the first of May, I hope. . . .

Let me know how everything is with you. I'll send you a copy of "Tobacco Road" as soon as I get one. Best wishes.

Sincerely,
Erskine Caldwell

To Maxwell Perkins:

[PRI.tls]
Wrens, Georgia
February 5th 1932

Dear Perkins:

I sent you a week ago the manuscript of a new novel called AUTUMN HILL. It is a story of present-day people in the cut-over pulpwood country of West-Central Maine. You told me last year that you preferred having the next novel about that section of New England to one whose scene was Georgia's, in as much as TOBACCO ROAD is purely of the South. I cannot say that this thought was foremost in my mind when I wrote it, but at any rate AUTUMN HILL is a novel about the country and people Down-East.

[Raymond] Everitt of Curtiss Brown wrote me that he had turned over to you all the paper connected with the Harcourt Brace -- Heron Press matter. I have no more confidence now in Harcourt than I have in the other publisher. I was assured by the former that he wanted to publish my stuff, but now I learn that he was waiting until I wrote a best seller before starting. I am anxious to hear what you have to say after you have made a study of the contract and option.

Is it about time for the publication of "Tobacco Road"?

I'll appreciate seeing a copy of it when it is ready. Best wishes.[78]

Sincerely,
Erskine Caldwell

---

[78] *Perkins responded three days later that "'Autumn Hill' (fine title) has come and, by a hasty scanning, looks to be very fine." He also reported that* Tobacco Road *was to be published the following Friday (Perkins to EC, PRI 2-8-32).*

To Alfred Morang:

[HAR.tls]

Wrens, Georgia
March 1st 1932

Dear Morang: I'm damn glad there was at least one reader of TOBACCO RD who could read it with understanding. Most of the reviewers in metropolitan newspapers understood it, too. But when you get out in the hinterland, there is where the fools begin. You saw the review in the Portland Express, didn't you? That's what I mean.[79] That reviewer not only could not understand the book -- he said it was obscene! -- but he could also not read the story that was in black and white. In the first place, there is nothing obscene or dirty in the book, because the people in it did not live consciously obscene lives. But Portland said <u>The Bastard</u> was obscene, too; I expected that to be said again.

I'm enclosing two or three reviews that you may keep if you want to. If you can say a good word for the book in Portland, I'd appreciate it, because I know I will never get anything else otherwise.

Have you seen William Carlos Williams new mag CONTACT? The first issue is out now. I shall have a story in the second number, which won't be out until May or June. PAGANY is still a good mag -- the new number is probably the best yet. CLAY is good, and so is STORY. transition is due for a come-back, but I haven't seen it yet.

Don't stop work because you don't get encouragement in the Portland Art School. To hell with them, if they don't like your stuff. I like it, and Idon't have to be an art critic or teacher to know a good thing when I see it.

I hope to get to Maine next month. I'll let you know. I'm anxious to see you again. Best wishes.

Sincerely,
Caldwell

---

[79] *The anonymous review sounded criticisms of Caldwell that would, in a very few years, become commonplace. The reviewer conceded that Caldwell had talent—even if the work betrayed "an unnatural, obviously deliberate style"—but found* Tobacco Road *essentially plotless, little more than "an animal story, the story of human animals, less intelligent, interesting and worth writing about than most other animals." And while the novel might be praised by those championing "the so-called modern school of writers," it nevertheless "tries too hard to delicately border on the frankly vulgar.... It lacks the courage to come out into the sunlight of honest filth and lurks in the shadows of implication, suggestion, intimation" ("Erskine Caldwell's Novel of the South,"* Portland *Express, Erskine Caldwell Scrapbooks, DAR 2-13-32).*

Caldwell maintained a long professional friendship with Milton A. Abernethy, editor of *Contempo: A Review of Ideas and Personalities*, the little magazine that advertised itself as "the literary newspaper" of Chapel Hill, North Carolina. Established as an alternative to "the standardization, stereotyped, stereoptician blah-blah-bleat book review magazines of today,"[80] *Contempo* regularly published (and promoted) the work of such major figures of twentieth-century literature as James T. Farrell, Kay Boyle, Wallace Stevens, e. e. cummings, Conrad Aiken, William Faulkner, Nathanael West, and James Joyce.

To Milton A. Abernethy:

[HRC.tls] Wrens, Georgia
March 2nd 1932

Dear Abernethy:

Many thanks for giving me the opportunity to read [Roy] Flan[n]agan's new book.[81] I am returning the galleys to you.

This is one of the novels that should have been written fifty years ago. There is a race problem in the South, and eventually it will color the Nation. Virginians, and Southerners, who have been holding their breaths all this time may at last take a deep sigh of relief. Their course has been set by Flan[n]agan: that course is not to prohibit but to delay the mixture as long as possible.

By all means let me see a copy of Henry Hart's piece.[82]

Sincerely,
Erskine Caldwell

---

[80] *"Editorial,"* Contempo *(31 Aug. 1932), p. 2.*

[81] Amber Satyr *(Doubleday, 1932). An anonymous review in the New York* Times *drew a qualified comparison of Flannagan to Caldwell, rather than "to Faulkner, with whom he has been compared": "If Mr. Flannagan lacks Caldwell's eloquence, his Swiftian bursts, his poetry and sudden sharp observation, he offers compensation by an adroit enough dramaturgy" ([8 May 1932], p. 6). Although Caldwell's remarks on the novel did not appear in* Contempo, *Abernethy featured an excerpt from* Amber Satyr *alongside Caldwell's story "Picking Cotton" on the front page of the magazine's 25 May 1932 issue.*

[82] Hart *had written a combined review of* American Earth *and* Tobacco Road *in which he introduced Caldwell to* Contempo *readers as "A New Star in the Firmament" of Southern writers. Grateful for the attention, Caldwell nonetheless thought Hart's piece amateurish, as he suggested in a letter to Abernethy on the publication of* God's Little Acre *(See EC to Abernethy, 11-27-32).*

To Milton A. Abernethy:

[HRC.tls]　　　　　　　　　　　　　　　　　　Wrens, Georgia
　　　　　　　　　　　　　　　　　　　　　　　March 7th 1932

Dear Abernethy:

Thanks for sending me the Henry Hart piece. It will help me get coffee -- I don't eat cake, anyway. I am returning it to you herewith.

Sorry I can't send you a copy of The Bastard; I haven't a copy myself now, and as far as I know it can't be bought. The bastards who published it vamoosed with all the copies and the money. A clever combination of Jew and Hungarian.

It looks now as if I can't get to Chapel Hill. I'm broke as hell to begin with, and in order to get to NY the first of April I'll have to take a bus on a non-stop ticket, which is the cheapest way of getting there. If something turns up in the betweentime, however, I will be able to make better plans. I want to come to see you while I am here this time.

What does Flan[n]agan think of my comment about his novel? I really liked it, and I wish I could have written something truely bright and sparkling. But, alas, I'm not that way. The best I can ever do is to transfer my thoughts to paper.

Don't forget me when the time comes to print that short story of mine.[83] -- Best wishes.

　　　　　　　　　　　　　　　　　　Sincerely,
　　　　　　　　　　　　　　　　　　Caldwell

In late March, Caldwell went to New York to meet with Perkins and, he hoped, remedy problems with *Autumn Hill*. Perkins had written that he was "doubtful" about the manuscript as it was, "that the book calls for a great deal more development, and could easily have it." Three days later, Caldwell replied that he was making plans to be in New York by the end of the month, and was willing to "do everything I can to make the book 'right.'" He explained that he had been preparing another volume of short stories and wanted to arrange their publication as well as that of the *Autumn Hill* manuscript, before turning his full attention to "the new novel I have in mind," probably *God's Little Acre*. Frustrated, he reminded Perkins: "Writing is the only source of income I have, and I must keep everlastingly at it like this. You will understand."[84]

During these very stressful times, Caldwell relied heavily on his wife Helen for moral support—and as this letter reveals, for her critical abilities.

[83] *"Picking Cotton."*
[84] *Perkins to EC, PRI 3-4-32; EC to Perkins, PRI 3-7-32.*

To Helen Caldwell:

[DAR.tls] [New York City]
April 4th 1932

Dear Helen:

I got your Saturday letter today with the enclosure. If you do leave Friday, you won't have time to answer this, because I'll have to leave here then also, or at the latest, Saturday. I was planning on going down on an excursion to D C; but I have not been able to find if there is one that day (Sunday). If there is not, I'll go on a bus to D C, and from there down the best way I can. If I can find the means to stay here another day (room is up Friday), I'll more than likely come down at thes same time I did last Fall. I don't know what time yet, so the only thing I can do is wait and let you know leter. If I can find out in time, I'll write a letter; otherwise I'll have to send a telegram. In either case be sure and meet me, and try to have something to eat. I've only had two meals so far, but I have prospects of two more before I leave. One with Henry Hart, and one with Marj [Morse] and Nannie.[85] The rest of the time I'm eating doughnuts, rye rolls, or chease pie twice a day.

I believe this new part of the book can be made as good as the rest. It may be a matter of time, but I'm positive that we can get it done within another month or six weeks. As soon as it is officially accepted, I get the money. That part has been settled. It's up to me to finish the thing, and I can if you will help me. But if you are going to keep that up like you did last winter, I may as well through the whole thing overboard now.[86] I can't do a damn thing while I know that youdoing soming I wouldn't want you to do. If a person can't be honest he at least can be fair and say he's not. There are too many goddamn deceitful women in the world now for me to perpetuate the lot. I'd rather not having anything to do than kind of thing. If I can't trust a person behind my back, I shall certainly balk at trusting him in front of me. [Al] Capone attributed his success, you know, to the fact that he always put double-crossers on the spot.

If you want to get out, go ahead; I myself do not. If I had not loved you I wouldn't have married you. I wouldn't live with anyone else. It's either you, or nobody.

Love,
Erskine . . .

---

[85] *Unidentified.*

[86] *According to Harvey Klevar, Helen had recently confessed to Erskine that she had "loved a man she somehow had met in Charlottesville ... and would have married the man had she been more selfish.... And again according to Helen, 'Erskine knew this' because she had not tried to hide it from him" (*Erskine Caldwell: A Biography *[Knoxville: U of Tennessee P, 1993], p. 117). Hereafter cited as Klevar,* Biography.

To Helen Caldwell:

[DAR.tls] New York N Y
Saturday [April 1932]

Dear Helen: I received your letters and the mail yesterday and today. One of the letters was from the Missouri State Prison; a fellow from Georgia wanted me to donate "Tobacco Rd". He said that all they had to read was "Gangland Stories", "Crime Stories", and such pulp magazines. He had been to the U of Ga three years. ### Johns came in yesterday with [William] Chapman[87] and took me downtown for a dinner, the first real one I've had here yet. He and William Chapman are both buying places in Redding (Ct). A new Pagany will be out about the 20th; even larger than the last one. Chapman said that someone in Scribner's told him that Tobacco Rd was one of the finest books the house had ever published; and he was also told that they expect my next novel to sell, really sell, as Tobacco Rd was planned as the foundation for promotion and sales. Hope he heard correctly. Anyway, that ties up with what Perkins is driving at: wanting Autumn Hill to be big enough and complete enought to warrant complete promotion. It is silly to think that I can't expand it; it can be done, and if you will help me, it shall be. I've made a draft of fifteen pages during the past few days; and with another fifteen we'll have something to work on. I am depending on you, though, to tell me if the new part is fine enough. Without your help I couldn't do anything with it. I never know until you tell me. ### Contact is on the edge; may not go to a second issue. The first was rotten enough; everyone I have seen thinks so too. Williams is unpredictable always.[88] ### What have you decided about leaving for Charlottesville? I don't know what else to do, than to go to Maine. I want to go there, and if we can get enough money for two or three months, we'll pull through. The world isn't going to stop turning, and once we get something going, all this will seem unimportant. For, after all, people have always had to buck the world. If you decide it will be better for me to stay here until the 15th, then all right; I'll let you decide what to do, only let me know as soon as possible. If I can get an extra ten dollar for another week after this, and you want to wait until the

---

[87] *Chapman, a professional journalist, was also a regular contributor to* Pagany. *According to his biography in O'Brien, "He fishes, plays golf, despises Byrrh and Chianti, admires William Faulkner, and lives in New York City" (*The Best Short Stories of 1932 *[Dodd, Mead, 1932], p. 289).*

[88] *With co-editor Robert McAlmon, Williams had founded* Contact *in 1920 to promote experimental writing, particularly imagism; it ran for just five issues, until June 1923. In 1932, determined to foster the literary* avant garde, *Williams alone initiated a "new series" of the magazine. Financial instability permitted the publication of only three issues at irregular intervals (Hoffman, et al., pp. 48–49, 258–259.)*

15th, then it will be all right. Personally, I don't hanker for a week or ten days in Virginia, but it may be the only way. I don't believe we should try to go to Maine until the 20th, or later, on account of the roads. It costs five dollars to get pulled out, and there are at least three bad places, you remember. I think, with a week's or two week's work on the new matter for the book that I can have something really done. That is the best time I'll have for at least a month to do it in, and if I have it ready when we go to Maine, it will be ready for you to help me with. I think sixty pages more will do the job as it should be. That will make about 300 ms pages. ### Don't let anything happen to Pixy and Dabney. If they get sick, let me know. Take care of yourself, and write when you can. Explain to Mother and Father how much money it costs me to stay here by the week, and about the fare down to Virginia. When you get ready to leave, ask them to give you what they can, including twenty for the suit if possible. Some day we'll get out of this mess.

Love,
Erskine

To Alfred Morang:

[HAR.tls] Mount Vernon, Maine
April 30th 1932

Dear Morang:

Did you get my letter mailed from Virginia? Wish I could have sent you a story for the magazine then, but I haven't got a thing ready. The magazine is coming through, isn't it?[89] Tell me about it, and if you still wish to have a story of mine. I wouldn't miss being in it for anything. . . .

I've just heard that O'Brien will represent me again this year; in "Best Short Stories of 1932". Personally I think he failed to select the best of them, but that is his business, not mine. The one he chose wasn't so bad, possibly.[90]

I like the countryscape you sent me. I believe I thanked you for it once, but I wish to thank you again, anyway. You are doing better

---

[89] Morang had proposed to begin a little magazine, but like many of his other plans, there is no evidence that it materialized.

[90] Edward J. O'Brien had selected "Warm River," which had appeared in the Winter issue of Pagany. Other stories published that year (or late in 1931) that he might have chosen were "Indian Summer," "The People's Choice," "The Corduroy Pants," "The Empty Room," "Hours Before Eternity," "Rachel," and "We Are Looking At You, Agnes."

work now, aren't you? What I mean is, this one seems to be deeper in conception than the former ones were. I don't know, though. It's hard for me to judge. I like a work, or I dislike it. That's as much as I can criticise. . . .

          Sincerely,
          Caldwell

Like so many of its contemporaries, *Pagany* experienced financial difficulties almost from the start, despite ample subscriptions and a steady flow of letters praising Johns' editorial acumen. Ezra Pound, Robert Cantwell, Edward Dahlberg, Norman Macleod, and Caldwell were among the many who strongly urged, even begged, Johns to keep the magazine in print—but also, if at all possible, to forward payment for their contributions.

        To Richard Johns:
[DEL.tls]   Mount Vernon, Maine
                 July 8th 1932
Dear Johns:
  Thanks for the note. Hell, you got me wrong. I didn't mean to give the impression I was dunning. I only wished to say that if you were paying these days, I'd like to be remembered. That was all. By all means salve the printer to the extent of the next number. Maybe something will turn up in the meantime that will insure getting out issues thereafter. For God's sake don't discontinue; there is something in the air -- can't you feel it? -- something of an impending revolution, actual or in theory, and that will mean new writing. PAGANY ought to be the mouthpiece. Writing now, to me at least, seems to be at the end of the current trend; after this calm there will undoubtedly be even finer stuff written. Possibly I don't know what I am talking about.
  Great! come on up; we eat in a kitchen -- more fully when someone catches a few fish. There will be three or four up from Portland next -- from Monday to Friday -- and you and the Chapmans will make a full house. There's plenty of room and plenty of air -- you are welcome. Try to arrange a trip then. We hope you will. Tell Chapman we expect them both; man and wife.
  Can't get any satisfaction out of Scribner's about the next novel. It is falling through. [Maxim] Lieber[91] believes he can place it elsewhere,

---

[91] *Caldwell met Lieber, his longtime agent, at a party hosted by the Macaulay Company in New York in 1931, just as he was completing the draft of* Tobacco Road. *A former editor for Brentano's, and a vocal sympathizer of the American Communist movement, Lieber was known for his aggressiveness and sharp business sense, and he pursued Caldwell as a client (*Experience,

and if so, why not? He will probably sound out Harcourt Brace. In the meantime, no book, no money, no nothing. . . .

Sincerely,
Caldwell

PS: Did you see that story anywhere -- "A Message for Genevieve"? If you can put your hands on it, I should like to have it awhile to work over some. Thanks a lot. EC

By September, Perkins had formally rejected *Autumn Hill*, and Caldwell's agent, Max Lieber, had begun talks with The Viking Press. Working with Morang, Caldwell's immediate project was the publication of a pamphlet version of his story "Mama's Little Girl," which William Carlos Williams was considering, and eventually accepted, for publication in *Contact*. Morang would provide the illustrations, and the pamphlet, limited to seventy-five copies, would be printed by Joe Bradford, owner of Portland's Bradford Press.

To Alfred Morang:

[HAR.tls] Mount Vernon, Maine
September 15, 1932

Dear Morang:

I don't know what to say about selling the pamphlet wholesale. I'm not in favor of signing them for this reason: we have started this thing on a co-operative basis and I should like to see it through on the same track. But on the other hand, we need the money, you and myself even if Bradford doesn't, and we ought to get all we can out of it. In our Communist State, one person has no right to sign the things unless all of us do. That's one reason I'm against it. But as for selling them unsigned, I'm tickled to death. . . .

I am enclosing the drawing I should use if I were you. It's the one without the three people. It's a superb drawing even now, and when you work it over, it'll be a jim-dandy. Don't you think the idea of not having the drawings peopled will be well to follow? I do. But if you think otherwise, do whatever you like, because you are the man who is doing them.

No, the story has not been copyrighted. We shall have to do that ourselves, as I indicated on the sheet I sent last time. Williams has the story, but whether he prints it or not will not interfere with what we are doing. The story is my property, no matter who prints it, until I

---

p. 105). Lieber managed Caldwell's affairs for twenty years, until 1951, when he fled to Mexico in fear of prosecution as a "spy" in the wake of the Alger Hiss trial (Miller, p. 350).

sign away the rights, and that is something I've never been fool enough to do yet, and I hope never. I'll write Williams that we're printing the story in a pamphlet, and he will probably send it back. But even if he does print it in CONTACT, there's nothing to keep us from doing the same thing. . . .

Maxim Lieber has had a nibble. He wrote me about it Tuesday. When it becomes a bite, he says he's going to pull up a contract. The Viking Press offered us $100 for an option, but I don't know what Lieber has done. If he can't get a contract the firest thing, he'll probably give them the option for two or three books for that amount. That will be something to put fat in the soup, anyway. God knows it's been lean long enough. I'll let you know what happens as soon as the thing comes to a head. I'm hoping this won't be my last year. If I can stave off starvation, I'd like to live many more years. The Viking Press can sell books if anybody can; maybe we'll live off the fat of the land yet. . . .

Best wishes
Caldwell

James Leippert was founding editor of *The Lion and Crown: A Quarterly*, a short-lived little magazine published in New York by undergraduates at Columbia University.

To James Leippert:

[CHI.tls] Mount Vernon, Maine
September 16th 1932

Dear Leippert:

Many thanks for your letter. I am greatly interested to hear that there is going to be a new magazine, and with the material you have in the offing it should be a good one. I wish by all means to see a copy of the first issue. Will you let me know the price and so forth?

You ask if I care to send something. I do. A story is enclosed -- "Crown Fire" -- for you to read. It is the only piece of work I have on hand at present that is complete. I've been working on a novel most of the summer, but that's finished now, and I hope to do some other work this fall. I've succeeded in squeezing a few dollars via a story from The Yale Review, and we'll laugh the wolf away for another several months.

Please let me know what you think of the story enclosed. Best wishes --

Sincerely,
Caldwell

Caldwell's story "Crown-Fire" appeared as the first item in the second issue of *The Lion and Crown*, in Spring 1933. The issue also included work by William Carlos Williams, Archibald MacLeish, George Oppen, and Gertrude Stein.

To James Leippert:

[CHI.tls] Mount Vernon, Maine
September 22nd 1932

Dear Lieppert:

I'm glad you liked the story. I never know whether a piece is any good, and I must rely on what others say, most of the time.

I'm looking forward to the first number. The first of anything offers more or less a track for what is to come. The improvements, and the degeneration, follow the grooves of the first without fail. You are sending copies to O'Brien, I hope; his annual for this year is very fine.

Yes, I've written a novel; in fact four books have been published. I'm willing to forget the first two; Scribner's published American Earth (short stories) in 1931, and Tobacco Road (novel) during the past spring. I expect to have a new publisher for the one I've just finished.

I'm afraid the list of magazines would be too long. It should be enough to say that I've had stories in the following: European -- This Quarter, transition, Story, and The New English Weekly; American -- The Hound & Horn, Scribner's, Pagany, and Contact. There are several others, to be sure: Nativity, Blues, Contempo, The American Caravan, Clay, Folk-Say, The Yale Review. And possibly others that I can't think of just now.

When I get something else finished, I hope to send you another story or two for you to read. Just now I'm getting over the effects of wringing a novel out of my system, and enjoying being lazy. I'll get over that, however, very shortly.

Best wishes -- and be sure and let me see a copy of the new magazine when it's ready --

Sincerely,
Caldwell

Caldwell knew Gordon Lewis from his days in Charlottesville, where Lewis, himself a writer, had owned a bookstore popular with University of Virginia students.

To Gordon Lewis:

[VIR.tls] Mount Vernon, Maine
September 23rd 1932

Dear Gordon:

Jesus, I was glad to hear from you. I've heard of you several times during the past few years. CC[92] said you were in New York, and someone else said you weren't. Let me know how to get in communication with you in Florida: 1st, I may come down to see you; 2nd, I may hear of something that you could find of use. Your letter, by the way, was held over at the University for about a week; people never are careful of others' mail, though.

Tell me about the novel. Have you got a publisher?[93] I'm out at Scribner's; had some good words in command that I made good use of. Now I'm looking for another publisher. I've finished another novel and Maxim Lieber (a damn good agent) has gone fishing with The Viking Press. I'm sitting here on eggs, waiting. God damn it. Lieber sold a story to The Yale Review (winter issue)[94] and that's all between us and the wolf. It will run out after the first of the year, and we may bum down to Georgia for a few months on the folks. We were there last winter two months (Augusta). Will you give us crawling space if we can get down to see you, if we can get down as far as Augusta, if the sheriff hasn't got me by then? The bookshop went skyhigh in Portland. Did you hear the bang? Jesus, we came out with our clothes, and several (many) hundreds hanging over our heads.[95] Now I'm trying to earn a living via writing. Have to give most of my short stuff away for lack of a market. (STORY, CONTACT, NEW ENGLISH WEEKLY, CONTEMPO, etc). If I can get an advance out of the new novel, we'll pull through the winter.

I wish you and Ruth had got up to Maine this year. Is it too late? What about next summer? We'll probably be here, or not far away in the county jug, at any rate. Suppose we could get down to Florida this winter, could we stay a few days around somewhere? (Your address, if/and when you give it to me, is under the hat; you can depend on that).

---

[92] *Probably Caldwell's classmate, the novelist Charles Christian Wertenbaker, who attended the University of Virginia from 1923 to 1925.*

[93] *Lewis never published a novel.*

[94] *"Country Full of Swedes."*

[95] *The Longfellow Bookshop had gone bankrupt due to inattentive management and dwindling sales. As Miller reports, particularly after the controversy over* The Bastard, *Caldwell's local "reputation as a 'writer of dirty books' kept respectable citizens out of the store" (p. 147).*

You must have been in New York this spring; I was there two months. Also the spring before, and the fall of 1931. I wish I might have run across you. I asked CC where you were, but he seemed to be in sort of a daze, possibly a coma.

What are you writing about? You've got one customer for the novel. I've been waiting and looking for something from the typewriter of G.L. for the past how-many years. Now, it's time not to disappoint me any longer. Do you get out many short stories? You ought to be able to make a name of sorts doing them, and all of a sudden cash in on them. But I haven't. I can give them away, yes; but who wishes to buy them, would you care to buy one? But maybe you'll have beter luck than I've been having. . . .

. . . If you are in want of a good agent, try Maxim Lieber. He can sell where all hope has been lost. He hasn't sold so much for me, but when he did sell, I fell down in amazement.

Best wishes from Helen and me -- and write soon --
Sincerely,
Erskine Caldwell

To Milton A. Abernethy:

[HRC.tls] Mount Vernon, Maine
October 19th 1932

Dear Abernethy:

It was swell of you to write Covici Friede[96] about my book. I received their wire today, and I'm having to decline. I should have written you sooner about it, but I only signed the contract last week through Maxim Lieber. The Viking Press has accepted one novel, and two more books are in prospect in the future (when I write them). The book Scribner's and myself got sore about (AUTUMN HILL) is laid aside temporarily, and Viking is publishing in March a novel called GOD'S LITTLE ACRE, which follows, in many ways (and I hope better), TOBACCO RD. Anyway, Viking seems to be nuts about the book, and Lieber says everyone says its good. GOD'S LITTLE ACRE is about a string of textile mills in Horsecreek Valley South Carolinia and a family in Georgia that does more digging for gold than farming. I know you are going to like it, if you liked TOBACCO RD, because it's a much better book.

I received my new number of CONTEMPO, and it's great. (When

---

[96]*A New York publishing house known primarily for its fine, limited editions.*

will you publish my story?) We've been living off the proceeds of the sale of a story to The Yale Review. There'll be something coming in from Viking shortly, and we hope to pull through the winter. I'm coming South after Christmas if possible. This time I am going to do my best to see you.

Thanks again for writing Covici Friede. I'm beginning to think that Scribner's was a mistake to begin with. Viking is much more decent about everything.

Best wishes, and let me hear from you ---
Sincerely,
Caldwell

To Milton A. Abernethy:
[HRC.tls]   Mount Vernon, Maine
                                                October 28th 1932

Dear Abernethy: . . . I wish you would print a piece in answer to Donald Adams; he needs to get wise to himself.[97] Now what in the hell will you say about AUGUST AFTERNOON??? (if you decide to print it, please writer to Lieber and ask him if he will release it to you. He told me he didn't have hope of selling it, so he may not object to you printing it. His version, as you will suspect, is far from being the same as this one.) It's not a shocking piece at all, but I can see how a [John S.] Sumner might dislike it.[98] It's up to you, whether you like it. Maybe you don't think it's worth a damn. Vic really intended to kill Floyd, when he got around to it; it was hot, and he was sleepy, and he told Hubert to be sure and wake him up.

[97] *Adams was editor of the New York* Times Book Review. *Likely Caldwell is referring here to his unkind words about Edward Dahlberg's recently published novel,* From Flushing to Calvary *(Harcourt, 1932): "... in time [Dahlberg] may be a Faulkner of the Coney Island proletariat, but at present the business of writing still seems too much for him" ("Sordid Lives" [23 Oct. 1932], pp. 6–7). Abernethy had published Dahlberg's "self-review" of this book as the lead item in the 25 October 1932 issue of* Contempo *(pp. 1, 2); in response to a critical firestorm surrounding the book, he devoted practically the entire 10 January 1933 issue to the controversies about its literary merits and the "authenticity" of its proletarianism. Caldwell admired the novel greatly and reviewed it for the* New Masses *(See EC to Richard Johns 12-5-32).*

[98] *An innocently ironic reference to the legal counsel and secretary for the New York Society for the Suppression of Vice, which in the spring of 1933 would file obscenity charges against Caldwell and Viking Press on the grounds that* God's Little Acre *violated the New York Penal Code prohibiting "the sale of literature that was 'obscene, lewd, lascivious, filthy, indecent or disgusting'" (see Miller, pp. 174–177).*

Hubert let him sleep, of course. Otherwise he wouldn't be drowsy, and singing to himself.[99]

Sincerely,
Caldwell

To James Leippert:

[CHI.tls] Mount Vernon, Maine
October 30th 1932

Dear Leippert:

Many thanks for the note. I am sending you the copy of "Mama's Little Girl". We are selling them for a dollar, if we can get it, but if you can't afford it (which I couldn't) we'll put it on the cuff. Let me know how you like it. The three of us did it cooperatively, and it's not a commercial job. Bradford had bought a new case of type from Europe and he wished to try it out. This is the result. The paper is American rag, the threan linen; you will have to judge the story and drawings yourself. We are thinking about getting out a cheaper pamphlet next month; longer story, no illustrations (save the cover), and sell for a quarter. I think it will go through. I'll let you know. I wish there could be a way to make pamphlets known, and sold through The Lion & Crown. The trouble with us is that we haven't any money, and can't pay for ads, much less the printer if he duns us too quickly. CONTEMPO is going to run an ad on it, I believe; but your idea would be ideal for the type of thing it is. What do you suggest?

This story was supposed to appear first in CONTACT. Williams said he was publishing it, but I can't find out when that mag will appear next.[100] Williams said to go ahead and print it, so here it is. Now what? I would have used another story, but I presumed that CONTACT would come out as stated.

When is The Lion & Crown coming? Will it be ready soon? Don't forget to let me know.

The Viking Press is publishing my new novel in March or April. It is called "God's Little Acre". I have left Scribner for better or worse. I think better, that's why I'm signed up with Viking for three books. Scribner had a chance to do something with "Tobacco Rd" (have you read it, by the way?) but they muffed it.

---

[99] *Abernethy did not accept the story; it was published for the first time in the Autumn 1933 issue of Esquire. Later, Caldwell either forgot that he had submitted "August Afternoon" to Abernethy or he couldn't resist a friendly jab about the rejection when, the following summer, he reported that one of his stories was to appear "in some god damn contraption called Esquire. Why is it I can't write stories for Contempo or some such decent magazine? I hate to see what I have written pied with parfume advertisements" (EC to Abernethy, HRC 8-25-33).*

[100] *The story did appear in the October 1932 issue of* Contact.

Let me hear from you soon.
Best wishes --

>Sincerely,
>Caldwell

To Milton A. Abernethy:

[HRC.tls] Mount Vernon, Maine
October 30th 1932

Dear Milton:

I'm sorry I can't write about the So. Writers Con. for you. I'm right in the midst of making final revisions of God's Little Acre before it goes to press, and it'll be a week before I'm done. And anyway, I'm not so hot as an article writer, anyway; everything I touch turns to fiction. This thing should be true and accurate, to say the least, because there will be some who will try to tear the piece to pieces. Do get a piece written, though; it's too good an opportunity to clarify the situation to let it slip. If they are so damn aloof, let's holler "Woof!" at them and it may scare them to death. Allen Tate and Caroline Gordon belong the the crowd; if they weren't there, they should have been. What I could say to CG in a roomful of people![101]

I can't find out a damn thing from CONTACT. Go ahead and review the pamphlet, if you are so minded, and run the ad for it if you will.[102] I'm sending two copies for the purpose. The price is one dollar postpaid, and we only have about 25 copies to sell (one of the three has sold and given all of his 25 away), and there are no more to be had. Call them The Mount Vernon Pamphlets; address in care of Erskine Caldwell, Mount Vernon, Maine. If possible, try to run the ad in a November issue, as we are planning to get out another one,

---

[101] *Abernethy must have extended the invitation when he found that Donald Adams, editor of the New York* Times Book Review, *was scheduled as one of the featured speakers at this conference (see EC to Abernethy 10-28-32). According to a brief news item in the* Saturday Review of Literature, *reported by South Carolina poet Josephine Pinckney, the event sounded more like a social affair than anything very serious: "... a certain group of Southern writers, which to the everlasting discomfort of reporters refuses to be classified with a name, met in Charleston on the twenty-first and twenty-second of October for purposes that would be hard to classify.... The program consisted of two group-discussions, visits to Magnolia Gardens and Middleton Place, a harbor trip to Fort Sumter, and other social diversions." In attendance were critics and editors, such as Adams, Fanny Butcher, Irita Van Doren, Laurence Stallings, and James Southall Wilson, plus a fairly homogenous group of writers, such as Mary Johnston, Julia Peterkin, Donald Davidson, and eleven Charlestonians, including Beatrice Ravenel, DuBose Heyward, and Pinckney herself, who "hosted a house party" ("News from the States," Saturday Review of Literature [5 Nov. 1932], p. 231).*

[102] *Mama's Little Girl.*

longer, priced at a quarter, for December. You'll get one of those for review hot off the press. There'll be no delay this time. But please blame CONTACT and not be for waiting so long. I've written half a dozen letters to them.

I sent you a story last weekk. If you got it, let me know what you think. Don't hesitate to send it back if you don't like it. But be sure to write to Lieber if you do like it.

Best wishes ---

Sincerely,
Caldwell

To Alfred Morang:

[HAR.tls] Mount Vernon, Maine
November 1st 1932

Dear Morang:

The two stories are fine. The shorter one may turn out to be the easier to get in print -- for various reasons. It benefits by its briefness, and its rings the bell. The longer one, for one thing, and the main reason, may be unprintable in America at present. That old devil censor. I'll tell you whatever criticism I have the next time I see you. They are both so good that I am a little inarticulate in my criticism. But I don't believe I have read anything so good since the beginning of 1930. They both went off to [Whit] Burnett and Martha Foley yesterday. It will be 25–30 days before a reply can reach us, considering the mails.[103]

... I'm making final revisions on "God's Little Acre" before it goes to the printer. The Viking Press was damn decent about the revisions. They wrote the suggestions they had, and said they thought so highly of the book that they would publish it whether I made the revisions or not. But some of them are damn good, and I'm taking advantage of them to try to get out the best book I've done yet. I wish you could read it in script. I'll have to send it back this week, though, and they also have the carbon copy. Seven editors and publishers' readers read the script, and there was not a single unfavorable report. And that, as Lieber wrote, is something in these days when publishers are so damn careful with their output.[104]

---

[103] *Caldwell forwarded Morang's stories with a note recommending them to the editors of* Story. *Burnett and Foley, two American journalists, had founded their magazine in Vienna in 1931 "because they felt that experiments in the story had received slight notice and almost no encouragement" in the United States. They moved the operation to this country in 1933 (Hoffman, et al., p. 303).*

[104] *Perhaps Caldwell was thinking here of Perkins' rejection of* Autumn Hill: *"I believed in it, I wish to say, and still more in you; and I saw that it was given every kind of consid-*

A friend of mine -- Gordon Lewis, a writer -- is living on an island off the coast of Florida, and he's asked us to come down and stay a while. If we make the Southern trip in January, I'm going to try to get that far. The only hitch is the money for the trip. God knows where it's coming from. But, what the hell, we only live once. There's a lot of world I've got to cover during the next twenty years. He says it's impossible to starve there, and no clothes, no people, and no trouble to live on nothing a year. He's got a brand-new wife, and that may be the cause of his joy. But he's writing on two books, and getting a lot done, he says.

Let me hear from you -- Best wishes -- Sincerely
Erskine

To Milton A. Abernethy:
[HRC.tls]   Mount Vernon, Maine
                                            November 8th 1932

Dear Milton:

I wish to God I were capable of writing the piece on the brotherhood of southern authors, but I know my limitations. Why can't you do it? You know more about their situation than perhaps anyone else, and you can express yourself; no one else can possibly do more. I wish you would write it. As for other suggestions, I am at a loss. The best critical mind, in my judgement, in American today is Matthew Josephson (care of Harcourt Brace.) Whether he could or would do the piece, I do not know. He is not a Southerner (maybe he shouldn't be for this article), and he may not know the situation; but on the other hand he is not tied up with a group (except Communism, which has nothing to do with the case), and he does know his social values from a to z. The only other man who comes to mind is Stringfellow Barr (ed. Virginia Quarterly); Barr, unfortunately, is tied up with the brotherhood (to what extent I don't know); and yet he is a violent enemy of the Nashville school.[105] We might see a good dog

---

eration. It was read by six people,—including those who necessarily consider more the business side of such questions, and who, in normal times would not have read it.— The sales of 'American Earth' and 'Tobacco Road' were against it. The fact is that this depression compels a scrutiny of manuscripts from the practical point of view such as never was before required, and it is very hard when confronted by the figures to resist the practical arguments. I cant tell you how sorry I am" (Perkins to EC, PRI 6-18-32).

[105] *The Nashville Fugitives had published their traditionalist manifesto* I'll Take My Stand: The South and the Agrarian Tradition *two years earlier, in 1930, with the contributors identified collectively, generically, as Twelve Southerners: John Crowe Ransom, Donald Davidson, Frank*

fight, in such a case, anyway. Of the two, Josephson is the better critic; Barr the better informed. With some outside help and information, Josephson would do wonders with the article.[106]

I was surprised to hear you say that about [William] Faulkner. I thought surely you had more respect for him. That's why I had not mentioned him. I can't see his short stories, not with a telescope. I read only one book, "As I Lay Dying", and that I believe is his best one. It's a good piece of work. I could not bring myself to read any of the other novels. I don't know why. I just didn't care for the scarehead ballyhoo, for one thing. . . .

I have word from New York that there is a report in circulation that I am "writing too much." What do you think? This is my ninth year; the total is 35 stories, two novelettes, and three novels. What's wrong with that? It sounds pretty lean to me. I fear the late unpleasantness on the east side of the street in midtown (NYC) has hatched a lot of eggs with a rank odor. I'm not calling names, but you know who I mean. Several have told me that they would try any means to save their face.[107] I'm willing to stand or fall on the work I do; I do not offer excuses for myself, and I don't care for the other fellows' either.

Best wishes ---

Sincerely,
Erskine

L. Owsley, John Gould Fletcher, Lyle H. Lanier, Allen Tate, Herman Clarence Nixon, Andrew Nelson Lytle, Robert Penn Warren, John Donald Wade, Henry Blue Kline, and Stark Young.

[106] *Josephson admired Caldwell and, in an essay soon to be published in Barr's* Virginia Quarterly, *praised him as "a younger, perhaps more naturally gifted, though less turbulent writer than Faulkner"—"a cool craftsman, thoroughly aware of his materials, imbued with a devastating sense of humor" ("The Younger Generation: Its Young Novelists," 9 [1933], pp. 251, 253). This was perhaps an intentional rebuttal of James Southall Wilson's statement about Caldwell in the pages of that journal, in a review of* Tobacco Road *and other new Southern fiction the previous year: "[Tobacco Road] has neither the surprising experimentation of Faulkner's studies in degeneration to recommend it, nor the shocking fullness of detail of naturalism. There is nothing that I can honestly find to commend about this book except a sort of drab sincerity of narration which suggests that the author might tell a really significant life story, if he knows one, with the powerful restraint of unemotional honesty" ("Back-Country Novels," 8 [1932], p. 470).*

[107] *A reference to Caldwell's recent separation from Scribners.*

In this unusually spirited letter, a response to the first issue of *The Lion & Crown*, the ellipses are all Caldwell's.

To James Leippert:

[CHI.tls] Mount Vernon, Maine
November 15th 1932

Dear Leippert:

Congratulations on a fine magazine. It is far better, in material and format, than I have been accustomed to look for. I hope it gets around.

There's not much I feel capable of saying. The opening essay is perhaps the best piece in the issue.[108] I say that because I enjoyed it the most. The two pieces of fiction are rather sketchy -- I believe there are two. Unless one can get down under the skin of life in the first two or three sentences in such a short piece, the rest is difficult. Not words words words make creation, but a feeling other than the writing of them. Another way of saying it: unselfconsciousness. The closer we get to that state, the nearer we are to pure creation. But I am not a critic, so why should I go on?

The poetry. . . . What is poetry? I feel very much about the present day poetry as Barzun does about the "new" biography. There is something about it that puzzles me. We have got away from the tight form of the past, which is very very good; but what have we got now? Is it better than the old? Can it go further? Will it be bound to earth by reason of its form and not be capable of rising into a more rarified plane? Art is a pixie . . . a will o' the wisp . . . a mirage . . . we never quite touch it, and for that reason it cannot be studied. But shouldn't art . . . creation . . . poetry . . . fiction give us a feeling of the godhead, of supernatural strength; shouldn't it swell our muscles? A poem (to me) should grip its fist, bare its arm, and slowly swell the bicep to the hardness of oak . . . and then to "show-off", to prove, to demonstrate, strike someone in the chest with the power of that muscle. All these poems now, since the days of "free verse", have been promising something. But the promise has not been fulfilled. Is it to be true that all these poets, the army of a promised creation, to be merely poet's poets? I am not a poet. But no one is writing poetry for me. Poets are writing poetry for poets. They understand, they feel, they comprehend . . . but what of us who are not poets by nature? Where are we to get our poetry? Will we be forced to go back to the 19th, 18th, and 17th centuries for poetry "for us"? The today's poets of the mind, the brain ("the fingers of my brain") are writing poetry for poets of the mind and the brain. I have no brain . . . I am not wise,

---

[108] *"The 'New' Biography," by Jacques Barzun.*

smart, bright, sharp, brainy . . . but I do have an emotion that every man has, and every woman. I can feel with that when my head is asleep. Can't we have poetry like a strong masculine pile of stone, mighty in strength, beautiful in design, and towering in height? Art in everything is art still. Buildings, music, writing, painting, . . . are art. Why not poetry? Why not give us poetry like we search for beauty? In a woman, in a scene, in a sound? Half the population of the world can feel beauty in woman . . . why cannot most of us feel it in poetry? For one thing, there is no beauty there in 1932.

This is no criticism of the poems in The Lion & Crown. They are perhaps better than you will find in a week's reading. I am speaking of "poetry". I've got that against it. And the reason I have that against poetry, is that it does not move me. Why should I sit through a play, or read through a novel, that bores me? There is too much else to do, for me to sit through such as those. I can stand on a street corner and feel the beauty in a woman, or lean against a building and feel its beauty, rather than be bored stiff by poetry of the brain ("the fingers of my brain"). What I must have is that swelling of the muscles, the quickening of the heart, the shortness of breath, that comes from feeling beauty . . . art.

I'm 'way off the track. What I meant to say was that "new" poetry ("the fingers of my brain" school) leaves me cold. The idea seems to exist in these poet's poets that men and women are emotionless; the fact is, men and women have brains only by courtesy. We are not gods, which poets take us to be; they should make us <u>feel</u> like gods, and for that reason they will have to stop being gods themselves. Only a man can understand man.

Forgive all this. I'm sorry I went off like that. . . .

All in all, the first number of The Lion & Crown is about the best of any magazine I've seen. The printing is very very fine, and the editing is all that could be desired. I hope it will be possible for you to continue without the shadow of debt hanging over you. I'll talk it up whenever I have a chance.

Best wishes, and with hopes for success,
                          Sincerely,
                          Caldwell

To Milton A. Abernethy:

[HRC.tls] Mount Vernon, Maine
November 27th 1932

Dear Milton:

Many thanks for the new number of CONTEMPO. How do you do it? It's one damn fine magazine. Many thanks for the ad.[109] I hope it sells us out, and with the proceeds we may be able to do another one soon, cheaper however (in manufacture).

Viking is publishing "God's Little Acre" about the middle of February, I hear. The galleys should be ready any week now, and I hope you will write (Marshall A Best, or [George] Oppenheimer) for a set. If you do review it, for God's sake get a better man than Henry Hart proved to be.[110] I don't know whom to suggest, but you will know of course. Since the thing is Southern, perhaps someone familiar with Georgia and the Carolinas; since the thing is somewhat revolutionary (cotton mill strike), perhaps someone like Mike Gold. But I do believe a man of the South will understand it better than even Gold. After all, it is not a revolutionary novel so much as it is a book about the people, and myself.

[F. Wright] Moxley's piece is the finest in the new issue (don't you think?) -- and Flannagan's the worst. God, how I hate that Richmond-Charleston school! Flannagan had the disadvantage of reviewing Ellen Glasgow's book, and that lets him out somewhat; but just the same the attitude he takes is enough to puke a cat.[111]

Whit Burnett is coming to this country in a week or so. I hope I can see him. I was in NY last week, and I won't be able to get away again for a while, but if possible I am going to try to see him. He runs a damn fine magazine in STORY.

Best wishes --- and drop a line ---

Sincerely,
Erskine

---

[109] *A boxed ad for the pamphlet* Mama's Little Girl—*wrongly titled* Mama's Little Daughter—*appeared in the 15 December 1932 issue of* Contempo, *which was mailed at the end of November.*

[110] *Hart's review of* American Earth *and* Tobacco Road *had appeared a few months earlier ("A New Star in the Firmament,"* Contempo *[15 June 1933], pp. 1, 2). Caldwell's criticism is curious, since Hart had only praise for him, particularly* Tobacco Road, *which he called a "short and perfectly integrated novel [that] reveals ... a really remarkable talent for authenticity" (p. 1).*

[111] *In the new issue, Moxley sharply criticized Abbe Dimnet's new guidebook for good living,* What We Live By *("I'm So Tired of Saviors, or The Salad and the Savant,"* Contempo *[15 Dec. 1932], pp. 1, 2). In an effusive review of* The Sheltered Life, *Roy Flannagan called Glasgow "a skillful storyteller" with a mature "social vision," "[t]he first able novelist to see the*

Caldwell's encouragement of Alfred Morang is always interesting for what it reveals about himself, particularly his understanding of the challenges and responsibilities of the writer. Caldwell regularly recommended Morang's work to editors who had printed his own stories, including William Carlos Williams and Milton Abernethy.

To Alfred Morang:

[HAR.tls] Mount Vernon, Maine
December 1st 1932

Dear Alfred:

Good news -- damn good! William Carlos Williams writes: "The Morang stories hit me right; I'll take the longer one (<u>Rust in Spring</u>) for CONTACT #4." I can't recall stories by their titles, and consequently I don't know if that is the right title. But, what the hell! he's taking <u>a</u> story, and what more could we ask? He returned the shorter one, which I am keeping for you. We'll do something with it and one or two other good ones when we can find a good place to send it.

I don't know about you, but I'm damn highly pleased. For one thing, you're lucky to batter down two inner doors of the sanctum sanctoriums right off the bat. But don't misunderstand me: I don't mean lucky to be printed, but lucky to get past the prejudice that always stands in front of a new writer. Most editors (and I do myself) are antagonistic towards first work. This shows, and shows conclusively, that you are writing good stuff. But don't get swell-headed (I mean this in fun) and go up-stage, or I'll have to remind you that I did some tall talking about you. That's silly; but I hate to see anybody get like Skolfield[112] and several others I know. Hell, genius is 90% hard work. A man's native ability is pretty small, and only hard work brings it above the common, or garden-variety of writing. But you have every right to feel proud of your work; and don't let anybody tell you different. This is something like it! I myself feel damn good over it! Don't cheat yourself of that pleasure.

About the pamphlet: if you have decided to carry it through, don't you think we should change all the '32 dates to 1933? For this reason: During the Xmas rush it would be hard to sell them to dealers, and if we wait until that's over, we'll have something new for a new year. Even if it gets ready within a week or two, I believe we should put the 1933 dates on copyright notice and title page; we can solicit orders in advance, and ship the pamphlets out for publication Jan 1st. What do you think?

---

realities of a recently Yankeefied south" ("The Yankeefied South," Contempo [15 Dec. 1932], pp. 1, 5).
[112]*Probably Raymond White Skolfield, a minor painter and lithographer who was born and lived much of his life in Portland, Maine.*

When are you and Dorothy coming up? How about coming up for a week or so at Christmas? We'll be damn glad to have you, such as it is. Could you put up with Russian plumbing? (We've had to cut the water off for the winter). Or better still, come up next week or later, and again for Christmas. . . .

I hope you are as well pleased over Williams' note as I am. You've made a damn fine start.

Best wishes -- and try to get up --

Sincerely
Erskine . . .

To Richard Johns:

[DEL.tls]   Mount Vernon, Maine
                                                  December 5th 1932

Dear Johns:

I'm damn glad to hear a new number of PAGANY is coming this month, and that more are to follow. Best of luck!

Here's a story submitted.

If you can come to a decision shortly, I'd be pleased. MEDDLESOME JACK is included in the script of a new collection of short stories I've just got ready, and if the piece is any good, I'd like to get it published before the book comes out -- if and when, of course. The book won't be published before next summer or fall, but I'd like to get this story a home before itt's too late. I haven't fully decided on a title for the collection, but I'll let you know.[113]

Perhaps you do know that The Viking Press is publishing a new novel about the middle of February. It's called: GOD'S LITTLE ACRE, and it follows TOBACCO ROAD in many respects, but a damn sight better. I'd like to send you a copy of it when the advance printing is ready.

I was glad to see your story reprinted in THE BEST SHORT SHORTS. It's a shame Putnams' and Anderson couldn't have chosen a less vulgar title.[114] Maybe nobody else dislikes "short short" as I do; I think it's a rotten term. My own preference is "brief story". What do you think?

What do you think of [Edward] Dahlberg's new book? I've just

---

[113] *The collection would be called* We Are the Living: Brief Stories by Erskine Caldwell, *published by Viking the next year. "Meddlesome Jack" appeared for the first time in that book.*

[114] *Paul Ernest Anderson and Lionel White, eds.,* The Best Short Shorts of 1932 *(Putnam, 1932).*

finished reading it for NEW MASSES (don't know if they'll print the review though), and it struck me like a ton of brick.[115]

Best wishes --

Sincerely,
Caldwell

To Alfred Morang:

[HAR.tls] Mount Vernon, Maine
December 15th 1932

Dear Alfred: Your two letters at hand. First of all, however: Samuel Putnam writes that he did not receive the story we sent The New Review last summer.[116] He says he's searched for it everywhere, but can't find it in the office. He's sorry, but that doesn't help much. Do you have another copy of the story? I hope you have. Bring everything you have ready when you come up and we'll send them out....

Whit Burnett is in this country now for a few weeks; he thought he and Martha Foley might get up, but now he writes that they can't make it. He's trying to make some arrangements to distribute STORY more nationally. I hope he succeeds. He didn't mention your stories this time, but I'll jog him up next time I write.

Williams is quitting CONTACT after issue #4.[117] Did I tell you? He didn't mention the future of the mag, so probably there'll be a new editor. Maybe [Robert] McAlmon. Ford God's sake!

PAGANY is coming out this month. So I hear. And it will continue through 1933. So I hear, also. I haven't heard from Johns, but we'll send him some stories, and then go down and break his neck if he loses them, as he did one of mine.

Viking asked for suggestions for a jacket; wish to God you had been here to draw up some sketches for the book. If you had had the script it would have been different; an artist can't do anything with a script he hasn't read, though. That's why I didn't call on you.

I've had three stories this week from would-be authors; God, what awful stuff. None of them knows how to tell a story. And that's what fiction is. Story-telling. Anderson knows. That's why he's the best writer in America. He's a story-teller.[118] What else is there to matter.

---

[115] *Caldwell called* From Flushing to Calvary *(Harcourt, 1932) "one of the best books I have ever read" (EC to Morang, HAR 11-26-32). His review was published as "Ripe for Revolution," New Masses (Dec. 1932), pp. 26–27.*

[116] *One of the many stories that Caldwell tried to help Morang place.*

[117] *A fourth issue was prepared but never published.*

[118] *Sherwood Anderson was the one writer Caldwell would freely acknowledge as an*

The best story-teller is he who tells his tale the most convincingly and beautifully. That's why God made words. Words are to tell stories with. They are delicate; we ought to handle them with the love and care a mother does her baby. . . .

        Sincerely,
        Erskine

To James Leippert:
[CHI.tls]   Mount Vernon, Maine
            December 31st 1932

Dear Leippert: --

  I'm afraid I must decline the honor you so gravely confer upon me. There are several reasons why I feel that I can not accept an associate editorship; but I assure you than I appreciate your having thought of me. Really, I believe that Morang should be the down-East representative, and both of us down here would be just too much. I hope you will consider him. I commend him to you.

  If you must have a specific reason: it seems to me that the true function of a writer is, simply, to write. I take myself so seriously that I would no more think of trying to criticise than I would think of attempting to pass myself off as -- well, an actor. If I have made myself clear, you will readily understand why I must decline. To me, at least, it is an important reason.

  I am looking forward to the pamphlet series.[119] Morang tells me that he has forwarded you estimates he got from a local printer; they seem reasonable to me, as little as I know about such things. Do let me know your plans for the series; the pamphlet form has always interested me, and your selections will be without a doubt very fine.

---

influence. As he said of Anderson in a 1967 interview, "I admired the way he could write a short story and get the feeling of life into it. Not so much what he wrote about but just the way he did it. I've always admired Anderson for that" (Alan Lelchuk and Robin White, "An Interview with Erskine Caldwell," Conversations with Erskine Caldwell, *ed. Edwin T. Arnold [Jackson: UP of Mississippi, 1988] p. 92). Collection hereafter cited as Arnold,* Conversations.

  Caldwell was more explicit in his admiration during a 1980 interview for the Georgia Review: *"In those days [the 1930s] there were plenty of novels in existence but very few good short stories. What interested me about Sherwood Anderson were his short stories. I liked the brevity. I liked the way he presented his people. His style was lean. It was not cluttered up with superfluous adjectives and unnecessary paragraphs" (Elizabeth Pell Broadwell and Ronald Wesley Hoag, "'A Writer First': An Interview with Erskine Caldwell," Arnold,* Conversations, *pp. 198–199).*

  [119]*Leippert, Caldwell, and Morang were planning a pamphlet series to be issued with the imprint "Caldwell & Leippert" and to be distributed through* The Lion and Crown. *The series never made it beyond some elaborate planning.*

You should have received our second one by now. It may also be the last one. . . .

Best wishes -- and do let me hear from you,
Sincerely
Erskine

When Viking published *God's Little Acre* in January 1933, Caldwell was disturbed by criticisms of the novel he would later describe as "the most satisfying experience I had had since I first began writing."[120] While visiting his parents in Georgia, Caldwell and Helen had made an excursion down to Florida to visit Gordon Lewis and his wife, Ruth.

To Gordon Lewis:

[VIR.tls] Wrens, Georgia
February 6th 1933

Dear Gordon:

Back, and sorry we're not at Indian Rocks with you and Ruth. It was a week I'll talk about the rest of my life, and I owe it all to you. I hope we can make your and Ruth's stay in Maine as pleasant as you made ours in Florida.

There's plenty of sunshine here, but it's as cold as the devil. Temperature, low, last night: 28. That's one reason why we wish we were back on the island.

I suppose you saw the review in The [New York] Times; not so much worse than [the New York Herald Tribune] Books', but still far from the mark according to how I see it.[121] I realize now how imperfect the novel is, and it sets me a-burning to do the next one better. The next time I'll not make the theme as prominent as a wart on the end of your nose -- I'll make it a boil under the seat of your pants. That'll make them stand up.

We had a wonderful reception here. I was confronted by a cold check for seven-fifty somebody had given Helen. Aint it fun?

I'm expecting great things of you. Send Maxim Lieber, 545 Fifth Avenue, NYC, some stories; he'll do right by you, I can assure you. And when you get the novel done, I hope to get a chance to read it. I like to think I could give some helpful criticism.

---

[120]*Experience, p. 130.*

[121]*In his review for the Times, Louis Kronenberger remarked, "The whole situation on the Waldens' farm reads like an elaborate off-color story skillfully combined with an enlarged comic strip"([5 Feb. 1933], p. 6). The same day, Horace Gregory complained in the* Herald Tribune, *"Mid-way through his story Caldwell shifts from violent, roaring humor to equally violent melodrama. The transition is too rapid, and in the turn-over, several of the characters lose something of their original vitality" ([5 Feb. 1933], p. 8).*

Let us know the way of the world with you. And accept our heart felt thanks for a week to remember you by.

Best wishes—to you and to Ruth,

Sincerely,
Erskine . . .

To Milton A. Abernethy:

[HRC.tls] Wrens, Georgia
February 13th 1933

Dear Abernethy:

Your note enclosing [Bennett] Cerf's review reached me today, and I'm hurrying to return it by the next mail, afraid it has been held up too long in transit.[122]

No, I haven't an answer to it. Why should I? The man may be entirely right in everything he says. Who knows? So let him say it. Of course I could defend myself and the book, but after all, I wrote the book and it will have to speak for me. However, the idea Cerf's review propounds seems to me to be wholly wrong. I couldn't expect to please everyone, and I did not set out to please anyone but myself in the beginning. I maintain, though, that he did not "get" the novel. And as for the pamphlets he objects to: he has the wrong idea there, too. We got them printed merely for the fun of it, not trying to sell them. In fact, of the first one, we gave away a total of sixty out of 75 even before we ofered any for sale. Maybe Cerf dislikes the idea of our giving them away.

I think Cerf would get a new set of ideas of life if he would form his impressions first-hand. No man can understand another man by reading about him. And as for there being no such people as the characters—if they are not convincing, let him say so. I've never been to the other side of the earth, but I do know one can get there by going in either direction.

Tell Cerf I am ashamed of the two noveletts[123]; but I am also

---

[122]*Abernethy sent Cerf's review of* God's Little Acre *for Caldwell's response. Cerf complained that the characters seemed more like "a foreign species" than recognizable human beings and that the novel repeated too much of the material of* Tobacco Road. *"For the man who has read both," he wrote, "there are too many striking parallels and too many unescapable duplications in characterization to further any original impression that Caldwell is a real man to watch for important contributions to American literature." Cerf also chastised Caldwell for the "petty business" of printing the pamphlets Caldwell had so often asked Abernethy to help him advertise: "unimportant little stories in overpriced and unlovely editions designed solely to gull . . . collectors." The review and Caldwell's response, excerpted from this letter, appeared in the 15 March 1933 issue of* Contempo *(pp. 1, 4).*

[123]The Bastard *and* Poor Fool, *which Cerf labeled "inexcusable junk" (p. 4).*

ashamed of "Tobacco Rd" now, and if I'm not ashamed of "G's L A" inside of six months, I'll never be able to write another book.
Best wishes ---
                              Sincerely,
                              Erskine . . .

Caldwell met the poet and translator I. L. Salomon in New York, perhaps when he was there the previous spring dickering over the *Autumn Hill* manuscript with Scribner's. Caldwell appreciated Salomon's interest in his work and solicited his opinion about the recently published *God's Little Acre*.

                    To I. L. Salomon:
[LOC.tls—postcard]   [Mount Vernon, Maine]
                                [February 20, 1933]
Dear Salomon:
   I don't know why I didn't get your note recently. I've been away from Maine for several weeks, but there shouldn't have been any trouble on that score. Anyway, I hope to get a chance to see you next time I'm in town. I don't know what the final verdict on the book will be; it all seems to be scrambled egg right now. I still have hopes of some day seeing the theme come out on top. Just now, the air is full of dust, and it seems to have got into everybody's eyes. What do you think?
   Best wishes --
                              Sincerely,
                              Caldwell

                    To Milton A. Abernethy:
[HRC.tls—postcard]   [Mount Vernon, Maine]
                                February 26th 1933
Dear Milton Abernethy:
   Sorry as I can be that I had to come back without seeing you. This makes the howmanyth time I've failed to show up in Chapel Hill? What do you say to my coming South for keeps, and not being able ever again to accept your bid? I wish I could; and, if/and when I get a place to live, I am coming back to stay (a while). The only review so far (out of the hundred I've seen) that gets what I drove at

in G's L A was [William] Soskin's review in NY Eve Post.[124] All the others missed the point entirely (or else they were afraid to mention it (which may have a lot to do with it). Cerf certainly missed it by a mile. . . .

>   My best,
>   Erskine

[VIR.tls]

To Gordon Lewis:

Mount Vernon, Maine
February 26th 1933

Dear Gordon:

We are back home again, and wishing we were still down with you and Ruth. In order to make it more emphatic: 14 inches of crusted snow on the ground; temperature at mid-day of 19 degrees, and only God knows to what depths it sinks after mid-night.

I am continually wondering if you have read the book yet, and constantly cursing myself like the dog I am for not having presented you with a virgin copy. It was inexcusable, as I see it now; I don't know how I can ever make up for it. Probably I can't. Anyway, I'm going to send you a copy from England (when and if they arrive), and I'd appreciate it if you would sling it into the Gulf, or else wipe your razor blade on the leaves one by one.

Now that Mister Gordon of the Sat Eve Post has made mention of God's Little Acre, I have no come-back.[125] You win. And whether or no that had anything to do with it, the thing has sold out the first edition and the second printing is now on press. You will be able to

---

[124] *Soskin commented that* God's Little Acre *contains "some of the best peasants and most lush and sluttish nymphs [Caldwell] has ever created. To me they seem more closely related to the Thomas Benton portrayals in pigment of rural America than to any literary creation. But back of all their comedy and back of their hilarious antics one senses an essentially ominous note. The farmer ... who has spent some fifteen years digging for gold on his property and devoting his and his sons' energies to making large holes and many heaps of dirt is something more than a clown. He is something like the [D. H.] Lawrence hero who puts the hard, self-seeking, commercial world behind him and goes off on dark exploits. Lawrence makes a subconscious crusade of it. Caldwell keeps his farmer on the ground digging only to satisfy his 'gold fever,' using his farm not for profit or for the immediate, practical advantages, but to satisfy his own emotional urge that will not be denied" ("Gold and Nymphs in Georgia," New York* Evening Post *[11 Feb. 1933], p. 7).*

[125] *Proclaiming Caldwell and Faulkner the founders of "a corn-likker classic school of fiction," Donald Gordon described* God's Little Acre *as "a drama of human animals shown more than ordinarily in the raw" ("The Literary Lowbrow: Who Reads for Amusement,"* Saturday Evening Post *[18 Feb. 1933], p. 61.)*

distinguish between them by looking at the title page. The first is printed in a reddish brown ink; the second will be a different color. If you ever do read the thing, I'd appreciate hearing what you have against it. I'm that way; I'd much rather hear what you dislike about it.

Again in Charlottesville I saw C C [Wertenbaker], but there is nothing more to be said. He was as abstract as usual, if not more so. He moans that he can't sell books because he hasn't any to sell and he hasn't any because he can't buy any and he can't buy any because he hasn't any credit. That's the cycle as I heard it over and over. He confided in me that he's engaged in doing a little scribbling on the side, evenings. Another bum for the breadlines. . . .

Write me a letter and say how your work in progress is shaping out. I'm deeply interested, even if I do appear casual. . . .

Sincerely,
Erskine . . .

To I. L. Salomon:

[LOC.tls—postcard] [Mount Vernon, Maine]
[March 10, 1933]

Dear Salomon:

I've been in New York a few days, and got back yesterday to find your letter. I wished to look you up, but had forgotten your address. I'm surprised, and pleased, to hear that anyone really "got" the novel. You are one of millions; I don't believe anyone else understands it as you do. It would be interesting to find out from others who have read it if they got what you did. I'm in a difficult position, and I can't go around asking people if they understood so-and-so. If you get the opportunity, I'd like to hear about it. That's what the book is, of course; the story of digging for gold is merely the web the spider spun to snare the innocent. And how many were snared! . . .[126]

Sincerely,
Caldwell

---

[126] *Caldwell used the same metaphor in a postcard to Milton Abernethy three weeks earlier: "I hope someone who reviews the book finds out what it is all about. Some of the reviewers (all I have seen) say the book is about some people who dig for gold. Which it isn't. The novel is about something else; the thing about digging for gold is merely the web the spider spun to snare the innocents. I hope you weren't taken in by the reviews before you read the book" (EC to Abernethy, HRC 2-11-33).*

With the exception of his willingness to monitor Alfred Morang's work, Caldwell always "disliked"—and was very uncomfortable—offering advice to other writers. Nonetheless, he repaid what he saw as Salomon's real attentiveness to *God's Little Acre* by agreeing to comment on a story Salomon was trying to place.

To I. L. Salomon:

[LOC.tls] Mount Vernon, Maine
March 26th 1933

Dear Salomon:
    First of all let's say this about the story --
    I dislike to say that I think this piece is good, that one rotten. Because no one may be able to judge thusly; no one man, that is. TRACKWALKER, I should say, as frankly to you as though I were judging one of my own stories, is perhaps too obvious in its whole. By that I mean the story's point or conclusion is in the bag, so to speak, from the start. See what I'm driving at? I have no fault to find with the conception, the writing, or the story-telling. All of that, I believe sincerely, is fine. The one exception is, as I said above, that the story is far too obvious. You may not think so; then well and good. For you, after all, know more clearly exactly what you are driving at than any one reader can ever comprehend. But if you care for my criticism, I'm pleased; if you don't, I'm no less pleased. But I would like to say that I think you're a damn fine writer. Your story in PAGANY will be with me as long as I live.[127] I can't say as much for any other piece I read in that mag. Please keep it up. . . .
    There's nothing much I can do about the novel now. I did my damnedest in the writing of it. What peeves me right now is the way so many readers and reviewers went blah-blah about what they said was comedy, and not a word about the theme of the book. Christ! Can't they read? Or after reading are they afraid to report what the thing is really concerned? Soskin was the only one who approached the idea, and he backed off immediately, long before he expressed himself.[128] The others were merely blah-blah. Why don't you turn critic? I'll write the first book for you to examine. A promise! . . .
Sincerely,
Caldwell

---

[127] *"Moon Awareness," in the Winter 1932 issue.*
[128] *See note, EC to Abernethy 2-26-33.*

Caldwell met *New Masses* editor Mike Gold in 1931 at a cocktail party hosted in New York by The Macaulay Company, publishers of *The American Caravan*. At the same party, Caldwell, who had just completed a draft of *Tobacco Road*, also met Max Lieber and other notables such as Robert Cantwell, Lewis Mumford, Georgia O'Keefe, Edmund Wilson, and, as he pointed out in both his autobiographies, Mae West. Caldwell would always deny any active participation in "politics," attributing his associations with Gold and other prominent Communists to his natural involvement in "the atmosphere of the time."[129] He would, however, admit the social interest of some of his fiction, as this letter suggests.[130]

To Mike Gold:

[CU2.tls]　　　　　　　　　　　　　　　　　　Mount Vernon, Maine
　　　　　　　　　　　　　　　　　　　　　　　April 11th 1933

Dear Mike:

I saw a copy of Saturday's World-Telegram today, and read what [Harry] Hansen had to say regarding your comments on [Albert] Halper's book.[131] I hope to get a copy of New Masses soon and read all you said. Hansen was pretty feeble in his come-back.

I don't know the author in question, although I once met him; neither have I read the book (I have seen a copy somebody sent), but I talked with him that one time for several minutes. He more or less informed me that everyone below 14th Street was sour on the world because they weren't in the money, and that as soon as they could make a killing, they would grab the first northbound subway. He said he had felt that way, too, before he started making some money with his book. I did not argue the point with him then, because I saw that he had deserted the revolutionary movement.

What I am trying to say is that the report Hansen gave of your

---

[129] Jac Tharpe, "Interview with Erskine Caldwell," Arnold, *Conversations*, p. 138.

[130] *In a 1968 interview Caldwell told Jack McClintock: "My interests are in social-economic subjects. Those are the basics of life. Politics spring from that. I'm not a political person, and you don't have to be a Democrat or a Republican to be interested in the basics of life. You're going to find flaws—because they're there. So that's a protest right there. But as far as agitating is concerned, no. I let the material speak for itself" ("Erskine Caldwell: Down South Storyteller," Arnold,* Conversations, *p. 107).*

[131] *In his daily column, Hansen quoted Gold's remark that Halper's new novel,* Union Square *(Viking, 1932), seemed clearly the work of one of the new "'generation of careerists [who] will drift in and out of the revolution, remaining long enough to acquire a certain verisimilitude for their anti-revolutionary yarns.'" Reviewing the book in the most recent* New Masses, *Gold had continued, "'Mr. Halper's book is the book of one who has no real social passion. The characters are stock figures of Hollywood and Bohemia. Not a worker in the novel. Not a person who suffers as the masses suffer today. Not one bitter cry of rage against capitalism!'" Hansen observed, "Mr. Gold's comment is along the lines of the Marxian rule that reporting is not enough," and seemed pleased to note that the same* New Masses *contained a piece in which "Granville Hicks severely rebukes Harry Hansen. Mr. Hansen feels very meek in consequence and realizes what will happen to him if Mr. Hicks ever becomes commissar of literature" ("Book Marks for Today," New York* World-Telegram *[8 April 1933], p. 19).*

criticism fits in exactly with my impression of Halper as a member of the movement. In other words, your criticism of the book conforms to my impression of him personally. I'll know more accurately of course, when I read your review. In any event, I know one of us is right; undoubtedly we both are.

Revolution needs numbers; there is no question about that. But it is also important that the members of the revolutionary movement be whole-heartedly supporting. The guts of the loyal ones will see that the flag is carried high; the falling out of the Halper's and the Harrisons [Hansens?] is nothing more than the shucking of coats by the movement.

My own work so far has been slow to reach what I am striving for. What I am trying to do is to work upward from the surface, and I may never reach the status of a revolutionary writer. If that is to be the case, the fault will be mine and not the material. Because if I know my material, there is a revolution in the whites and blacks of Georgia. The trouble I find (which I try to show in what I write) is that the masses have been damn near killed by the lack of education and by starvation. The two forces together make a situation where protest against hunger and mistreatment is without a voice. A Negro in Georgia is lucky if he can attend the four-month school for four or five years; he is exceptional if he learns to read and write in that time. The white is hardly better off; he usually learns to read and write, but he has been given no incentive. In most cses the illiterate teachers kill the native incentive. The need, for both peoples, before there can be an audible voice of protest, is instruction. There are millions in Georgia (four out of five or six) who think that hunger, illiteracy, cruelty, and oppression are the natural laws of nature.

Best wishes --

                     Sincerely,
                     Erskine

Censorship troubles with *God's Little Acre* emerged when John S. Sumner, secretary and attorney for the New York Society for the Suppression of Vice, brought charges of obscenity against Caldwell and Viking Press, arguing that "the sale of the book is a violation of section 1141 of the Penal Law and that the book is, within the meaning of that statute, 'obscene, lewd, lascivious, filthy, indecent or disgusting.'"[132]

---

[132] *"People v. Viking Press, et al.,"* Rpt. in MacDonald, Critical Essays, p. 28. The charges were filed in Manhattan on 2 May 1933.

To Milton K. Abernethy:

[HRC.tls] Mount Vernon, Maine
April 15th 1933

Dear Milton:

No doubt you know by now of the death a few days ago of Kathleen Tankersley Young Ellinger in Torreon, Mexico. It is always sad of course to lose a friend, but aside from that she was, for a woman, no mean poet. What I have now to say is that you might be inclined to consider my suggestion that several of her poems be printed at an early date. You may not care for the idea; I am merely making the suggestion. . . .[133]

The new book is having Sumner trouble, as you have perhaps heard. The preliminary hearing takes place Tuesday, and the trial will undoubtedly come upon its heels. I am enclosing a copy of a sheet Marshall Best sent me.[134]

We have been looking for a new issue of Contempo. Try not to with-hold it any longer.

Best wishes --

Sincerely,
Erskine

To Milton A. Abernethy:

[HRC.tls] Mount Vernon, Maine
April 26th 1933

Dear Milton:

I'm starved for a damn good "Southern" novel, and I'd like to write a few notes upon it in exchange for reading. But none of your goddam Hervey Allens, DuBose Heywards, [Ellen] Glasgows, [James Branch] Cabells, etc. I swear I'll ship it back to you via freight collect if it's by one of those sires. I'd rather not undertake [Sherwood] Anderson's, for many reasons, no single one of which is strong enough --- I'd just rather not. If [Robert] Cantwell's book gets out, I

---

[133] *A friend of Caldwell's, Kathleen Tankersley Young was the editor of* Modern Editions Press *and contributed poetry and fiction to such little magazines as* Blues *and the* Hound & Horn; *her poetry was collected in two notable volumes,* Ten Poems *(Parnassus Press, 1930) and* The Dark Land *(Dragon Press, 1932). Her work had appeared previously in* Contempo, *but Abernethy did not acknowledge her untimely death in its pages. Helen Caldwell apparently suspected her husband of having an affair with Young (see EC to Helen Caldwell, undated [late June/early July] 1933).*

[134] *Missing.*

wouldn't object to it, either.¹³⁵ But, aren't there good writers in the So Atlantic? When I read a book to comment on, it must be a novel, (sometime stories), American, conscious artistry, economic (or social) necessity, creative experience, and that's all. But that's enough -- more than I find in a book three or four times yearly.

The preliminary trial was postponed till May 2nd. As far as I know, down here down east, it's a toss-up between Sumner and us. I've been assured he can't win his case, but I'm pessimistic. . . .

If you ever wish a good critic to take a book apart and put it together again, ring up Matthew Josephson. Jesus christ, the fellow has got a mind like God Himself.

I haven't written a story in six months. This damn novel takes the blood out of me.¹³⁶

Sincerely,
Erskine

Like many of his Depression-era contemporaries, Caldwell spent time, off and on, as a contract writer for Hollywood. His first job was for Metro-Goldwyn-Mayer, a three-month deal at the fantastic salary of $250 per week, replacing William Faulkner as screenwriter for a movie being made in Louisiana, *Bride of the Bayou*.¹³⁷ Caldwell would always be disturbed by the need to seek out such work, but he did so "for the sake of my family welfare." As his letters reveal, the M-G-M work induced nearly as many strains—personal as well as professional— as it alleviated.¹³⁸

---

[135] *Anderson's new book contained the stories that many critics now regard as his last truly exceptional work,* Death in the Woods, and Other Stories *(Liveright, 1933). Cantwell's new novel,* Land of Plenty *(Farrar, 1934), concerning a Western lumber mill strike, would not appear until the following year, by which time* Contempo *had ceased publication.*

[136] *Caldwell was drafting* Journeyman.

[137] *In an earlier letter Caldwell had told Helen that he had been hired to replace Faulkner, who was to be fired because he "wouldn't work." "Faulkner was to write the dialogue, but he stays drunk most of the time," Caldwell wrote, and "the producers don't like him" (EC to Helen Caldwell, DAR "Saturday" [May] 1933). Eventually the title of the film was changed to* Lazy River *(1934).*

[138] With All My Might *(Atlanta: Peachtree, 1987), p. 133. Hereafter cited as* Might. *Several sources have been particularly useful for annotating the letters Caldwell wrote during the periods he worked in Hollywood: David Quinlan, ed.,* The Film Lover's Companion *(Secaucus, NJ: Citadel/Carol, 1997); Andrew Sarris,* The American Cinema: Directors and Directions, 1929–1968 *(New York: Dutton, 1968); Robert Sklar,* Movie-Made America: A Social History of American Movies *(New York: Random House, 1975); Paul Trent,* Those Fabulous Movie Years: The 30's *(New York: Crown, 1975); John Walker, ed.,* Halliwell's Film Guide *(New York: HarperPerennial, 1995); and an internet source, the International Movie Database Website (<http://us.imdb.com>).*

[DAR.als]

To Helen Caldwell:
[Roosevelt Hotel stationery, New Orleans]
5/8/33

Dear Helen --

I've just got your Saturday letter. I'm writing Father to wait till the 20th so he will be in Mt. Vernon to look after things when you need him. . . .[139]

Of course, buy the fertilizer. You can get it in Augusta the next time you go there. The garden won't grow without it, even if it costs $5 a sack. Have the hot water fixed, of course. Don't let the lawn & garden get ahead of Clifford. Grass grows fast. . . .

I understand Faulkner is going home tonight. Anyway, the synopsis has to be finished & sent to Hollywood for O.K., & that will mean the end of the week before anything is done. However, I hear that I may start on dialogue. Nobody knows a damn thing. But what do I care? My pay started May 5th, & I'm not worrying about M-G-M's picture.

Don't get foolish & think all kinds of silliness. You know why I came here, & you know what I'm going to do.[140] I'm trying to get some money for you, & I don't give a damn about anything or anyone else. If I did, I'd tell you. But I don't, & that's all there is to it. Just because I don't say a lot of things, don't think that I never feel them. You know that all I'm doing is putting in time, & the minute that's done, I'm coming back to stay. I don't wish to be here, but it can't be helped. I'd lots rather stay there. When you discover that I care a hell of a lot more for you than you do for me, you won't be questioning my faith any longer. Don't forget that.

It's too damn hot here for white people. You can count Florida out. I've got my fill of the tropics. I'll take Maine 9 months of the year. I'm hoping I can go to Culver City soon, because So. Calif is a little cooler than this furnace. Write to tell me how everything is, & if you still love me.

-- Love --
Skinny[141]

---

[139] *Helen was then pregnant with their daughter Janet.*

[140] *Helen regularly—and with good reason—suspected her husband of being unfaithful: e.g., see Klevar,* Biography, *pp. 91–92, 118–119, and 139–140; and Miller, pp. 182–184.*

[141] *Caldwell's nickname, a derivative of Erskine.*

[DAR.tls]

To Helen Caldwell:
[Roosevelt Hotel stationery, New Orleans]
Saturday [May 13, 1933]

Dear Helen:

I haven't heard from you since Thursday, but there must be a reason for it. Probably I'll get a letter tonight or in the morning.

I've been working for two days on dialogue. Together with [Chandler] Sprague's continuity, we have 15 pages done now (the first sequence of scenes). We are to meet [Tod] Browning tonight, and he'll read it and have his say.[142] As it works out, about two thirds of the script is dialogue, and that means I did 10 pages, Sprague 5. Sprague does most of the camera directions, and the rest of the technical work. My job is to make people talk, and with a reason; motivate their action and direct so-and-so to raise a window, light a cigarette, and shoot his brother. Do you catch on? I may be fooled after Browning reads the script tonight, because he'll probably say it's rotten; but just the same I think it's an easy way to get rich. And don't think I'm not going to stick up for what I have written, even if I'm fired (which nobody can do till August 1st).

I don't think much of the system, which gives Browning the absolute say. His idea so far has been to tell me what to write, though I haven't done it all that way; but he is a good director, even if he may not be a good inspiration for a story. A director should interpret the script, instead of trying to write the story, or rather say how it should be written. If I have my way half the time, it'll be a lot different than he said it should be.

I've got a new Remington Noiseless, which isn't so good. Smith-Corona is 50% better than this. And, by the way, I heard today that my hotel bill will be paid as long as we are here. This is considered location, and when I get to Hollywood it will be the company's idea of home. But now, my bills are paid.

The business manager wired the home office last night in his nightly letter asking about my check, and he'll have an answer tonight. No one here had authority to pay it, and I'll know tonight when I'll get it. If I don't get it by the first of next week, I'll put Lieber on the trail of it, and he'll raise hell. So I'm not worried.

We were to leave for the bayou tomorrow, but now it's uncertain. I won't know until I see Brow[n]ing tonight. Everyone but Sprague and me goes out there every day now. I'd much rather stay here the rest of the time, because I don't like all those insects they talk about;

---

[142]*Sprague and Browning were both veterans of the movie business by the time Caldwell met them. Browning in particular had had several recent successes, namely as director of* Dracula *(1931),* Iron Man *(1931), and the cult-classic* Freaks *(1932).* Bride of the Bayou *was released in 1934 as* Lazy River.

mosquitoes, flies, ticks, redbugs, and anything you can think of in the South. But Browning is the boss, and what he says goes.

It hasn't been cool here yet. I know it's not been as low as 70, and most of the time, night and day, it's around 85. I've got enough of the tropics, already. Keep the house in good repair, because I'm coming back there to stay. I'm wearing a linen suit ($3.00), but it is still hot. . . .

Don't work too hard, and don't let anything happen to yourself. I'd be in a pretty fix without you. What could I do without you there all the time? There wouldn't even be any use in going back there. You ought not to think you can get by with it; let somebody else do all the work.

Write soon -- it's pretty bad sitting here all day, and again another day, and not getting a letter from you.

Love,
Skinny

[DAR.tls]

To Helen Caldwell:
[Roosevelt Hotel stationery, New Orleans]
5/15/33

Dear Helen:

I worked all day yesterday, for the third day, and I'm tired, what with this heat, and cockroaches that look like Irving Thalberg (MGM head).

I've just found out that my weekly check is payable in Hollywood, and that means, I suppose, I'll have to wait until I get out there to collect in whole. However, I can draw any amount up to the limit weekly from the business manager here. I am enclosing ten dollars, out of fifty I drew this morning. When you send me that figure of money you need to take you up to June 15th, I'll send it. In the meantime, this ten will help.

I hear we're moving out to Grande Isle tomorrow, where the location is. I hate like hell to go, but what can I do; the company is paying my expenses, and I have to live where everyone else goes. Send all mail here until notified, and I'll see that it is forwarded. Hold the book (and work on it some more) until I let you know. I don't believe I'll be able to work on it till I get to the West Coast. But I'll let you know more later.[143] Don't send any magazines; keep everything for me.

---

[143] *Caldwell was worried about being distracted from his revisions of* Journeyman *and, as usual, expected Helen's editorial assistance. Helen admitted that she frequently helped Caldwell edit his writing, and according to Eugene Joffe, a writer whose work often appeared in little*

I've got another typewriter this morning. The other one did not have a tabulator key, and in writing script for the screen story, three or four different columns must be used (one for dialogue, one for camera direction, one for exposition, and etc).

Writing this stuff would be all right, but there are so many taboos (1000s of them), and five or six people have to be pleased, instead of myself alone, and yet it probably is good training. I haven't seen Browning in three days, but have an appointment with him tonight. He'll read what we have done, and then we'll know if the work is satisfactory.

I bouthg another wash suit this morning, blue striped seersucker. It's impossible to wear my wool suit here. But Sprague says it's cool in California at night the year around and I hope we get there soon.

I had a note from father, advising me not to eat much in this climate. He's right. I can't eat lunch, and very little at supper. Maybe I'll sweat some of the fat off of me.

Sprague is lazy as hell. He never gets up until 10 or 11, and I have to wait for him everymorning to talk over the work with him before I go ahead. That throws us back, and it's seven or eight before we get through for the day.

I haven't had a good drink of water since I left home. The water here is hot, and ice water tastes like chemicals. I'd give anything to have a gallon of water out of the pump or spring now. (have someone clean out the spring)

Don't bother to write me what to do -- go ahead and do it as you think it should be. And it will be right.

Send Whit Burnett fifty cents for a copy of Story. Tell him you can't do without it, and also that I can't buy it on the newsstands in N.O.

I had a letter from Morang. The fool sent [Eugene] Joffe some stories for that childish thing of his. Joffe sent the first ones back, and M is sending him two more. Looks like M would have enough sense to stay out of such business. I told him, but it did no good. He'll learn, though.[144]

We have a draft of 20 pages now waiting for Tod's OK. That

---

magazines with that of Caldwell, that assistance was common knowledge among his contemporaries: "Caldwell lost a vital critic when he divorced Helen [in 1938] (and her feather duster that she'd take to his manuscripts as they came out of the typewriter)" (Klevar, "Interview," p. 91; Eugene Joffe to Robert L. McDonald 3-23-98).

[144]*Joffe published stories in* Clay, Contact, Pagany, *the* Windsor Quarterly, *and* Outlander *among other places. He recollects helping José Garcia Villa with the publication of* Clay— *which was mimeographed in order to save on production costs—and suspects that this is the little magazine that Caldwell refers to in this letter (Eugene Joffe to Robert L. McDonald, 3-23-98).*

takes in the first two sequences of scenes (about ten). And that is about 1/5 of the whole. The script when finished should not be over 110 pages, and not under 100.

Take care of yourself and all the others for me. If there is any danger, don't hesitate to call in better doctors. This money is no good if it can't do something for us. That's what I'm getting it for. . . .

Keep on writing, and don't spare the air mail. If I didn't hear from you, I couldn't stay here five hours.

       Love,
       Skinny . . .

[VIR.tls]
    To Gordon Lewis:
    [Roosevelt Hotel stationery, New Orleans]
                5/16/33

Dear Gordon:

It was good to hear from you, but I must say your luck is something I couldn't even dream of. About the only way I could ever get to Europe would be to enlist in the Swiss navy.

But don't envy me -- pray for me. In this gang of cut-throats anything is liable to happen. -- With just about as much protection as a house cat in city traffic, we're leaving to live for god knows how long on location on one of these mosquito-tick-redbug, ant-lice-snake bayous. I hope to get out of this hole by the first of June and get to the Coast, where it is at least cool at night.

Don't ask me anything about the picture -- it's a mess. M*G*M bought a play script from somebody; the director and a studio hack rewrote it; and now my job is to rewrite that, with sound. I don't know a damn thing about it, and neither does anyone else. But we'll have a [John] Barrymore -- [Barbara] Stanwyck picture, even if my dialogue is tossed out. . . .

I attended the hearing in New York two days before leaving for here. Sumner thinks he has a water-tight case against us, but everyone else thinks otherwise. The decision will be handed down May 23rd; and it is then we will know whether Viking will be held for jury trial, or the case dismissed. . . .[145]

       Sincerely,
       Erskine

---

[145] *New York Magistrate Court Judge Benjamin E. Greenspan dismissed the case on May 23, calling the novel a fair literary representation of the "truth" and therefore rejecting the*

To Helen Caldwell:
[DAR.tls]   [Roosevelt Hotel stationery, New Orleans]
5/19/33

Dear Helen:

I've got so many letters from you to answer, I won't be able to remember all the questions I'm supposed to reply to. For one thing, don't worry about money: I sent you ten last week, and I'm enclosing another ten with this letter. As soon as I can get a check cashed, I'll send you some more. If possible, take all you can get out of the checking account, and use that. We might lose most of it, if the bank does not open (which it undoubtedly will).[146] Draw ten a week as long as you can, but I beg you not to give anybody checks on it. Do all the drawing yourself (or send for it).

Marshall Best writes that Viking is going to put a book on the fall list. He asks for the novel, if it's ready; otherwise the stories.[147] I am writing him that the novel is not ready, and won't be before July or August. Since that will be too late, it will then be the book of stories. Keep the novel until later. I may not even write for it. If nothing happens, I can wait until I get home to work on it, and have much more time to revise it. However, I may write for copies of two or three stories, in case I decide to substitute some.

I'm out here at Manila Village now. We left Wednesday, and have been here two days; we'll probably stay another week, maybe ten days. My address remains the same until I leave for the Coast. It will be a day or two's delay in sending and receiving mail, as it comes

---

description of it as "pornography": "This Court has carefully read the book in question. It is an attempt at the portrayal, in a realistic fashion, of life as lived by an illiterate Southern white farm family.... They are of a simple nature, and savage passion is found close to the surface.... The author has set out to paint a realistic picture. Such pictures necessarily contain certain details. Because these details relate to what is properly called the sex side of life, portrayed with brutal frankness, the Court may not say that the picture should not have been created at all. The language, too, is undoubtedly coarse and vulgar. The Court may not require the author to put refined language into the mouths of primitive people" (reprinted in MacDonald, Critical Essays, pp. 27–31).

The following day, Marshall Best wired Caldwell: "DELIGHTED TO REPORT GODS LITTLE ACRE TRIUMPHANTLY EXONERATED GREENSPANS OPINION IS A LANDMARK OF LIBERALISM AND THE PRESS HAS BEEN FULL OF PRAISE FOR THE DECISION AND THE BOOK SORRY WE COULD NOT REACH YOU YESTERDAY" (DAR 5-24-33).

[146] On 4 March 1933, the day after he took the oath of office, Franklin Roosevelt declared an emergency "bank holiday," halting the country's financial business. Five days later, Congress passed the Emergency Banking Relief Act, providing for federal monitoring of a bank's fiscal strength, and the strongest banks began reopening.

[147] *Journeyman* was near completion; Caldwell was also planning the collection that would be published as We Are the Living: Brief Stories.

and goes only thrice a week. However, I think there are arrangements for sending out telegrams daily. So continue sending everything to the Roosevelt Hotel, NO.

We are living on stilts out here at this shrimp fishing village. There is no solid ground, only marshes; houses, paths, and platforms are built on twelve-foot stilts; and even then, when there is a bad storm, water rises almost to the top. Everybody is Chinese, Malay, and Cajun. The storekeeper is the only white man on the platform. A larger crew of 15 arrived from the Coast Wednesday, and shooting has been going on now for two days in dead earnest. All together there are about 25 here in the company. All meals and room is furnished gratis. That's a help. I'm living in a converted houseboat, made from a scow. It is resting on the marsh now, but when the water gets high, it floats. But it's anchored good. It's hard to tell one race from another. The chinks look like the Maylays, and the Cajuns look like the cross between Indian and Canuck.

By all means hire the nurse for as long as needed. The important thing is to have somebody to take care of you. You do not wish to run the risk of getting infected. That seems to be the greatest danger to guard against, and by having a capable nurse, there is no danger.[148] I'll send the money.

Roark Bradford was here yesterday. He's living on a fishing boat, and he stopped here to get supplies. He's all right. I don't see how anybody could help but like him. I promised to go to his house for dinner when I go back to NO, but we'll probably be there only a day or two, and I may not have time.

My duties are to write dialogue, and nothing else, for this picture. Sprague is writing the continuity, and nothing else. We have a first draft nearly half done now. But I can imagine how it might take another two months to put the script in finished form.

I won't be able to send Dabney and Pixy anything until I get back to town, which probably will be ten days from now. But assure them that I shall send them each a present as soon as I can. I did not have time before leaving for here.

This is 40 miles from NO. We drove twenty miles in a car, and came the rest of the way in a speed boat (sedan), at 45 miles an hour. Browning, Sprague, chief cameraman, business manager, and myself rode in the sedan, while the reset came on a slow packet that took them all day. We got here in two hours after leaving the hotel. Three barges full of equipment (lights, props, cameras, etc) got here yesterday. MGM is hooting a bankroll on this picture -- and they did not even have a story until we started writing it. I still can't see

---

[148] *Helen's pregnancy was near term.*

why a story cannot be bought, and filmed; this is the opposite process. . . .

These little Cajun and Chinese boys never go to school and never touch the ground with their feet. They go barefooted, but there is no ground for them to stand on. There are several cats and dogs, and neither no they ever get on earth. Under us is nothing but marsh grass and swampy mud. The boys fish nearly all the time, and they can land 50 pounders as easily as I can a sun-fish. Tell Pix and Dee to learn how to be good fishermen; never hurt a fish that has to be thrown back. If they do tear its mouth too much with a hook, it bleeds, and the other fish try to eat it. Tell them not to hurt fish, just as we do not hurt cats and dogs. . . .

Max [Lieber] says the Shuberts asked to read the novel to see if they could find a play in it.[149] They probably won't, if they are anything like the movie people. A play is there all right; and I'm certain [Patrick] Kearney would have got it, if he had stayed to write it. . . .[150]

I got a telegram yesterday from M-G-M, dated Culver City, and signed Sam Marx, as follows: "When do you think your contract ought to start?" I showed it to Tod [Browning], and ignored answering it. I've been here two weeks, and they wire asking me when I wish to start! The signed contract is dated May 5th, and I'm not worrying about it as long as Lieber is my agent. He raised hell with M-G-M for not paying me promptly the first week, and now the business manager here has orders to pay me every week.

Take care of yourself, and don't do anything foolish, and write when you can. . . .

Don't forget why I'm here -- for you and nothing else.
          Love
          Skinny

---

[149] *Legendary theater producers Lee and Jacob Shubert eventually promoted the first road companies of Jack Kirkland's adaptation of* Tobacco Road. *They did not option* God's Little Acre.

[150] *Among Kearney's successes were his original play* A Man's Man *(1925) and a dramatization of Theodore Dreiser's* An American Tragedy *(1926); he was always more committed to the theatre than to the movie business.*

To Alfred Morang:

[HAR.als] Culver City, Calif
5/25/33

Dear Alfred --

Just a note to let you know my new address. I left N.O. Monday night & got here this morning (Thursday).

I have been given an office, typewriter, & phone, & am probably expected to turn out 6 or 8 masterpieces. I had no assignment today, & so I do not know if I am "on" or "off" the Bayou story. Either way, I don't care -- because I'm already itching to get back to Maine.

Perhaps you've heard in some way, however, Helen & the new member are both doing fine.[151] It was hell to have to be out here at such a time -- but what in hell can a man do in this capitalistic society but try to earn a living? But you can depend on me to get all I can out of these bastards -- the trick, I've found, is for one of us to "do" the other before he gets "done". Well, I'm getting mine, & then I'm getting out.

You might like pictures. And if you think you would, I'll talk to you about the possibilities when I see you in August. The thing to do now is to make a name for yourself with stories, & later novels. These people are knocked cold by names, & if I were you, that's what I'd strive for now -- write the best stories -- then the best novels & then you can make your own terms. You've got a far better start than dozens of writers I know -- just keep at it.

Drop a line --

Sincerely,
Erskine

P.S. Sorry about the scrawl -- I'm going to rent a portable in a day or two for my personal use.

To Helen Caldwell:

[DAR.tls] Culver City, California
May 26th 1933

Dear Helen:

... I wish I could write a longer letter now, but I won't be able to this time. I do not have a typewriter in my room yet, and this is being written on the company's time. I may have to stop at almost any moment.

I am enclosing a twenty dollar bill with this letter. Yesterday I

---

[151] *Helen had given birth to Janet the previous day.*

wired you fifty, and before leaving New Orleans I sent twenty. This makes ninety all told, and it will see you through the month, won't it. Pay up all the bills at once. Don't let any run over. . . .

It looks as if i have talked myself out of the bayou picture. It was "suggested" that the dialogue be made a sort of dog-Spanish. I maintained that the Cajuns were French, not Mexican; but somebody here had decided it would make a good picture if a Spanish technique were used. Result: I refused to do a damn fool thing like that. Who with any sense wouldn't? You, and anyone else with any sense, know damn well that the Cajuns (Acadians) speak French. I was there, and I heard them speaking french just as plainly as we heard it spoken in Quebec. I do not know now if I am still on the story, or off; but nobody in Hollywood can make me, even for $250. a week, write dog-Mexican dialogue when the people who do the speaking are French.

The pictures are fine. Those kids are going to grow up so fast I won't know them when I get home in August -- and I will be there in August, you may be sure. I've come to the conclusion that this business is nothing more than a glorified newspaper office; and it is no place for me after August 5th.

If there is ten dollars that you will not need for ten days or two weeks, take it out of this money and use it to buy whatever you wish for yourself. Don't save it to buy things for the house -- it is for you to keep for yourself.

I've got a room in a hotel five or six blocks away. It's cheap, and I will be there only at night, and it suits. I can't see paying out $25 dollars a week, when a room for ten is just as good for the little time I'll be there. I'll be here from 8:30 or 9 in the morning until 5 or 5:30 in the evening.

I was being shown around a little this morning on the sound stages, and saw Robert Montgomery. He's an ass. There were five or six other players around, but he was the only one I talked to. I think I'll like my office better now, after seeing the so-called stars.

You don't have to worry about my being taken in by the glamor of this place. I made a good beginning when I talked back to them about changing the dialogue for the bayou picture; and I'm going to be even more frank. These people are too silly to take seriously; the only real writing is being done in the East anyway; out here it's not what you write, but how much money you make.

I'm afraid I'll have to stop till tomorrow. I'm supposed now to be reading two or three scripts, in order to see how the thing is done; but even if I'm not going to do more than look at them, I want to make some show of earning my pay. You may be sure that when and if I write a script, it will not be a copy of someone else's. And if they don't like what I write, I can't help it.

Don't get up until the doctor says you may. And take care of yourself. Tell Pixy and Dabney as soon as I can get into Los Angeles (I'm ten miles from there now, northward towards the sea and Venice) I'll send them postal cards.

Don't worry about the garden or anything else. Tell Clifford to keep the lawn mown, and the weeds and grass out of the garden. Let him do those things, and you stay where you belong. . . .

        Love,
        Erskine

    To Helen Caldwell:
[DAR.tls]   Culver City, California
            May 28th 1933

Dear Helen:

At last I've got a typewriter in my room, and I won't have to rush through a letter again. I rented it for two months and my that time I'll be getting ready to leave. And it can't come too soon to suit me, either.

I haven't been able to see a World-Telegram clipping yet, but the Wednesday papers are due to come in today, and I'm going into Los Angeles this afternoon to buy one. I saw the Times and Herald-Tribune, which I sent you yesterday. If there were notices in the other papers, I won't be able to see them for a while, as all of them are not to be had here. . . .[152]

Did you know that O'Brien has gone over to Houghton Mifflin with his Best Short Stories? At least that's what I read somewhere. I don't know why, unless he had a better offer there. Maybe he'll pay for stories now, but it's too late for me, because my three times is all that I wish. I haven't heard anything about Harry Hansen's book, so I suppose I'm out. I had hoped to get in one time, but probably because I've been in O'Brien this many, and the Uzzell book, Hansen was scared of me. He wouldn't follow the lead of anyone else.[153]

I think I've discovered the mystery of writing for pictures. It seems that a script passes through five or six stages, and each time, a new writer works on it. That explains why I was taken off the bayou picture after I had made a draft, and put on another one, this time a

---

[152] *Caldwell was keeping up with reports of Judge Greenspan's ruling on* God's Little Acre.
[153] *Hansen did select "Country Full of Swedes," originally published in the* Yale Review, *for his anthology,* O. Henry Memorial Award Prize Stories of 1933 *(Doubleday, 1933). Thomas H. Uzzell had included "Indian Summer," reprinted from* Story, *in his* Short Story Hits, 1932: An Interpretive Anthology *(Harcourt, 1932).*

timber picture in Washington (state). Anyway, I was assigned to work on it yesterday. After I have done something on it, I'll probably get another one to work on. However, Sam Marx (head of writing department) asked me if I would like to write an original story, and I told him NO. Any original stories I have will go into books, not movies to be worked over by six or seven different writers after I've finished it. In other words, picture writing is nothing more than glorified newspaper work. And I had my fill of that in Atlanta.[154] The only difference is that writers here work forty hours a week, and receive ten and twenty times as much pay. There are no regular hours for writers: just so long as 40 hours a week is got in. Most of them go to the studio about ten in the morning, take an hour or two for lunch and leave around 5:30. However, if one wishes, he can go at night and work, or anytime whatever. The studio is open all the time.

This country is no fit place to live, except for old people. There is no soil, nothing to put your feet on. I don't see how anything can take root here. And I would not be surprised to see the movie business blow up here some day. There is no stability. A magazine like Scribner's has a tradition behind it; a publishing company like Harper's has also; there is no picture company that is a part of people's lives. If any one company moved or dissolved, other companys would make the same kind of pictures without anyone knowing about it. They all do the same things, work alike, and do anything under heaven to make money. It's not necessary to make good pictures, because there's no name to uphold. In other words, every picture company here is on the same footing with The Macaulay Company. They can't hurt their names by making cheap pictures, because they have no name to injure. . . .[155]

I may have to ask you to send me carbon copies of several stories. I'll let you know when I receive the script from Best sometime this week I think. I'll probably wish to substitute several stories (Masses of Men, The Man Who Looked Like Himself) for some that

---

[154] *Caldwell worked as a cub reporter at the Atlanta* Journal *for over a year, beginning in the spring of 1925. He was frustrated by the constraints of newspaper journalism, however, and left to concentrate on becoming "a professional writer"* (Experience, *p. 47). Later, he would acknowledge the influence of this work: "The newspaper style helped regarding simplicity, and the simplicity led to formulating a literary style that was as precise as possible" (Edwin T. Arnold, "Interview with Erskine Caldwell,"* Arnold, Conversations, *p. 268).*

[155] *Known primarily as publishers of inexpensive popular literature, the Macaulay Company had provided Caldwell with national exposure by publishing his story "Midsummer Passion" in the 1929* New American Caravan, *edited by Kreymborg, Mumford, and Rosenfeld. Caldwell's comment in this letter is ironic, of course, since fantastic sales of cheap paperback reprints of his books would later make his reputation as "America's Best-Selling Author."*

are now in the book. The carbons should be in the box that was on the table in my room. I'll let you know later which ones to send. I'm glad they are publishing the stories. I really think it should come next, in spite of what Best said last winter. But now that they think they can sell it, they are willing and anxious to publish it.

I'll ask Best to send you a copy of the new edition of the novel containing the judge's decision.[156] I don't know when it will be ready, but I should think within a week or two. . . .

When you get through paying up all the bills, let me know how much you have left. Estimate how much you will need a week to run the house, including everything. Then I'll send you the money in advance so you will not be bothered about such things. . . .

Love,
Skinny . . .

To I. L. Salomon:

[LOC.tls] Culver City, California
May 28th 1933

Dear Salomon:

Now, what in hell can I say for myself! Three weeks ago I was seeing you in New York, with hardly a care in the world, and now I'm out here, worried because I'm on the way to getting enough money to pay off my debts and have a clean start in life (for the second time since December 17th 1903).[157]

Perhaps you've already heard about it. Anyway, I have not gone Hollywood. I can assure you of that. I thought when I left there might be danger, but since being here three weeks, I know damn well it's not my pie. I'm disgusted, dissatisfied, and disgruntled. It's nothing more than a glorified newspaper job, and I had my fill of that in my youth. When my three months' contract expires, I'll be on my way East before nightfall -- and to stay.

I was delighted with the verdict on the novel. Viking is going to reprint the judge's decision in a new edition that will be ready soon. I have not seen it yet, and I'm anxiously awaiting it. But what is still

---

[156] *For many years Judge Greenspan's decision was included as an appendix in reprints of God's Little Acre.*

[157] *Caldwell was inconsistent in providing the year of his birth, sometimes indicating the year as 1902. Klevar explains that this could have been due to his father's erroneous dating of the birth in family records, but concludes nevertheless that the correct date was 1903* (Biography, pp. 418–419).

more pleasing, Viking will publish a book of stories this fall. The title, now, is WE ARE THE LIVING. Do you like it, or what do you think?

That piece you wrote for Abernethy was damn fine. The truth is, I was so disgusted with the reviews and letters, that I told him about you, and suggested that he write you to find out what the book really was about. He knows now, and I hope he runs it, not alone for me, but for you, because to me you have read my mind in the novel. And as you know, no one else has succeeded in doing that.[158]

Tell me how you are getting along. I hope Story uses something of yours soon; if they are to continue being as good as they started, they will have to print you. . . .

Sincerely,
Erskine

To Alfred Morang:

[HAR.tls] Culver City, California
May 29th 1933

Dear Alfred:
It developes that Metro considers my rough draft of the bayou story finished as far as I'm concerned, and I've been handed another one to work on. I'd thank God for a chance to complete a story, but it seems that is not the way things are done in this racket. A story travels from one writer to another, until the script editor decides it's about time to shoot the picture, and then he calls it in. That's how pictures are made, and now you know why they are so consistantly rotten. It's a wonder that occasionally there are two or three good pictures.

But I'm not kicking. I've decided this is merely a job, and nothing more. In other words, it's a glorified newspaper office with ten and twenty times the pay. And that's why I know it isn't my pie. I'm coming home the first of August to stick to my last.

There's a big bunch of writers on this lot -- fifty or sixty at present. Most of them are hacks in the business. Occasionally I come across a decent person. For instance, Phil Stong turns out to be a "literywhore"; but John Howard Lawson is damn fine. I don't know what to say about Vicki Baum yet. Laurence Stallings, of course, is all right. Anita Loos is what you might expect. . . .

---

[158]*Abernethy did not publish Salomon's "piece," which was perhaps a rebuttal of Bennett Cerf's review in the 15 March 1933* Contempo. *See EC to Abernethy, 2-13-33.*

As a job, this isn't so bad. The company doesn't ask for more than forty hours of work a week. Writers drift in about ten in the morning, take a couple of hours off for lunch, and leave at five or five-thirty. Being used to working like hell, I feel a little ashamed to take their two-fifty checks on Saturdays; but I'll probably get up to my neck in work one of these days and wish I were clerking in a drug store. However, when I collect all that's coming to me, and take it home to pay off the mortgage on the old homestead, I'll feel like really doing some honest-to-god work. And it will be for myself, then; not for somebody else.

I hope you are getting some more stories out these days. A story at the time seems small and insignificant, but in the end they'll look like a mountain to you. That's they way it should be.

Drop a line when you have time --

Sincerely,
Erskine

To Helen Caldwell:

[DAR.tls] Culver City, California
June 1st 1933

Dear Helen:

I got today the letter you mailed Tuesday. I hope everything is all right now for a while. You should receive this letter not later than Monday, and so I am enclosing twenty dollars for expenses of the coming week. I do not know if this is enough, too much, or not enough; but try to save all you can against the year starting August 5th. After that date there'll be no more easy money, and all that we can save now will keep us that much longer. Do not fail to get the carriage, though, or some clothes for yourself, either. . . .

This fellow Phil Stong makes me sick at the stomach. I moved into the office he vacated the same day. I asked him about the revolution in Iowa (where he lives), and he said there was just a handful of Communists there who did not amount to anything, and nothing was the matter there. In other words, he's completely capitalistic. He's made a lot of money with his book, more out here, and he's all against admitting that people in his own country are starving.[159]

---

[159] *Stong's first novel,* State Fair *(Harcourt, 1932), was made into a popular film in 1933 (screenplay by Paul Green and Sonya Levien). A new novel,* Stranger's Return *(Harcourt, 1933), had just been published to good reviews.*

I heard today that Laurence Stallings bought up his contract and pulled out of here. He got completely disgusted with the whole mess, and told everybody that Thalberg and [Louis] Mayer on down to go to hell with their infantile pictures. I think Stallings had something to do with my getting the job, via Jed Harris. Anyway, he was here ten days ago, getting four figures a week; and all at once he bought up his contract, costing him nearly ten thousand dollars, and left for North Carolina. I'd heard a hint of it in New Orleans; Browning said that Stallings had told him he was disgusted with the way money was spent on nothing, while the rest of the country was down and out. Browning had no sympathy for him, and probably no one else out here either. Anyway, he has gone home to North Carolina. I hope I can meet him soon.[160]

I'm beginning to see how pictures can get a writer. All this easy money, no hard work, would appeal to anybody who was out to make money by writing. That's what is called "going Hollywood", I guess. But By God they'll never get me. I get a little sicker of it each day. And each day I thank God that I've got one day less to stay in this factory. If anyone ever had a good story, it would be talked to death ever before it could be put down on paper. I've been listening for two days to a story that has not yet been written, and the main concern seems to be to invent something new for it every half hour. The way it is now makes me sick. I've listened but have not agreed to anything so far, and when it does get to the point where it is to be put down on paper, I'll either be so repelled by it that I'll say so, or else vomit right on the floor in the "conference". I don't believe these fools realize that there are good stories in books; but no, they buy a book, and then begin making up a new one, keeping only the title. When the picture is made, they send out notices that they'll pay fifty dollars for a good title for the picture. What a rotten mess. . . .

I'm expecting the script of the stories from Marshall [Best] soon, and when it comes, I'll send for the carbons that I wish you to send me. I won't know until I have a chance to see the script and decide what stories to take out and which ones to put in their places. I hope they get the book out early enough so it won't be killed in the Christmas rush. . . .

---

[160]*A native of Macon, Georgia, like Caldwell Stallings's first job had been as a reporter for the Atlanta* Journal. *For years he reviewed books for the* New York World *but achieved notoriety when he collaborated with Maxwell Anderson on a popular play based on his experiences in World War I,* What Price Glory? *(1924). Intermittently throughout the 1930s, Stallings worked in the movie business, though he continued to make his home in Yanceyville, North Carolina. The origins of Caldwell's friendship with writer/director/Broadway producer Jed Harris are unclear, but Caldwell's respect for Harris eventually led him to enlist him in a failed effort to adapt* Georgia Boy *(1943) for the stage (see* Experience, *pp. 220–222).*

I haven't been anywhere yet, except into Los Angeles twice. I may go in again this afternoon to get a [New York] Times Book Review. I haven't even been to Hollywood. There is nothing out here except stores and cafes, and studios; and I stay at home at night and read. There's nothing else to do. As asson as it gets warmer I'll probably go to Venice (a coney island) and see what it looks like. Other than that, I'll be in Culver City most of the time.

When you are up and able to walk, have Clifford wash the car and keep it polished with the polishing cloth. If nothing goes wrong, we can trade it it when I get back, and we wish to get as much as possible for it.

Tell Pixy and Dee to take good care of you and their sister for me.

Love,
Skinny

P S: A Variety reporter just came in to chew the rag, and so I guess I'll make a line of "Chatter" for next week.

To Alfred Morang:

[HAR.tls] Culver City, California
June 1st 1933

Dear Alfred:

Your story came this morning; I hastened to read it through; and now that it is fresh in my mind I'll try to give you my reaction (which, you must remember, is merely one in a hundred and twenty thousand).

There's no sense in my saying it's a good story. It is a fine story, and the kind that I wish to see you write.

Now, after getting that over and done with, I'll say what I dislike about it. As a critic I may be a pumpkin, but I was born this way, and I can't help the way I think. My principal criticism is that the story is perhaps a little too obvious. Your symbollic apples will probably strike the tabloid-snappy story public as hot stuff; to me, it is not subtile enough for my old bones. Perhaps I'm too arty, if you wish to put it that way; but just the same I see writing as an art, and not as a pastime or amusement. The artist in you knows how a thing should be done; when you over do it, or even under do it, you cease to be an artist and become a salesman to the public that likes over ripe, or as the case may be, under ripe, fruit. Me myself, I like fruit in its state of natured ripeness.

There is no way of drawing the line: the artistic draws its own line. There is a certain imperceptible hair-line between good and bad, perfect and rotten. In this case, I should say that the story barely escapes perfection solely because it stepped a fraction of an inch over that line, thereby making it not quite so good as I'd like to see it.

To put it another way: I'm convinced that you have got on the right track, but in this one case you missed getting off at the right station. I mean that: I really think you've progressed a hell of a lot since a year ago, and I honestly believe you are headed in the right direction.

But that's enough. I did not say exactly what I wished to say, but I hope I've said enough to make it of some help. Maybe I can tell you a little more clearly when I see you.

This time a year from now I expect to see you writing the best stories in America. After that comes the novel. And after that a damn long pull for the rest of your life. . . .

I hope you sent O'Brien a copy of the story. It will put him on the look-out for you in magazines. There's no way in the world of keeping you out of his Best Short Stories after this year. O'Brien can't make any writer, but he can give you a push in the right direction.

Viking is getting out a new edition of the novel, which will include the text of the judge's decision as handed down on the 23rd. I haven't seen the complete decision yet, but Marshall [Best] says it makes good reading. Marshall, by the way, plans to come to Mount Vernon sometime in August, and it might be well for you to met a publisher. It could do no harm, anyway. Someday you'll have a book, and -- well, so it goes. . . .

You'd like a visit on the lot (don't stay more than one day, though, I beg you). I watched the shooting for a while this morning of Tug Boat Annie. Marie Dressler and Wallace Beery are working in it. I also looked in on the set where Another Language is being shot, and also at Night Flight. The studio cafe is the place to see everybody. Everyone comes in there some time or another. You can go in to eat lunch and look up to see a Barrymore perched on a stool across from you; while beside you will be a clown or an Indian eating soup. The next day you'll be eating your apple pie and a cornfed who has been running all morning from the "villyan" will come in to eat a sandwich before going back to the set to get seduced. You see everyone except [Greta] Garbo; Garbo brings her lunch in a paper bag and eats it in the ladies dressing room -- so they say. . . .

Thanks a lot for sending the story. I hope you don't think I didn't like it, because I did. My trouble is that I always try to see how a piece of work could be made better. In this case I may be wrong;

maybe it is perfect. The main thing, though, is to progress, and that's what I attempted to help you do. . . .

Sincerely,
Erskine

To Helen Caldwell:

[DAR.tls] Culver City, Calif
June 5th 1933

Dear Helen:

I got a bunch of letters from you today, and I'm glad to know you are getting better and better every day. I'll be really pleased when you write that you are up. I'll know then that you won't have to lie in bed all day, and can sit on the porch when the blackflies have gone.

Max [Lieber] has sold "Horse Theif" to Vanity Fair! It was unexpected, but I'm glad. And it is more than The Mercury paid, too. It will be a big help. I cut out only a hundred words, and told Max that it was enough. They think only of crowding their advertisements, I suppose; but the story was written with the right balance to begin with; I know, and William Harland Hale, the bright boy of Yale, cannot tell me otherwise. There is no excuse for throwing the story off-balance merely because it would take six inches more space in their shiny magazine.

Did you get a copy of the fifth printing [of <u>God's Little Acre</u>]? Mine came today, and it was the first time I had see the complete text of the decision. If you did not get a copy, write a note to Marshall [Best] and ask him to send you one.

Until we get this money thing straightened out, I won't know where you stand. I sent twenty five Friday, which you should have had Monday. I'll send twenty tomorrow, which should reach you not later than Saturday. Now, is that, was that, enough (by the time you get this), enough to carry you through Sunday, June 11th? . . . Don't hesitate to tell me when you do not have enough, because all I have to go by is what you write. And I can only judge by the lump sum you state for the weekly expense. The main thing is to pay up all bills to date, as they come due, so that there will not be a penny of debt.

George Oppenheimer called me up this morning, and I'm going to have something to eat with him Wednesday night.[161] I couldn't go tonight, because Metro is having a private showing of two new pictures on the lot tonight, and Sam Marx sent me a notice of it. I presume

---

[161] *An accomplished screenwriter, Oppenheimer had just completed work on the musical comedy* Roman Scandals *(1933).*

it to mean that my presence is called for. Perhaps he thinks I'll learn something and go and do likewise. Anyway, I'll go once; the next time maybe I'll know better. . . .

You don't write as though a sick person would; and I am glad you are feeling all right

Love,
Skinny

[marginalia] Keep the Best Short Stories -- But what happened to the two other stories in <u>Story</u>, The Yale Review, & one or two more? Weren't they any good?[162] Don't be silly -- You know damn well I'd a hundred times be there than here -- Where do you get all these notions, anyway? You know about me, so stop being crazy.

To Helen Caldwell:

[DAR.tls]   Culver City, Calif
                                                                               June 6th 1933

Dear Helen:

I am enclosing twenty dollars, which I hope will reach you before all your money is gone. The twenty-five I sent last Friday should have reached you on Monday.

It looks now as if I'm going to write an origional story after all. It happened like this: Harry Behn was called to the carpet this morning by Sam Marx because Howard Hawkes did not like the Cascade Mountain story Behn had done.[163] He was told to have a woods story within a week, or get out. And as I understand it, Marx told Behn that I was to tell him a story, and he was to put it down for Hawke's approval. At least, that is what I got out of Behn. And so today, I've been telling Harry a story, and he has been trying to put into it the picture angle. Tomorrow we'll try to work it out, and the next day it

---

[162]*Edward J. O'Brien included "The First Autumn," reprinted from the Summer 1932 issue of* Pagany, *in* The Best Short Stories: 1933 *(Houghton Mifflin, 1933). However, because he had not yet begun the practice of selecting stories from the calendar year in which they were published, he did not mention several of Caldwell's stories that appeared late in 1933—including "August Afternoon," "Masses of Men," "Yellow Girl," and "Country Full of Swedes"—in that volume's "Index of Distinctive Short Stories." Caldwell was aware of O'Brien's practice but evidently forgot about it in a typical moment of worrying that his work had not been "good" enough to merit notice.*

[163]*Behn had worked on a string of successful movies in the late 1920s and early 1930s, including* Sin Sister *(1929) and* Hell's Angels *(1930, dir. Howard Hughes). Caldwell consistently misspells the name of director Howard* Hawks.

will be put down on paper. If I have guessed right, it amounts to my doing an original story, with Harry finishing the technical work. And if Hawkes does not like it, the story will then be given to Sam Marx, head of the story department, for him to say whether some other director will do it or not. You now know just as much as I do about it. It seems as if it is up to me to save Harry's job; and it does amount to that; because if I can't work out a story that either Hawkes or Marx likes, Harry has to bow out. I'm going to do the best I can, because I wouldn't like to see someone else lose his job merely because I could not think up a story that would save it for him. It may not be so bad as all that, but Behn was pretty low this morning after his talk with Marx, and it is serious for him. The outcome cannot effect me personally, because I'm a contract writer, Behn a salary writer who can be fired at will.

I went to the forty-seat theatre last night and stayed from eight till twelve. There were two full-length pictures and six or eight short ones. It's a good way to see a show without having to pay for it; and besides only forty persons can get inside, and the seats are almost as comfortable as the morris chair.

This new story we are doing is, naturally, since I know nothing about any other woods state, about Maine. But the odds are 100 to 1, even if it should be acceptable, that the locale will be changed. That's the way things are done. But I'd be a fool to try to write a story about the Canadian woods, or even about the Northwest. And when it is finished, if it should still be acceptable, it will be given to one or two other writers to adapt for the screen. And so in the process, there is not a chance in the world of it's ever being made as I am writing it. . .[164]

An agent in Hollywood wrote me a letter which I got today asking if I had any stories suitable for pictures, and if so would I send them to him to read. To hell with him. Anybody who knows me also knows where to find the stories I write. I think he is the same agent who wrote while I was in Maine about sending him a copy of The AAcre to try to sell to a picture company. I think it's a lot os waste time; when/and if any company wishes to make a picture of anything I have written, they'll know enought about the piece without having to listen to an agent talk about it. . . .

Write whenever you can, and tell me how all the kids, and yourself, and the cats and dog are.

Love,
Skinny

---

[164] *Caldwell is probably speaking here about his work on a screenplay entitled "Timber," for which he signed a contract on 1 June 1933 (GU1 Ms 1653). It was never produced.*

And don't get any more crazy notions in your head. You ought to know better by now.[165]

To Helen Caldwell:

[DAR.tls] [Culver City, California]
June 9th 1933

Dear Helen:
   ... Maybe you'll be better now that Mother and Father have left; Father is enough to keep anyone nervous with his constant going somewhere. But if you are getting well, they won't need to be there. Keep Ethel as much and as long as you need her. The money does not matter so long as we have it. The idea is for you to get well and have a good rest at the same time, and let someone else do all the work. I mean for you to keep for yourself all the money that's left over from expenses. So far there evidently has been none left over; but as soon as I can determine your average weekly expense -- maybe I'm too dumb to figure out how much you need -- you will get enough each week to have some left over for what ever you wish to get. What I'm trying to do is to get as much money in the bank as possible as quickly as possible. And after we get it there, then it is for you to use. The reason for my wishing so much to get the cash on hand is that every damn thing out here is uncertain. For instance, in case of an earthquake, the company is automatically released from its obligations to make its weekly payments. And quakes, oil well explosions, and such things are continually in the air out here. I hope you can appreciate the situation; I'm merely trying to play safe so that nothing can prevent us having when we need on August fifth. It would be hell to have the company go bankruptcy next week, or something equally as dire. . . .
   A certain Charlie Smith, from some agency, came in today. He's the first agent out of some five or six that I liked, and I told him I'd tie up with him, thorough Lieber, if Lieber agreed. He thinks he can sell the new novel to a company that has been interested in it. I told him I would not take a penny less than twenty-five thousand. He said that if it could be sold at all, he'd get that, maybe more. It's just one of those things, so don't take it seriously.[166] People out here take such

---

[165] *Again, Helen was questioning Caldwell's fidelity.*
[166] *God's Little Acre was not made into a film until 1958 (dir. Anthony Mann, screenplay by Philip Yordan). In an interview that year, Caldwell said he approved of the movie, since it "is based on the novel's central theme, which is the attempt by the leading character, Ty Ty Walden,*

things seriously, and that's what's the matter with them. They live in a state of constant excitemnent, such as suddenly making fifty thousand. But I have no idea in the world that the thing will be sold; and so I'm forgetting it. However, he claims that he can arrabge a four figure contract, weekly, if I'll come back. I told him to submit all offers to Mount Vernon Maine after August fifth.

The first editions of the new novel are selling out here for five dollars. Several bookshops are asking and getting that. I know, because Harry [Behn] yesterday bought firsts of all three books at a premium.[167]

Marshall [Best] has written about the book of stories. He thinks sixteen stories will be enough; I'm going to hold out for twenty, and anyway, I don't think since such a small number are being used, that I'll substitute any of the new ones. So now you will not have to send any. We can use those written since Christmas for a new book two years from now. Strangely enough, Marshall (he rated the stories A B C & D) (D stories recommended to be left out), considered two stories that I think are punk, A stories. These two were A Lover of Horses and Crown Fire. I had intended leaving them out. What do you think? Surely they are not A stories. He rated The First Autumn as B, We Are Looking At You Agnes as D, Mama's Little Girl as D and Summer Accident as D. Do you think they should be left out? If you know any good reason why they should be in, please tell me -- and write him your reason, too, if you wish.

I'll get the book straightened out someway, but write and tell me what you think about his rating. I've got to get it back not later than July 1st. The reason I'm asking you is that I wish to be sure of these D stories, so that if I override him, I'll have full confidence in the stories' worth.

Marshall says the book sold 400 last week, bringing the total close to 5400. That's not bad, but I hope it goes higher.

Write me about everything. I'm looking forward to the pictures as soon as you are able to be up. Tell Pixy and Dee we'll get something; we may not be able to afford a bicycle, but we'll get somethinG. Tell them to makes second choices, anyway. It would hardly pay to buy a second hand wheel in poor shape; but we'll see what we can do. Tell them in the meantime to be good and help you. Tell Pixy he is the man of the household now, and to run things right. I hope

---

to hold his family together under all circumstances ... " (Carvel Collins, "Erskine Caldwell at Work," Arnold, Conversations, *p. 39).*

[167] *Publicity surrounding the New York censorship trial had caused a sudden flurry of interest in Caldwell first editions. Bennett Cerf had commented on this in his 15 March 1933 review of* God's Little Acre *in* Contempo *(p. 4).*

you can get some wood and make arrangements about the new part of the porch. Don't go to any trouble, however.

Love,
Erskine

To Alfred Morang:

[HAR.tls]

Culver City, Calif
June 11th 1933

Dear Alfred:

... You should have a pile of work in print before the close of December 31st. And I hereby lay a dollar that you'll be hearing from Edward J O'Brien asking for your biography for his Honor Roll not later than January 1st. And if you don't make it next year, I'll admit that I don't know a good story when I see one. And after you get a start there, you'll find swimming's easier.

I've turned in my second piece of work. Last Tuesday morning I got a phone call asking for an original story by noon Friday! That was all: no other information. I got hold of Harry Behn, an experienced scenario writer: I then reached up and pulled a tale out of the blue sky, told it to him, retold it twice: Harry churned it in his head for half an hour, and then told me the story in terms of continuity. At one o'clock we called in a girl, and Harry started dictating. While he was dictating, I was writing out a draft of the next sequence of scenes; that continued until Friday morning at ten o'clock. At 10:15 the girl wrote FADE OUT and dashed across the lot with it to the mimeograph plant; at 1:20 the thing was mimeographed, bound, and distributed. And now that we've worked the hair off of our heads, we probably will never hear of the story again. Howard Hawkes was the director who asked for it; but Hawkes, like all the rest, will probably never mention it again, even if he reads it. But what the hell! That weekly check comes in every Saturday morning on the stroke of 11. And I should worry if they never read what I write.

I've got a typescript of the book of stories that Viking is publishing in the fall. It got here yesterday, and it has to be back in New York by the 20th. I've decided to take out five stories, leaving twenty in the book. There is no extensive revision, but I can't send it back until I go over the stories again. I'll have to work every night this week to get it done in time. I told you the title, didn't I? WE ARE THE LIVING.

Well, our old friend Vanity Fair has stepped down from it's high perch and asked if I'd object to cutting five hundred words from a story.[168] Max [Lieber] sold them a story last week, and now they say it's too long for them. It was already a very short piece, and I couldn't see how the story would amount to anything after five hundred words were taken out. I struck out a hundred, and sent it with a note that I couldn't agree to its being shorter. I haven't heard from them since then: but I swear I'll sue them if they print the piece with more than a hundred words deleted.

Nearly everyone out here who's worth a damn as a writer seems to agree that it's suicide for anyone to stay longer than three months a year. Most of them work on that basis. I think myself that anyone who pretends to be a serious writer ought to work on the basis of nine months in the East, three months here, if he's got to have picture money. I wish I were not in the position of having to work here for the money, and I'll think twice before I come back again. The ideal arrangement would be to write an original story at home on a contract basis; but a writer has to know how to talk back to them before they'll agree to that. However, if anyone is going to write for pictures, he should come out here for one trip to begin with, merely to find out that the racket is not to be taken seriously.

I've got only eight weeks more of my term to serve, and then I'll be a free person again -- with a new suit of clothes, a five dollar bill in my pocket, and square with the world.

As you probably surmise, I'm holding out tooth and nail against going Hollywood. Most of them think I'm a "funny" person because I won't fall in with the crowd. The ninety-dollar tailors are shocked because I won't let them in my office,; the crowd is speechless because I refuse to buy a car, rent a four-room apartment, and keep a couple of girls. And to knock them completely speechless, I only have to add that I drink nothing stronger than beer. . . .

Sincerely,
Erskine

To Helen Caldwell:

[DAR.tls]   [Culver City, California]
June 12th 1933

Dear Helen:

. . . Howard Hawkes, the director, did not like the original story. His comment was that the people were too realistic. He then said, for the first time, what kind of story he was looking for. He wishes to take the plot of a picture he made called "Red Dust" and superim-

---

[168] *"Horse Thief."*

pose it upon a Northwest background. I told him I had not seen that picture, and besides could not take a plot from an already produced picture and use it ubder my name. That puts an end to that business. I wouldn't mind, but it's hard on Harry [Behn]. His job was depending on whether Hawkes liked the story or not; and now Harry may have to leave this week. However, he took copies of it to King Vidor and Clarence Brown, both directors, for them to read. If neother of tjem like it, Harry's job may be gone. The story editor is really the one to keep or throw out a story, but Sam Marx hasn't read a script since 1931, and the chances are the story will be put on the shelf and never heard of again. Me, I don't care one way or the other; because my weekly check will keep coming until the contract expires regardness.

I've learned that as long as a writer says "yes", he is kept on a picture; but if he answers "no" to any director or supervisor, he is immediately taken off and given another assignment. I have yet to say "yes". This morning I went with King Vidor to see "rushes" (preview) of a picture he is making now. A colt was tied to a stake with a rope, while the mare roamed freely. I told him on a farm a young colt was never tied, because it would not run away from its mother. Vidor was silent after that, and refused to say anything more. Later he sent his secretary to my office to ask if I had ever been on a farm. The secretary said "Mr Vidor wants to know what farm you lived on"....

That was not really a Maine story I wrote. Instead of placing the scene, I merely said "in the north woods", and there was no other identification. However, in my mind as I wrote it, the story was Maine; but I knew directors never followed such suggestions, and that if it were made, it would probably be called Northwest anyway.

I wish Harry Hansen would come across with a story in his book this fall. Still, he makes no sign of doing that; and we'll probably just have to forego O'Henry....[169]

It's good to hear that you're getting up a little now. You'll be all right soon, but no so all right that you can do any other work. There is no need for you to do it; that's what the others are for.

It is warm here today, too, for the first time. But I don't suppose it is as hot as it has been in the East. As soon as the sun goes down it turns cool, and there's always a breeze from the Pacific. But nothing can take the place of soil; God did not intend for people to live here on this desert -- anyone can tell that.

Write me all about everything. There's nothing much I can write, becuase every day it's the same thing, and that has not been interesting yet. I stay here all day; go home about six, eat supper, go back to

---

[169] Hansen included *"Country Full of Swedes" in his* O. Henry Memorial Award Prize Stories of 1933 *(Doubleday, 1933). See note 153, EC to Helen Caldwell 5-28-33.*

the room and read until it's time to go to sleep. I wouldn't be able to stand it if there was not always the knowledge that I'm getting paid for it. . . .

                    Love,
                    Erskine

To Helen Caldwell:

[DAR.tls]   Culver City, Calif
                                                          June 17th 1933

Dear Helen:

    . . . I'm still assigned to Lost Laughter.[170] I've had one conference, and have another this afternoon at 2:15 with the supervisor. This morning I had to sit through an unreeling of a Jean Harlow picture, alone; because Luhan[171] wished me to visualize Harlow in the lead for Lost Laughter. I'm opposed to such methods of writing a story or book, and likewise making a picture. Naturally that is why there is so little originality in pictures. If everything goes right, I'll probably start Monday making a rough adaption of scenes. There is no other writer at the moment assigned to the story, and it looks as if I'll be alone for a while. . . .

    Max [Lieber] writes that Viking has marked up $1300. expenses for the trial. That means I'll have to pay up $650. I agreed to the first $300. to begin with you remember; and all above that had to be earned by the book before I would authorize it. Not know now what the sales have been since May 1st, I don't know if it's come up to that. However, I don't intend to let them get away with anything; I'll put up a fight for that extra $350. if it has not been earned in royalty to date. But I think Max can straighten things out. However, I'm going to stick up for the contents of the stories; I'm just about decided on my selection. I'll send you a copy of the list tomorrow. I intended sending it today, but I have to stay here on the lot this afternoon to see Luhan about the story for Lost Laughter.

    S. J. Perelman just called me up and tried to get me to come to his place this afternoon or tomorrow. I got out of it by saying I had to work here this afternoon, and that tomorrow I had some other work to do. I don't care especially about seeing him; but I wouldn't mind

---

[170]*Caldwell was assigned to write for this project immediately following the rejection of his original script,* Timber.

[171]*Probably the director, producer, and screenwriter Albert Lewin.*

meeting him. I refuse to run over to Hollywood every day or two. If I have to keep on saying I drink nothing stronger than beer, and that only once or twice a week, somebody is going to think it's a joke. But it is no joke -- no more than my refusal to sit in overstuffed chairs in directors, supervisors, and Sam Marxes office. If there is no hard bottomed chair, I ask for one. And you should see the queer looks I get. I suppose most of them think I'm half, if not wholly, cracked. But today I saw [Lynn] Riggs,[172] and accidentally discovered that he also refused to sit in overstuffed chairs. Perelman introduced himself by saying that he was [Nathanael] Pep West's brother-in-law, and that West had told him I was out here. West's book was taken over by Harcourt, he sold the film rights, and he got a contract to write an original for Anna Sten. At least that's what I've heard; he's certainly getting his share of luck....[173]

I haven't heard or seen Harry [Behn] since Thursday night, and I hope they don't call me up to go to the beach tomorrow. They asked me to, and I said I couldn't; they said they were going to call me up again. But tomorrow is the last day I'll have for the book, maybe. I've got to get it back by the first. As soon as I send you the list of stories, write me at once and tell me if you agree with my selection, and if not tell me what to substitute. Back On The Road is out; both Viking and myself dislike it. Marshall [Best] marked Lover Of Horses "A", but I wish to leave it out....

Max [Lieber] sent a check today for the Vanity Fair story, and I suppose that means it will be printed without the 500 word cut.[174] But it is too soon to be certain; they may go ahead and cut it themselves. The check was for $135. -- the sum after Max's commission was taken out. I'm banking it Monday morning. And I'm sending you twenty dollars Monday morning....

                       Love,
                       Skinny

---

[172]*A fellow screenwriter, later famous for adapting his play* Oklahoma! *for film (1955).*

[173]*Caldwell met Nathanael "Pep" West in the fall of 1931 when West, as manager of the elegant Sutton Hotel in New York, offered "attractive rates" to aid struggling writers like himself (Experience, p. 110–112). Caldwell stayed at the Sutton for three weeks, drafting* Tobacco Road *and, on occasion, visiting with West about his own new work-in-progress,* Miss Lonelyhearts *(Harcourt, 1933). In a comment solicited for Harcourt's advertisement for the book, Caldwell called* Miss Lonelyhearts *"a neat piece of work.... I haven't read such good satire on life and living in this era of the twentieth century in a long time" (as published in* Contempo *[25 July 1933], p. 7). Humorist S. J. Perelman was married to West's sister, Laura.*

[174]*"Horse Thief" appeared in the November issue of* Vanity Fair *and was selected for inclusion in Edward J. O'Brien's* The Best Short Stories of 1934 *(Houghton Mifflin, 1934).*

After belabored consideration, exacerbated by his inability to understand Marshall Best's opinion about some of the stories, Caldwell sent Helen his selections for *We Are the Living*.

To Helen Caldwell:

[DAR.tls]   Culver City, Calif
June 18th 1933

Dear Helen:

    I'm enclosing lists of the stories. One list is the choice I have decided upon: if you believe I am wrong in any story, let me know. The other list is marked as Marshall listed the 25 stories. You will see that I do not agree with him in several instances; but I do believe I'm nearer right than he is. You will have to answer right away, so I'll get your letter by Saturday. The MSS will have to be shipped back not later than Monday in order for it to get to NY by the first of July. . . .

    It surprised me a little to find out that Vanity Fair had taken the story without the 500 words taken out. However, there is nothing to prevent them from still doing it, I suppose. But before I would give them my permission to cut it, I'd rather not have them publish it. It will probably come out in about two months' time. Yesterday I got a note from a new magazine in Chicago that offered to pay $150 for a story if it was not over 2200 words. I sent the letter to Max [Lieber]. I don't believe he has one that short; but even if he did have one, they probably wouldn't like it. It doesn't matter anyway. I'm more concerned about getting the best 20 stories in this book than I am in anything else at the present. Marshall said 16 stories were enough; I can't see it that way, and I'm going to insist on 20. Surely there are 20 good stories in the lot. . . .

    Tell Pixy and Dee I wish I could stay out in the sun all day and get tanned. But I have to work in a building.
Love,
Skinny

[Attachment 1]
Contents: WE ARE THE LIVING/Scored by Marshall Best/
1. Warm River. -B-
2. We Are Looking At You, Agnes. -D-
3. The People's Choice. -C-
4. Indian Summer. -A-
5. Rachel. -B-
6. The Medicine Man. -C-
7. Picking Cotton. -B-
8. Summer Accident. -D-
9. Meddlesome Jack. -A-

10. The Picture. -B-
11. Yellow Girl. -A-
12. August Afternoon. -A-
13. Mama's Little Girl. -D-
14. Back on the Road. -D-
15. A Lover of Horses. -B-
16. The First Autumn. -B-
17. The Cold Winter. -C-
18. After-Image. -B-
19. The Empty Room. -C-
20. Crown-Fire. -A-
21. Over the Green Mountains. -C-
22. The Grass Fire. -C-
23. The Midwinter Guest. -D-
24. A Woman in the House. -C-
25. Country Full of Swedes. -B-

A--first-rate
B--good; retain
C--preferably omit
D--omit.

[Attachment 2]
This is my choice/
Contents: WE ARE THE LIVING.[175]
1. Warm River
2. We Are Looking At You, Agnes
3. The People's Choice
4. Indian Summer
5. Rachel
6. The Medicine Man
7. Picking Cotton
8. Meddlesome Jack
9. The Picture
10. Yellow Girl
11. August Afternoon
12. Mama's Little Girl
13. The First Autumn
14. After Image
15. Crown-Fire
16. The Empty Room
17. Over the Green Mountains
18. The Grass Fire

[175] *This arrangement was used for the book.*

19. A Woman in the House
20. Country Full of Swedes.

Caldwell's prolonged absence—and Helen's persistently suspicious readings of his letters in an effort to detect how he might be spending his free time—strained their marriage terribly. If the past were any measure, Helen's insecurities were probably justified. But increasingly her accusations irritated Caldwell, who with less than a month remaining on his contract was not holding up well under the stresses of work he hated. He vented his frustrations angrily and bitterly.

To Helen Caldwell:

[DAR.tls] [Culver City, California]
[June/July, 1933]

Dear Helen:
    I just got four letters from you, including the registered letter. You have written more than I can answer. But I tried to make it plain to you that you've been a damn fool, and that you ought to behave with some sense. You jumped at the conclusion that I was angry with you for going to the Beales.[176] All I tried to say was that personally I should think you could find better company. You do know that people rot when they get to the top; that's why I never wish to get there as far as money is concerned. Why don't you forget Kathleen [Tankersley] Young? She's dead now, and it won't do anybody any good to try to bring people back. I never had anything to do with her, as I told you. That ought to be enough, (which it nearly always isn't). But I said it long ago, and that's all there is to say. How much money do you owe on your bills? I wish to Christ you would try to pay them up instead of trying to cover them up. You can't pay them that way. I don't think you were born with much sense. But if you'll listen to me I'll teach you some, and you'll pay all that you owe by August first. I have no way of knowing how much it is unless you tell me. And if you ever charge another dime I'll wring your neck off. Or else insert a no-responsible ad in the paper. . . .
    I'm not taking up with anybody here. If I were to, or did, I'd say so. And I wouldn't stop at that, either. I'd probably bring them home with me just to show you that any liking was second to you. And even that would probably be a different kind of liking -- I know it would. But I could like anybody under 150, and you'd

[176] *Unidentified.*

better not refuse to step on the scales when I say I don't believe it.

                              Love,
                              Erskine

To Helen Caldwell:

[DAR.tls]   [Culver City, California]
                                                    July 1st 1933

Dear Helen:

The letter I wrote yesterday[177] did not get mailed because when I got to the post office I found I had left it in the desk drawer. It will be mailed with this one this afternoon.

From the way you write about your self, I think I see the cause of some of the trouble (but there shouldn't be any more). It's probably like this: while you are being one of yourselves, you are being remembered as one of the others. When you are thinking and acting as Helen A, I remember you as Helen B; those times when you are Helen C, I recall you as Helen D. In other words, you are so many people that you change from one to the other without my being able to determine at the time just which one you are. So when you are being A, B, C, or D, remember that I am probably thinking of you as one of the other three. The best way to settle that is to select a color for each of yourselves; red today, and I know you are A; blue tomorrow, and I know you are B; and so on.

It's a good thing you are many people. One person becomes tiresome. The Mormons and many others took care of that by have half a dozen, each different; since it's against the law now, you've got it on most other women by reason of having the gift of being abel to be as many as you wish. You probably made the mistake of thinking that I remember you as so-and-so; I don't. When you are reading a story, I know you as a critic; when you are cooking dinner, I know you as a housekeeper. But out here, you are not being any of those; out here, I remember you as somebody getting naked when I want you. Maybe this is the real reason why you misunderstood everything I wrote. Anyway, it can easily be the reason. It shouldn't be any more.

I saw Paul Green leaving the lot this morning as I was coming in. He's leaving today for Chapel Hill. He came to Metro a month ago

---

[177] *Possibly the previous letter.*

from Fox to adapt The Fountain. When he found out that the producers demanded a triple picture, he told them nothing doing. But he has a contract to write two stories for another studio at home, and he's not out of pictures entirely. I think he is going back to teaching in the fall, but I don't know.[178]

It looks as if Vidor won't make the picture; or if he does, not for this company (and if so, I probably won't be assigned to it).[179] This happens because I read in a paper last night that he has signed a new contract with RKO for a picture. He was only on this lot for a loan, and RKO is his home studio. I haven't heard today if he's leaving here, but the item in the paper makes it look that way. Miriam Hopkins is not an M-G-M player (she was on loan here for Stranger's Return), and she has gone back to her home lot. Vidor will probably make a picture for her at the other studio, since they are going to be married I hear. . . . I'mm probably go back to my assignment with [Albert] Lewin to work on Lost Laughter. And even that is not a certainty. There is no certainty in this crazy spot. Every time I hear the Culver City fire department send out an alarm, I'm all ready to accept the burning down of M-G-M, because in such a case, all salaries and contracts are automatically stopped. If not an earthquake then an oil well explosion; if not a fire, then pictures can think up some other "act of God" to enable them to void all contracts. You probably don't see it that way, but out here there is nothing but pins and needles to live on from day to day. The whole thing can easily turn out to be a dream (with the help of the scenic department).

There will be no holiday on this lot Monday, but I don't look for much to do until Wednesday. Most of the producers and supervisors take a four or five day vacation this time of year, and it's only the hired help who has to check-in and check-out. . . .

I read some more stories in O'Brien last night. I still think Sleet Storm is the worst one (it couldn't be any worse if intended). I didn't care for Cantwell's either. The Boyd story is too much tailor-made to suit me. It has all the crafty elements of magazine fiction cleverly disguised. If you read it closely, you'll see that it was built

---

[178] *A native of North Carolina, Green had built his reputation as a playwright, primarily in works dealing with racial prejudice, such as* White Dresses *(1923) and* In Abraham's Bosom *(1926). He also taught at the University of North Carolina at Chapel Hill, first in the philosophy department (1923–1939), then in dramatic arts (1939–1944), and finally in the department of radio-television-motion pictures (1962–1963).*

[179] *Caldwell worked briefly with King Vidor (who had just completed* Stranger's Return*) on plans for a film "about life in the Northwest wheat country," tentatively titled* Let the Hurricane Roar! *As he wrote to Alfred Morang, for once he was enthusiastic about an assignment: "It has genuine life in it—none of this goddam trip[e] of [love] triangles and such" (EC to Morang, HAR 6-23-33).*

up on a frame to begin with. The Farrell story is fine; Joffe is rotten. I haven't read Villa. I think I read most of the others when they were first published.[180]

Take care of yourself --

Love, Skinny . . .

[HAR.tls]

To Alfred Morang:

Culver City, Calif
July 11th 1933

Dear Alfred:

Nothing much that's new to write about, except that more than ever I'll be damned glad to get back East. If I could go for the Hollywood way, I have no doubts I'd be content to stay here and perhaps never come back; but, alas, it's not my pie. I couldn't get any fun out of acting and think like a twelve-year-old with ten times too much money; you could write my epitaph for use two years from now without mistake. They don't print stories about people here who blow their brains out, you know; it's only about those who are in the money, and to be in the money you have to have a weekly check of at least fifteen hundred. After this, I don't think I'll ever again try to make a dollar above what I actually need. . . .

This should be pleasing news to those fools who have been raising such a cry about rag paper and such goings-on. Marshall writes me that they will get out a limited edition of WE ARE THE LIVING, rag paper, signed, special binding, and such, in addition to the regular trade edition of the stories.[181] There are twenty stories in it, all of which were written and published prior to Jan 1st, last. That excludes, of course, the stories written and published this year: they are The Mercury story, New Masses, Story, Vanity Fair, and Esquire.[182] Have you heard about Esquire? It's a new magazine coming soon which is written by and for men. I hope it's not another Vogue. It's probably

---

[180] *Caldwell always claimed publicly that he did not read the work of his contemporaries. However, he obviously studied the contents of Edward J. O'Brien's* The Best Short Stories: 1933 *(Houghton Mifflin, 1933), which included his own "The First Autumn." He refers here to: "Sleet Storm," by Louise Lambertson, reprinted from* Country Gentleman *and* Cornhill Magazine; *"The Land of Plenty," by Robert Cantwell, reprinted from* New Republic; *"Elmer," by Albert Truman Boyd, reprinted from* Harper's; *"Helen, I Love You!" by James T. Farrell, reprinted from* American Mercury; *"In the Park," by Eugene Joffe, reprinted from* New Republic; *and "The Fence," by José Garcia Villa, reprinted from* Prairie Schooner.

[181] *Still capitalizing on Caldwell's vogue among collectors following the* God's Little Acre *case, Viking issued this special edition of* We Are the Living, *limited to 250 copies, which were numbered and signed by the author. Caldwell dedicated the book to Morang.*

[182] *Respectively, "The Man Who Looked Like Himself," "Slow Death," "Yellow Girl," "Horse Thief," and "August Afternoon."*

a little too soon for you to submit there, since they go in mostly for names and the like; but your time will come as soon as you get firmly started on your career of sin and shame via the little magazines.

You must read a story or two by Senora Babb, in Story and other places. Anyway, I found out the other day that she is a well-known Hollywood Boulevard character.[183] The kind that is kept to the tune of a thousand a month by the Stetson hat money, and who, in turn, keeps a friend to the tune of three hundred a month. And to carry the damned cycle to its logical conclusion, they do say that the last named friend keeps his girl to the tune of a hundred a month. That's far enough. But I am glad to hear that the Stetson money is giving so many boys and girls well-paid jobs. -- Now, turn me out a flaming screen script on that!

Pep West is here in all his glory. He's called me up two or three times, but I haven't had a chance to go over to Holly to see him. He's got a four weeks' writing job; and, too, some studio bought his book, Miss Lonelyhearts. What a little luck will do for a fellow![184]

A girl who sat next to me at lunch yesterday, who is the secretary to some supervisor, told me that the reading department had just sent for a copy of Tobacco Rd.[185] I don't know how she found it out, unless it was through her boss. But that doesn't mean anything: all books that get above the average are read and synopsized(?) by M-G-M and most other studios. God's Little Acre was given the same treatment two months ago, but all directors and supervisors turned thumbs down on it. I did not see the synopsis, but someone told me the reader had given it this comment: "Too brutal". This business goes so far away from reality that most pictures even attempt to deny a man his stomach: have you noticed that in pictures people as a rule don't eat? But SEX SEX SEX.

I don't know when the Vanity Fair story is coming; maybe August or September. It's called "Horse Theif"....

Best wishes --

Sincerely, Erskine

---

[183] *Caldwell misspells her name: Sanora Babb made O'Brien's "Roll of Honor" for the first time in 1934. In the autobiographical statement she submitted for that volume, she described herself as "Living alone in Hollywood, and planning to escape as soon as possible" (*The Best Short Stories: 1934 *[Houghton Mifflin, 1934], p. 359).*

[184] *The film based on West's novel,* Lonelyhearts *(dir. Vincent J. Donehue), starring Montgomery Clift in the title role, was not produced until 1958.*

[185] *The movie of* Tobacco Road *did not appear until 1941 (dir. John Ford, screenplay by Nunnally Johnson). Caldwell did not care for this adaptation of his novel. For an excellent consideration of film and stage adaptations of his work, see William L. Howard, "Caldwell on Stage and Screen,"* Erskine Caldwell Reconsidered, *ed. Edwin T. Arnold (Jackson: UP of Mississippi, 1990), pp. 59–72.*

To Helen Caldwell:

[DAR.tls] [Culver City, California]
July 12th 1933

Dear Helen:

Did I make a mistake in english in the letter I wrote to Jack Conroy? CONTEMPO came yesterday, and it reads: "The two poems are the best poetry, etc". To save my life I can't figure out the right or wrong of it. I still think it should be "is", but I'm unable to prove it to my satisfaction.[186]

At last I'm going to see Pep West. He called up this morning at nine o'clock and asked me to come to dinner tomorrow night. I think he lives with the Perelmans. Anyway, I'm going. He's called me a half a dozen times before, but I missed them on account of the defense system I've installed. I wish to see West, but I don't wish to see anyone else. The system got me out of going to dinner at some friends of Harry Behn's, a Miss and Missis Smith in North Hollywood, where I went with Harry about a month ago. The system is working fine now, thanks to the supervisor's secretary who is taking my calls. She tells them that I'm something-or-other, and that usually discourages them -- all except Pep West. He rings the phone like a bull-dog.

I'm a little worried about the money you didn't get when I intended for you to have it. If you had wired me for some, I would have sent it. . . . As time draws to a close, I'm more and more concerned about how much money we will have left over to live on. But it doesn't really matter. Even if there is nothing coming from Viking in August or September, which there should, we'll get by all right. As long as we have a place to live, and a little to eat, we're far better off than millions. Even out here where money is king, there are perhaps a million persons living on five dollars a week or less. I don't expect the book of stories to make any money, at least not much over the two-fifty advance already received. But maybe there will be another book soon.

Which reminds me to ask you if you have looked at Journeyman lately. Maybe if you would go over it again sometime within the next two weeks, you could find something wrong with it. Your mind

---

[186] *The 25 July 1933 issue of* Contempo *contained an advertisement for Conroy's new leftist literary magazine,* The Anvil*: "This is not a magazine for everybody. It publishes fiction and verse by writers internationally known, but its chief concern is with the courageous vanguard of proletarian writers usually barred even from* avant garde *reviews because of their revolutionary affiliation." Included were comments on the magazine's first issue from Heywood Broun, Granville Hicks, Edwin Seaver, and Caldwell, who offered: "Tell the kickers to go to hell! The two poems by Langston Hughes in the first issue are the best poetry I ever read!" (p. 6). Caldwell eventually lent his name to the masthead by agreeing to become an "associate editor" of* The Anvil.

should be clear after this lapse of time, and you will be able to almost read it with a first impression. It's been so long since I read it, that I can't decide whether it's any good or not. Two or three chapters still stand out; but that many pages doesn't make a book. When you read it again, write me the same hour and tell me what feeling it gave you. If bad, all right; if indifferent, all right; if etc, etc. . . .

Is the little kid growing any? You haven't written much about her lately. She should, if you give her all the milk she can eat, and all the sunshine she can stand. Sun will do her more good now than later; there won't be any sun after September, and you should keep her outdoors and let her store it up for the next six months to come.

The two Monday letters that came this morning give me to understand that you may be waking up. I hope so. A person's personality matters more than the way he may look; but it acts the other way, too, because a person who looks sluggish is usually sluggish in behavior. There is such a thing as being alive and awake. You know damn well the only reason I ever liked anybody else (momentarily) was because it was the contrast. It's just that I couldn't help being a fool about anybody (no matter whom) with what you lacked. Call it round breasts, firm legs, or mental and physical agility. It doesn't matter what you call it: the fact was that you were abnormal.[187] And I can only stomach normality. In other words, aside from having those basic qualities (which you've always had), you must also display them. Isn't that being normal? I myself think it's perfectly normal for a normal person to like normal things. You will be normal when your mind and body reacts to my conception of naturalness, and I don't think my conception is warped. I like healthy people: men and women. I can't stand perversion in people, in writing, or in life: I won't have anytjing to do with any of it, because I know it is more satisfying to be natural. That comes out of the earth, or whatever you call it, and it endures. If you are to be abnormal, then I wish none of you; if normal, then I'll have to take all or nothing.

It's silly to get all up in the air about nothing. You ought to forget it. I don't change over-night, you know. . . .

I told you with whom I was at the beach. I've been three times;

---

[187] *Caldwell's precise meaning in calling Helen "abnormal" is not known. He was probably rendering a judgment of her mental stability, based on her relentless suspicions about how he was spending his free time in California. A little over a week later, he would apologize for "writ[ing] all these damn fool letters," and attempt to explain away his frustration (and guilt): "Some persons would masturbate I suppose; I won't, because it isn't the real thing, and I would feel even worse (if that's possible). And I wouldn't take anybody unless I asked or told you first, and gave you a chance to forbid it. And the only kind of girl I would take—no matter if you did say I could have the other kind—would be a prostitute. She would have to be the kind of girl I'd never seen before and would never see again. I couldn't take any other kind of girl, because she would be too much like you—and I'd be dissatisfied" (EC to Helen Caldwell, DAR 7-22-33).*

twice I went and came back alone. The last time, I went alone, and saw some people I knew. They made me stay and eat supper with them, and then they brought me home. That's all there is to that.
        Love,
        Skinny . . .

To Alfred Morang:

[HAR.tls]   Culver City, Calif
                       July 17th 1933

Dear Alfred:

 You're right about not listening seriously to haphazard and other stray advice. Don't let anyone tell you how to write or what to write about. A serious writer can never be anything more than an echo if he once begins listening to someone else. A man knows what he feels, and since that is the basis of art, he's a fool to take second-handed mouthings no matter how earnest or best-intentioned the advice may be. But it can never be anything except that; writing is an individual act, like going to the bathroom, or kissing your wife. All else is 100% bunk.

 My present assignment is on a piece of tripe called, naturally, "A Wicked Woman". The thing is scheduled to begin shooting August 5th, and since I've never done anything on it, I don't know what the hell it was assigned to me for. It's just like this business, though, to be called up the day before shooting starts, and informed to prepare a version to be handed in at 9 a.m. the next morning. That's one reason I've had a lot of bad dreams lately. And, queerly enough, supervisors are always the villyans in these torid nightmares of mine. (A supervisor is a non-creative worker who presumes to tell writers and directors how scripts should be written.)

 I had dinner with Pep West last week. He's as unsettled as I am. He said he'd like to stay another term or two after his contract is up August 1st in order to get enough money to live on at home. I have an idea that West would like to make one hell of a lot of money. Maybe I'm wrong, as usual, though.

 The new book is scheduled for publication Sept 18th, I'm informed. I hope I have a copy to send you long before that date, however. As yet, though, I haven't even received the galleys.

 My time is up in three weeks, thank God, and I'll be on my way home by the night of August 5th (if luck is with me). I won't reach Mount Vernon until about the 11th or 12th. I've paid up the biggest

bill in Portland, and the other one will be paid up soon. After all this I won't have any money left, over enough to live on a few months, but I'll have squared myself with your Portland sons-of-bitches. They can now, one and all, go straight to hell and roast there. . . .
                    Sincerely,
                    Erskine

Despite the financial rewards, Caldwell's impatience with Hollywood and its "business" obsessed him during the last days of his contract. He wrote Helen on July 20: "I'm getting goddam tired of this business. I'm not sorry for having had the chance to get the money to pay up; but I hate it none the less. It gets worse every day. If we can manage to get by, I'll be satisfied never to come out here again." A few days later he told her about a sound technicians' strike that threatened his "last two weeks' salary checks." He was distressed at the thought of losing the money, but explained: "I'm siding with the strikers, of course; but I also realize that the individual in the present constituted society has to fight for existence. If he doesn't do it, there's no one just yet to fight for the individual collectively."[188]

To Helen Caldwell:

[DAR.tls]   Culver City, Calif
                                                                                                        July 26th 1933

Dear Helen:
    It looks today as if the strike might pass away. There has been nothing in the paper about a settlement, but it is said that Columbia resumed work today, and M-G-M stopped hiring men this morning. So, it looks as if the strike is over. It was probably started, to begin with, in order for the various studios to shake off undesirable men. The companies, like all capitalists, work together in more ways than one.
    Last night I went over to a canyon in Hollywood and had dinner with West, his sister, and Perelman. West had called me three or four times since Sunday, and I thought I'd better go and get it over with.
    West's sister claims that she has a producer in New York interested in Kirkland's play. I don't know his name, but it is the one who is going to produce Perleman's play in New York this fall.[189] The only trouble, she said, is that the producer thinks Kirkland's piece needs doctoring before it is ready for the stage. I promised her I'd get Kirk-

---

[188] *EC to Helen Caldwell, DAR 7-20-33, 7-24-33.*
[189] *Jack Kirkland had been working on an adaptation of* Tobacco Road *since May 1932. S. J. and Laura Perelman's new play,* All Good Americans, *opened at Henry Miller's Theatre in New York on 5 December 1933.*

lan's permission to rewrite it, if she'd get the producer and money for the play-doctor. I don't think much will come of it. But they seem to think that it would make a good play. I don't like the play as it is now, and I don't see why Kirkland wouldn't agree to letting someone else work on it.

They asked me to come back to dinner one night next week, but I'm not going. By that time I'll be getting ready to leave this godforsaken place, and I can't be bothered with going places to dinner.

I worked all day yesterday on revisions for this two-reeler, and now I'm waiting for a chance to see the director. The thing is done as far as I'm concerned, and if they ask for more rewriting, I'll tell them no soap. Let them bring in another writer, if they aren't satisfied. I can't see any sense in writing a thing "away"; and that's what happens when a picitre script is over-written.[190]

It's getting really hot here now. Yesterday it was 90 at noon, the hottest day so far. Today started out just as hot as yesterday, and it feels now that it will get hotter. I suppose this is the hot season now, and I'm glad to be getting away.

West talks as if he would stay another month if he gets an offer. He's going back to live on his farm this fall, and he probably needs the money. Perleman said, though, that he wished he (himself) had never seen Hollywood. The trouble is that he's been here too long, I guess. And now it's too late for him to break away. A person probably gets so that he can't give up the two-fifty and five hundred a week, always promising himself to leave after he saves the next two thousand. The trouble, like dope, is that you can't make yourself shake it off.

I had to change to the New Orleans seersuckers. I've got two suits, and they'll last me until the end of next week, if it doesn't get cooler. And this cold I caught somewhere doesn't make me feel any better. I've been taking pills, but they don't seem to help much.

I suppose all these fellows who got jobs Monday to take the place of the strikers will be fired. That's rotten, too; because some of them haven't had a job in two years. This was the first chance some of them had to work in all that time, and two days after starting, they'll be fired to make way for the men who walked out last week. There's no justice in that. . . .

Love,
Skinny . . .

---

[190] *Caldwell earned one of his only screen credits for his writing on* The Express Train Robbery, *an episode of the film series* Crime Does Not Pay *which dramatized cases from actual F.B.I. investigations (Experience, p. 146).*

As scheduled, Caldwell departed California on August 5. Before leaving he dashed off a letter indicating the relief he felt at the prospect of getting back home—and back to his work.

To Milton A. Abernethy:

[HRC.tls]
Culver City, Calif
August 3rd 1933

Dear Milton:

I go off tomorrow afternoon at 5 p.m.; leave L.A. Saturday night; arrive Chicago Tuesday; see the [World's] Fair, the fan dancers, rhumba girls, etc a day, and get to Mount Vernon Friday of next week. Thank God!

... I've only completed two scripts in all my three months. One an original story (which no one after two months has read), the other an adaption for a two-reel short about crime-doesn't-pay or some such hoke. Anyway, I'm glad now that I didn't have to turn in more. I turned down seven assignments, was taken off three, and completed two. That's my record. But the debts are paid off, by God, and we'll have about three hundred dollars clear. We can live on that till kingdom comes if necessary.

WE ARE THE LIVING is now in galleys. I returned my set, revised, last Monday....

Aren't you going to tell me more about the new magazine, or is it a secret? But if you think you're going to drop CONTEMPO, you're mistaken; because I'm enclosing a buck for a year's issues, and you'd better by a damn sight send them.[191]

I had dinner with West the other night, at the home of his sister and Perelman. I don't know when he's leaving, as he hinted he might stay another four weeks.

I'm sorry but I can't see this Joffe person. I can't see anything in Villa, either.[192] Why do I have to be contrary! Goddamn it I can't help it. I just don't think the stories they write is <u>writing</u>. A story, poem, novel should be an experience; the things they do merely confirm my belief that they can't write. Now, a fellow like Alvah Bessie, Jack Conroy -- they <u>write</u>! ...

Sincerely,
Erskine

---

[191] Contempo *published just one more issue after the date of this letter: a special issue on James Joyce (15 February 1934). Abernethy had recently moved to New York, but his plans for a "new magazine" are unknown.*

[192] *The most recent* Contempo *(25 July 1933) contained a brief story by Eugene Joffe, "The Unmarried Couple" (p. 5). A widely published writer of minimalist fiction, José Garcia Villa had founded the short-lived little magazine* Clay *in 1931. He published two of Caldwell's stories that year, "Rachel" and "We Are Looking At You, Agnes."*

Back home in Mount Vernon, Caldwell went immediately to work on completing the draft of *Journeyman*.

To I. L. Salomon:

[LOC.tls]　　　　　　　　　　　　　　　　　　　　Mount Vernon Maine
August 29th 1933

Dear Salomon:

I haven't been so hot myself. Putting up with the Hollywood idiots for three months sort of wrung me dry, and I'm just getting back to normal. And this novel that I've been working on since last January has had me worried. I'm beginning to find a little satisfaction in it now, though -- as little satisfaction as I ever find in what I do -- and I hope it will soon be done and off my hands.

The last time I heard, the book of stories was due for Sept. 25th. Half of them are punk, and if the book gets by, it will be by the skin of its teeth. Honestly, I haven't seen so many rotten stories since I heard Jose Garcia Villa was publishing a book.

All my debts are paid up through the courtesy of M-G-M Studios, and I'm back at scratch again. I don't owe nothing, and I aint got nothing; but I'm even with the world, thank God. Now, if somebody would buy a few copies of a book, I'd feel rich as hell. . . .

　　　　　　　　　　　　　　　Sincerely,
　　　　　　　　　　　　　　　Erskine

To Alfred Morang:

[HAR.tls]　　　　　　　　　　　　　　　　　　　Mount Vernon, Maine
August 29th 1933

Dear Alfred[193]:

I've been doing some thinking about your work. I've got an idea that you ought to [?] your time, so you will not try to go too fast. This [?] I mean: instead of trying to see how much work you can [churn?] out, or how often; try instead to limit yourself to a [certain number?] of stories within a time-limit. In other words, [?] the story less than you actually can. In that way, I [?] you will build up a reserve. And on the other side, [try to?] keep your things from being pushed into print. If [you will?] set, say three years, as the time to publish in a commercial magazine, rather than trying for it now, you will gain in the end I am convinced. In other words, devote yourself now to

[193] *The original of this letter is damaged so that parts are unreadable.*

building up a wall of water, daming it up so to speak, so that when three years are up, you will have enough force to break through all the magazines that naturally hold out against a new writer. Two years from now if you have twenty fine stories (unpublished), you will have what very few writers ever have. On the other hand, if you write two or three fine stories now and publish them in commercial magazines before the two years are up, you will be handicapped, for the very reason that you will have none to follow them up. You see, it's the force a writer can bring to bear that counts, and the more force (fine stories) you have at the right time, the more impress you will make on editors and readers alike. Seriously, three years is none too late to offer your wares to the great American reading public. By that time (two years from now) you will have progressed enough to stand face to face with any writer: [it?] does not pay to be a second-rate writer merely because personal vanity calls for quickness. For, after all, your stories, and mine, will be here to be read a long time after we are [gone?] and we wish to leave the best behind. -- I may be all wet. This is merely a thought that came to me. I thought you'd like to think about it. (And by setting the limit at two years from now does not force you to stick to it: later, if your stories turn out better than you hope for, you can set the time up a year, which would make it a year from now.)

I may be way off the course; [?] don't accept what I say. Things like this have to be adjusted to a person, not to a theory.

And one more [thing?] that came to me. If I were you, I'd try to cast my work more and more into the form of the *story*. A short story is a *story*. People read to hear about something that happened. The short story writer should tell people what happened once-upon-a-time. If you go too far in the extreme, you will be writing what is called "prose poems". Too far in the other direction will be writing "plots". You [should not?] wish to write either one, because neither are *stories*. The golden mean is the short story, a telling that relates what happened to somebody, somewhere, sometime. And the artistry appears when the telling is done in such a way that the reader is moved by the feeling the author has for [the?] subject.

This may be all wet, [?] don't accept a damn word of it without thinking it through. I'm no goddamn fountain-head of wisdom. . . .

I'm looking for the book sometime next week. I'll send your copy pronto.

Best wishes --

                    Sincerely,
                    Erskine

To Milton A. Abernethy:

[HRC.tls]
Mount Vernon, Maine
September 17th 1933

Dear Milton:

... I still have my like and dislike since the last time. I think Jack Conroy is one of the best writers, and I know damn well that J G Villa is one of the worse. I've been trying for two years to find something about Villa's work but to save my life I still see nothing of merit. The fellow is punk.

Did I write you about the reception committee that waited upon me when I got home from the Coast? Two creditors met me at the train, even willing to shake hands because I was back on the soil over which the State of Maine has rule. There would have been three, but one dropped dead while I was gone. However, two lawyers representing his estate called on me the next day. I paid off all the bastards, and I no longer have to dodge into doorways when I walk down the street of Augusta. Thank God. My only worry now is eating.

I read [Louis] Bromfield's "The Farm". Skim-milk.[194]

How about asking all the Guggenheim Fellows in Creative Writing for the past six or seven years what they have written and published since getting the money? [Thomas] Wolf[e], no book; [Caroline] Gordon, no book; [Katherine Anne] Porter, no book; [Jonathan] Daniels, no book; in other words, does it pay to get one of the fellowships? [Hart] Crane went off the deep end. What the hell? There must be something wrong, somewhere.

Listen: the South (S. Atlantic; S. Central; S. West) is the place where the best writing is going to come from during the next several years. The rest of the country hasn't any life; it is in-grown. A writer in the South has everything to gain, nothing to lose; therefore he can cut loose and write like a damn fool. In New England he can't do that; he has to fall into a school; he has to make money out of his writing; he has to have an income to live on. A writer in the South has a future.

Hurry up with CONTEMPO.

Best wishes ---

Sincerely,
Erskine

---

[194]*Reviewer Mary Ross described Bromfield's new semi-autobiographical novel (Harper, 1933) as being "filled with scores of portraits and scenes that have the full-bodied charm of a Currier & Ives print" (New York Herald Tribune Books [20 Aug. 1933], p. 1).*

To Alfred Morang:

[HAR.tls] Mount Vernon, Maine
September 18th 1933

Dear Alfred:
 . . . It's good to hear that you've had another story taken. Struggling through the mass of readers and writers to the top of the pile sometimes feels like butting your head against a brick wall. But there's plenty of room at the top, and the only way to get there is by means of a slow, laborious process of working upward step by step. Every story printed is just such a step. Flashy, sensational work never lasts any longer than it takes to explode flashlight powder in a fourth-of-july skyrocket. . . .

Sincerely,
Erskine

To Alfred Morang:

[HAR.tls] Mount Vernon, Maine
October 5th 1933

Dear Alfred:
 Don't let the Woodman matter worry you any. Such things mean very little after all. What he told somebody else was probably stretched a little, and by the time I heard it, it had been stretched to the limit. I had something of the same nature come up, and I disposed of it by saying I was not a member of the Communist Party, but that I was almost wholly sympathetic with its aims and ideals. This was for TIME magazine, and when the thing came out in print last week, it read in such a way that I was put in the position of being practically reactionary. But there was nothing I can do about it now. Someday I'll probably join the party if for no other reason than to be able to say, and say proudly, that I am a Communist.[195]

---

[195] Caldwell had reported a rumor that Morang had "renounced Com[munism]" in order to be an associate editor for Lawrence C. Woodman's little magazine, American Scene. "That can't be so," Caldwell wrote, "and I hope something can be done about it" (EC to Morang, HAR 9-30-33). In his own experience with misrepresentation, the past week's issue of Time carried an unsigned review of We Are the Living, for which Caldwell must have been contacted. Though he was not quoted, the reviewer described him as one of "the young writers who frisk it in their new-found freedom" from censorship: "Essentially a humorist, and of the earth earthly, he has not yet settled down to his rôle. Left wing critics have dragged tempting herrings across his track, calling him a heavyweight Red hope and trying to lure him into the ranks of the proletarian propagandists" ("U.S. Humorist," Time [2 Oct. 1933], p. 51).

On the other hand it means something to have people talking about you (if you are not cast in too much of a bad light). Nearly everyone I talked with knew who you were. That means a lot. By keeping at it all the time, hammaring away at magazines, dropping an occaisonal stick of dynamite in a complacent shirt-front, you will force people to take notice. That means that you will have to be considered where ever writing is mentioned. Burnett thinks you should lean a little heavier on the story element; that is, bring a little more force to bear on the storytelling part of the story. God knows you've got something to write about; Burnett himself admitted that. The thing to do now is to cast your material into the storytelling form as generally accepted. That does not mean you have to copy somebody else. That would be fatal. By all means, do the thing as you wish to do it. That is what sets one writer apart from the run-of-the-mine.

I think I wrote you that George Antheil is writing an opera around the novel. Max Lieber thinks that Kirkland's adaptation of the play will get produced. The producer who is interested is trying to get Kirkland to make some changes. Probably everything depends on that. But I'd lots rather see a play made of the other novel.[196]

Nothing has been decided about the new novel yet.[197] I'm waiting to hear what Carl Van Doren thinks of it before I decide. I'd hate to publish it if it's not good; and I'd hate not to publish it if it's going to leave a gap in my work. So you see, I'm plainly up a tree. I made that mistake with AUTUMN HILL, I think now; and I'd hate to repeat a mistake. I'll probably have to call a town meeting in order to reach a decision. What to do! What to do!

I've just had news that TOBACCO RD was published in London on September 19th; and also that [Martin] Secker has taken the book of stories for publication there. That sounds good, but it doesn't mean much to me. All that's done with as far as I'm concerned. The things that are yet unwritten interest me more. Another thing is that I can't visualize England reading anything I have written. My conception of England is a land where everyone wears tight collars and talks like Rhodes scholars. . . .

Instead of writing Scribner's a letter about Villa's book, I went in to see them and told them all, from Charles Scribner Jr on down, that I thought they were damn fools for publishing a book of his when they had the opportunity of publishing Alvah Bessie.[198] You can

---

[196]*God's Little Acre was dramatized by E. J. Basshe but was never produced in the United States. No opera based on either novel was ever produced.*

[197]*Journeyman was still in manuscript.*

[198]*Scribner's had recently published José Garcia Villa's* Footnote to Youth: Tales of the Philippines, and Others *(1933). Caldwell had been following Bessie's work at least since they had both appeared, each for the first time, in Edward J. O'Brien's* The Best Short Stories of

imagine how they liked that. Bessie and Conroy are the two outstanding new writers. . . .

                          Sincerely,
                          Erskine

Earlier in the month, Caldwell had agreed to write an article for the *Daily Worker* on conditions for blue-collar workers in the Ohio Valley. In the meantime, he had been sorting out his own feelings about Marshall Best and Viking's lukewarm response to an early draft of *Journeyman*.

    To Alfred Morang:

[HAR.tls]   Mount Vernon, Maine
                                                      October 29th 1933

Dear Alfred:

Because of some dirty work at the crossroads I'm back home a little sooner than I had anticipated. Helen showed me Dorothy's letter, and we're tickled pink to hear that you will have at least one three-star story catalogued in O'B. What more could you ask for the first year's work?[199]

While I was in the Ohio Valley it seems that Max Lieber was trying to locate me, and when he finally did, I had to go to New York to see him. And I came home from there. The gist of the matter is that I politely told Viking to go to hell. But not before I had received an offer of $2000 advance from a hell of a lot better publisher.[200] And, so, there you are. I could not reason out why I should let Viking publish the novel when they didn't like it, and at the same time when another

---

1931. *Politically a leftist, and inclined toward minimalist experimental fiction, Bessie published extensively in the short story during the early 1930s; in 1935 he won a Guggenheim Fellowship to complete his first novel,* Dwell in the Wilderness *(Covici Friede, 1935).*

  [199] *Edward J. O'Brien rated the stories in his annual "Index of Distinctive Short Stories," an appendix to each* Best Short Stories *anthology. Three asterisks (as opposed to two or one) qualified exceptional stories for his "Roll of Honor." Morang was included in O'Brien for the first time in 1934, with three out of six stories cited as exceptional: "Bright Saws," reprinted from* Windsor Quarterly; *"Bust of Balzac," from* Fantasy; *and "Hunger," from* Blast.

    *First-time honorees were invited to submit autobiographical statements. Morang's described him as "a violinist. Studied painting, but found the painted surface inadequate, as he had to tell a story, and in his opinion that is not the mission of painting. Erskine Caldwell urged him to try sending out his work, and he has had very good success so far. Has had the usual hard knocks in various cities, playing anywhere from dance halls to symphony orchestras. His whole interest now lies in trying to write. To him short stories are the fullest expression of this time and its life" (*The Best Short Stories of 1934 *[Houghton Mifflin, 1934], p. 363).*

  [200] *Despite their earlier disagreements over the merits of* God's Little Acre, *Bennett*

publisher was anxious to hand out that much money even before he read the book. I was swayed partly because you and Max and Helen all urged me to publish it regardless of what Viking said about it. I hope to christ you three are right. All this is confidential, and I ask you to keep it under your hat. It's a personal matter, and I don't wish to hang out my wash on Main Street.

I've just finished reading Jack Conroy's book, and it is damn fine.[201] It will be recommended by the book-of-the-month club, and that will help sales a little. But even so, it won't get around as much as it should in the beginning. It's the kind of book that lives a long life, though; we'll be hearing about it for several years to come. I've got an extra copy in case you can't get your hands on one.

Little magazines are getting as thick as molasses. There's been two or three new ones since I looked the last time. If they don't stop printing the same stories over and over again, they are going to get it in the neck. Every little magazine from here to Carmel-by-the-Sea print the same stories dozens of times. there's no excuse for them any longer, if that's what's going to happen. We'll just have to close the book on them, and look somewhere else for print. The only ones with any purpose now are such proletarian ones as THE ANVIL. It wouldn't be a bad idea for good writers to standardize on these latter ones. There's no danger of such persons as Jack Conroy making a mess of print.

Jack Kirkland's show was scheduled to go into rehearsal last Wednesday. If it ever reaches the boards, I'm convinced it will be a fizzle. However, I promised to go down and help stage it as soon as they have rehearsed a week. I don't know if that means I'll have to go this week or not. I'll go when I'm sent some traveling expenses, but not before. I hope something happens to it so it will be better, but I don't see much hope. Pat Kearney was the fellow to write a play; I had more confidence in him than in twenty Broadway playwrights. I can't figure out why it is that fellows such as Kearney do suicide, and the others live.[202]

If I have to go down to help with the play this week, why not let Dot take your classes,[203] and go down with me? It will only be two or

---

Cerf, of Random House, had recently "become a close friend" of the Caldwells (See Klevar, Biography, *pp. 142–143).*

[201]*The Disinherited (Covici, 1933).*

[202]*Pat Kearney "died of gas poisoning in his apartment" on 4 April 1933. According to his obituary in* Variety, *"Despondency was believed to have been the cause, the recent bank holiday having prevented the production of his most recent play, 'Veiled Eyes'" (Chuck Bartelt and Barbara Bergeron, eds.,* VARIETY Obituaries, 1905–1986, *Vol. 2, [New York: Garland, 1988], np).*

[203]*While writing and painting, Morang paid his bills by teaching art.*

three days, and we could break a lot of ice on your behalf while in town. The bus trip doesn't cost much, and finding a place to stay is easy, if you don't mind sleeping in 11th Street hallways.

I've got your copy of the London edition of Tobacco Rd and I'll get it off tomorrow if possible.

Best wishes --
Sincerely,
Erskine

Rehearsals for *Tobacco Road* began in early November, under the direction of Anthony Brown. At Brown's invitation, Caldwell was present, but he was distracted by the still unsettled matter of *Journeyman*.

To Helen Caldwell:

[DAR.tl] [New York City]
Friday a.m. [November 18, 1933]

Dear Helen:

I've just got your two letters and the contracts. It's no fault of yours or anybody else's, unless mine, but I can't do a damn thing with all this hell going on. The book is enough, but the play makes it worse. Untill both of these things are gone through with and over, I don't see how I'm going to get any decent work finished. Right now I'm ready to quit and try to put everything aside until something is done about the book. I don't care what it is, just so it's put in it's final resting place. Probably the best thing I can do now is to go see Lieber and Marshall [Best] and settle the thing one way or another. I've been working two days on this story, and I haven't much done; and now I don't see how I'm going to be able to get my mind and feeling into it while this book is raising so much hell with my nerves. I can't help being shaky all over from it. Maybe if we can do something: burn it up, or publish it, it'll be off my mind.

It's about 10:30 now, and the only thing I see to do is to go down and see Lieber and Marshall and ome to some decision. In that case, I'll offer my help for the play Monday or Tuesday, and be home Wednesday. It's the only God damn thing I know to do. This story isn't getting anywhere. It's a combination of worry over whether the play will make any money for us to live on, and what in hell the book is going to do. If I go down town at all, I'll go before noon today. I'll say that I happened into town, and am on my way out.

I wish to god I knew about the book. If I *knew* it was good, I'd let it be published. I think it is, and I feel it is, but how can you be sure.

Don't tell anybody anything about me, however. If I do make myself known to Lieber and Marshall, it will be in such a way that I won't have to deal with them any longer than today or tomorrow. If I go downtown today, it will mean that I'm giving up this try this time, and am coming home Wednesday. I'll write you tomorrow and let you know, so you can expect me Wednesday.

I wish you were here to tell me what to do. It's hell to have to take the book on my head when there are so many yeses and noes.

The way I feel now, I won't be able to do anything on the story today, and maybe not tomorrow. And then by that time, or Monday possible, there';; be something else about it comibg up that will put the skids under me for fair.

If we can get any money from the book or play, maybe the best thing is to go to Georgia or Florida for a couple of months and steam the book and play out of me. That is if everybody could go. It would be hopeless for not all of us to go.

By this time I know the only thing is to go down and see Lieber and get something done. I'll write you tomorrow and let you know what happens, and if you are to meet me Wednesday, where and when. . . .

Love,

Erskine
(no ink)

To Helen Caldwell:

[DAR.tl] [New York City]
Saturday p.m. [November 19, 1933]

Dear Helen:

. . . I got the play check today, and I'll keep them both until I get back. The play is due to open Thanksgiving week, cold. I've been to two rehearsals, and I'm going to one more Sunday night.

This "Journeyman" is a hell of a mess. I went to Viking to find out what they would do. They will contract for it, one thousand advance now, but won't publish it until I write and publish another novel. That's not so good. I don't know what Cerf's offer is, but I understand he will pay Viking a thousand, and give us a thousand. That's better. And now [Pascal] Covici makes this offer: Fifty dollars a week for three years ($7500.), charges or maybe not the Viking thousand, and agrees to take over all Scribner and Viking books. Now what in hell am I to do? Covici, by the way, would publish the book next Spring. If you care to figure the thing out and send tye answer by one p.m. Monday in care of Max [Lieber], collect, it would be a solution. I don't know what to do. I wish the book published, there's no doubt about that; but I'm afraid if we take up Viking the damn book will hang over my head so much I can't write another one. If Cerf could be induced to duplicate Covici's ofrer, I'd be inclined to take it, but I don't believe he would. That fifty a week for three years sounds good, but I'm not sure that Covici-Friede is the right place. And, in face, I don't know where the right place is. Maybe you can determine in half an hour and let me know what I haven't been able to decide in 48 hours, and maybe never will. I haven't signed any contract yet, though Viking is drawing up theirs for Monday I suppose. I'm going to try to see Marshall tomorrow and find out just what they are prepared to do now and in the future. God knows I don't know and unless you or Max can convince me, I'll probably just have to stay at Viking. I'll have to say something definite by Monday afternoon, because Viking expects me to sign there. I'll send a night letter tonight.

Virginia[204] called up this morning at Max's. She insists on both kids coming down when we do. You'll have to decide that. Personally I think Dee is enough. If you wish to come for the opening Thanksgiving night, we will; or we will wait one week or two. The thing may close up in a week, and if you really wish to see it, it would be best to come to the opening. Whatever you say.

I don't think Covici has much backing; Cerf has. That has to be considered in coming to your decision. Or make it Viking? What in hell!

Be home Tuesday. . . .

Love,
Erskine

Tobacco Road premiered on Monday, December 4, at the Masque Theater in New York. The Caldwells attended the second night's performance.

To I. L. Salomon:

[LOC.tls—postcard] [Mount Vernon, Maine]
[December 9, 1933]

Dear Salomon: I'm sorry I couldn't get down to see the show at the time you did. Helen and I went down and saw it Tuesday night from the balcony, which I think is the best (in order to study). You are

[204] *Helen's sister.*

no doubt right about it. Of course, I didn't have a thing to do with it, except furnish the novel, but I like the material Kirkland used, even if I would have used it in other ways. But maybe it will help picture the book a little better to those who thought it was rotten. I hear that the play is improving every night; if it runs another week, it may be something like it after all. I'm glad you got the tickets; being off up here, I was afraid you wouldn't in time. I'm hoping Kirkland will hurry and finish revising, and maybe we can get the script in book form. I've never had a chance to study the play since he wrote it.

      Best,
      EC

Ever alert to opportunities for free publicity, particularly those in which Caldwell could refine his growing reputation for having a social conscience, Max Lieber referred Caldwell to an item in the most recent issue of the *Nation*. In a lengthy letter, the Agrarian John Gould Fletcher warned against any rush to judge the South for its actions in the recently infamous Scottsboro Case, in which nine black youths were prosecuted on trumped up charges of raping two white women on a freight car passing through Alabama. Fletcher conceded potential injustices but blamed them on Northern "interferences and interventions on behalf of the Negro," which had only "stiffen[ed] Southern resistance" to reform in race relations. "We in the South do not legislate against the Negro as a class," Fletcher asserted. "And I believe I am speaking on behalf not only of Alabama but of the overwhelming majority of the Southern people today." An editorial note invited other Southerners to respond, "Is This the Voice of the South?"[205]

To Maxim Lieber:
[*New Masses*]   [c. January 30, 1934]
                                                                         Wrens, Georgia
Dear Max:

    I have read Fletcher's letter to the Nation and I find it unusual only in so far as it is probably the first composed statement of the ruling class in this section of the country. The state of mind he makes articulate is common. It is the type that sits in power in a dozen state capitols, but its power gains whatever strength it has by being backed up by thousands of petty minds holding petty offices, including that humane marvel of all ages -- the county chain-gang boss.

[205] *"Correspondence: Is This the Voice of the South?"* Nation *137 [27 Dec. 1933], pp. 734–736. Since the original of Caldwell's response does not survive, the letter is reprinted here as it was published, along with an excerpt from Fletcher's letter, in the 30 January 1934 issue of the* New Masses *(pp. 20–21).*

As for myself, I hasten to protest against the implications of this letter to the Nation. I myself am a Southerner, I was born here, I have lived here most of my life, and I shall probably die here. But if being a Southerner carries with it the implications of Fletcher's letter, then I will renounce whatever birthright and heritage I may have, and give my allegiance to some other country. However, I prefer to remain here, and I shall do so; and if anyone would like to coin a name for those of us who are opposed to what Fletcher stands for, then under that name I shall live. I have taken my stand, and I intend to keep it; but, to draw sharp this necessary dividing line, it is on the other side of the fence from Fletcher and his "millions of Southerners."

By his own words, Fletcher represents an obnoxious majority of people in power; he does not, however, represent a majority of the population. The Negro, the tenant farmer, and the mill worker have contributed, involuntarily, to the power of those holding the whip-hand; but the hand grows weak, the oppressed gains strength, and the outcome of the coming struggle cannot be in doubt. Fletcher and his "millions of Southerners" demanding injustice over the Negro will find that it is impossible to confine steam within a boiling kettle: sooner or later the lid is going to blow off.

Erskine Caldwell

Caldwell's immediate interest, however, was more financial than political: initial reviews of *Tobacco Road* were lukewarm, and there was some concern about how long it would last on Broadway. But in January, a series of reviews by *Daily News* editor Joseph M. Patterson urged theater-goers to see the play. As Caldwell would later boast, "By the end of the first year, the play had become an established institution on Broadway, and when it finally closed, it had had a continuous run in New York of seven and a half years, setting a record for being at that time the longest run in the history of the New York theater."[206] It had also made Caldwell a very wealthy man. Helen never forgot how the income from the play made their life "different": "You know, I could go to Duff-Goodman and get a $700.00 dress without bothering."[207]

---

[206] *Experience*, p. 151. Though road companies performed the play consistently for years afterward, the play closed on Broadway in March 1941, setting a Broadway record with 3180 performances. See C. Michael Smith, "The Surprising Popularity of Erskine Caldwell's South," Journal of Popular Culture 16 (Winter 1982), pp. 42–46.

[207] Klevar, "Interview," p. 94.

To Alfred Morang:
[HAR.tls] Mount Vernon, Maine
February 15th 1934

Dear Alfred:

We finally got here Tuesday, and now I'm down with, of all things, mumps. Can you beat it? I don't know how long it is going to last -- it may be a couple of weeks before I'm able to leave the house. I'm coming down to see you as soon as possible.

The play was going like wild-fire the last time I heard, but I haven't heard from last week and it may have slumpt all to hell. Sub-zero weather and the taxi strike hit NY last week and put everything on the bum. Tony Brown, Kirkland, and [Sam H.] Grisman all said when I saw them ten days ago that the play would run to May. That's putting high hopes on it -- but who can tell? I'll be satisfied with a lot less, because now I think all the critics who rushed into print the morning we got there have had to eat their words. I knew it was a good play even before it was through rehearsal, and it came close to the edge of closing during those first four weeks. If Kirkland had not had faith in it it would have closed.

Don't forget: if it runs another month or so, we are going down to see it again.

I'm going to try to stay here at least a month without leaving. I've got some work to do. There are three offers for this month that I'm trying to get out of accepting: Princeton, University of Georgia, and Bennington. I'd rather write a short story any day than make a talk.

The Bartow business isn't over yet by a long shot. The state's going to call me back in May, and some of the bastards have started a civil suit against me. If they all go through with it, I'm going to raise hell sure enough this time. I can break a few heads in Georgia.[208]

There are a bunch of magazines here, and I see your name here and there, but I haven't had time to even open one yet. The little magazine business seems to be picking up: but the little magazine of today isn't what it used to be, thanks God. They have got life in them that the others never had. Of them all, I think Pagany for two years was the best. But Pagany's day is over; 1934 called for something different -- and it looks as if we've got it. You should keep on trying

---

[208] *On assignment for the* New Masses, *Caldwell had visited Bartow, Georgia, in order to report on recent racial violence and lynch-mob activity there. He sketched a stinging indictment of the general cloud of horror and fear under which local blacks lived, and the townspeople's tolerance for brutality. They responded with threats on his life ("'Parties Unknown' in Georgia," originally published 23 Jan. 1934; reprinted in Joseph North, ed.,* New Masses: An Anthology of the Rebel Thirties *[New York: International, 1969], pp. 137-141). Volume hereafter cited as* North.

New Masses. Not only do they pay, but by getting in there you will have got on a rung that nobody can knock you from.

Dean Jagger (Lov Bensy) went out of the cast Saturday night to go over to the Theatre Guild. He got a better offer from them, and none of us wished to hold him back in the face of the Guild, especially when he is on his way up. He should make a name for himself someday. The new player we cast promises to be even better in the part than Jagger was. We'll have to wait and see, though.

[E. J.] Basshe's work on the other book is just about done.[209] I haven't read his play yet, but from what hear, it should be better than the present one. We are going to try to interest the [Theatre] Guild in the new one. And, naturally, we'll give [Henry] Hull[210] the script to read, too. I think, though, that he would rather do another person's play next.

Out of twenty-six plays that opened in December, TR is the only one now running. Jed Harris' "The Lake" was a flop, with his Great Dame [Katharine] Hepburn, too.

I've got contracts for a book in France and for another one in England. That ought to be enough to satisfy me for a while. But who wishes to be satisfied? When you get satisfied, you may as well close up shop and dig yourself a hole in the ground. . . .

                Sincerely,
                Erskine

Caldwell met Frank Daniel in 1925, when they were both young reporters working on the Atlanta *Journal*. The following year, when Caldwell decided to quit the newspaper in order to devote his full energy to writing fiction, Daniel supported the move and over the years wrote articles recommending Caldwell's fiction to an always skeptical, often hostile Southern public. Virginia Caldwell Hibbs recalls Daniel as "a friend who had enormous respect for Erskine and his writing. A sensitive man who regretted that he had visited the poor in the outlying areas of Atlanta countryside and he had treated them as a joke, whereas Erskine had so much empathy for them."[211]

To Frank Daniel:

[EMO.tls]   Mount Vernon, Maine
                                                          February 16th 1934

Dear Frank:

You are a hell of a fellow! I went to Atlanta expressly to see you, and where were you? Somebody in the city room sent me chasing out

---

[209] God's Little Acre.
[210] *Then playing Jeeter Lester in* Tobacco Road.
[211] *Virginia Caldwell Hibbs to Robert L. McDonald, February 1994.*

to the Fox Theatre in the rain, and when I got there, I was told there was no pre-view today. They sent me to the Fox Film Exchange -- and still nothing doing. That's how I spent my time when I went two hundred miles to visit you!

And now it's your time to come see me. I'll treat you to the best show in town if you'll come to New York expressly to see the play at the 48th Street Theatre. And I mean it, too. You owe it to yourself to see a real-honest-to-god drama; you'll get rotten on a diet of movies. Or don't you think I know after stinking in Hollywood for three months? Don't take me too seriously! . . .

I should have answered your letter I received in Wrens, but I was rushed to death most of the time, what from trying to keep out of Georgia's jails -- or off the chain-gangs for all I know. And they say a fellow will get his head cut off in Georgia if he walks down the street with a copy of the Moscow Daily News in his pocket. And, so, don't you think I had a right to keep moving all the time I was there?

If you don't answer this letter by return mail, I'll know you've got a grudge against me. Let me know what you are doing, with samples of same. . . .

                         Sincerely,
                         Erskine

To Alfred Morang:

[HAR.tls]   Mount Vernon, Maine
                                               February 22nd 1934

Dear Alfred:

I'm on my feet again and trying to get a story done. I won't be able to get away this week end, but I hope to be able to get down to see you next week if I can get this work off my hands by then. It looks as if I won't be able to get out of going to Princeton, since I apparently made [Maurice] Coindreau a promise in one of my damn-fool moments. But thank God it won't be a lecture, anyway; it's one of these things where you sit around and drink beer and whistle through your teeth if you have a mind to. If Coindreau were not translating the book,[212] I'd pass it up; I'll be gone most of week after next.

Don't let anybody rush you, whether it's a novel, a story, or a funny joke. But when you are ready to do it, don't let anybody stop you, whether it's the janitor, Roosevelt, or God. The only way to get

---

[212]*Gallimard (France) published three of Coindreau's translations consecutively:* God's Little Acre *(1936),* Tobacco Road *(1937), and* We Are the Living *(1938).*

anything done is to do it your own way; advice is a damn good thing to listen to if you can forget it a minute later.

The play will be 99 performances old Saturday night. I don't know what keeps it going, but I can't hear any rumors of its stopping. Brooks Atkinson in last Sunday's Times was the latest critic to masticate his review of last December.[213] They'll all have to do it sooner or later, and now then there is talk in the air about the Pulitzer Prize for the year, most of them are trying to find the right pew before it is too late. The play doesn't need the Prize to my way of thinking. I think it will be a better play in spite of it. In the same way, I hope the movies never get it. [Theodore] Dreiser and [Carl] Van Doren sent copies of letters they wrote to the Committee recommending it for the award. It'll be a shame for the play to get it, because I know just how bad the people of Maine and Georgia will feel. If the play were making some money, I'd probably be better off; it is making a little, or it could not run and pay Hull a thousand a week, not to mention the rest of the cast. . . .

Sincerely,
Erskine

Carl Van Doren appreciated not only *Tobacco Road*, but also Caldwell's short stories, and requested permission to include "Meddlesome Jack" in his new anthology, *Modern American Prose* (1934). Instead, he eventually printed an excerpt from chapter seventeen of *God's Little Acre*, retitled as "Death of a Hero." Caldwell took the occasion of Van Doren's letter to thank him for his kind words about the play, as well as to press him further about his opinions of *Journeyman*, which Van Doren had read in manuscript and whose fate remained undecided.

To Carl Van Doren:

[PR2.tls]   Mount Vernon, Maine
March 1st 1934

Dear Carl Van Doren:

    I have been ill for some time and I have not been able to reach

---

[213] Calling it "shabbily directed," though with "spasmodic moments of merciless power when truth is flung into your face with all the slime that truth contains," Atkinson had initially found Tobacco Road "clumsy and rudderless," "more like a soliloquy with variations than a dramatic character sketch" ("Henry Hull in 'Tobacco Road, Based on the Novel by Erskine Caldwell,'" Erskine Caldwell Scrapbooks, DAR undated 1933). Now he described it as "the one play of the season that has enriched our knowledge of the American people," and noted particularly how Kirkland's adaptation "has preserved Mr. Caldwell's demoniac genius" ("Reverie in an Attic," New York Times [18 Feb. 1934], sec. 9, p. 1).

my typewriter until today. I had someone reply to your letter for me, and I'm not sure that my wishes were made clear to you.

Maxim Lieber at 545 Fifth Avenue handles my work for me, and I have written him that you wish to reprint a story of ours. I'm sure that he will take care of this. Naturally, the Viking Press has as much to do with such matters as any of us. I like your plan for the anthology, and I am sure it will be a fine one. You please me a lot by selecting the story about the jack. We tried for two years to get a magazine to print it, but like the Yale Review story, which was accepted after two years, we finally gave up hope for it.[214] And incidently, this two-years business is getting on my nerves. I've almost reached the point where I think it saves nerves to put a piece of work aside for two years before trying to get it published. The new novel ("Journeyman"), which I understand you read, has been infected by the two-years germs, or, at least after one year it shows symptoms of it. I still can't see what there was for you to find wrong with it. Everyone I've asked has carefully evaded a swift reply. At first I thought perhaps the person did not wish to "hurt my feelings", whatever they are; but even after trying it on my worst enemy, even he thought a long time before deciding not to say anything. And, so, I remain in the fix I am.

I read what you had to say about the play, and it was good to hear you say you liked it. If you had had occasion to read the eight or ten newspaper reviews of it after the opening, you would wonder how it has survived as long as it has. It took one of the world's worst pannings.

You are having weather in New York, I know; but did you know that here we take off on snowshoes from our second-storey windows!

Best wishes --

Sincerely,
Erskine

---

[214] *"Meddlesome Jack" appeared first in Caldwell's collection* We Are the Living; *"Country Full of Swedes" had been rejected several times before it was accepted by the* Yale Review, *and went on to win their annual $1000 prize for fiction in 1933. Caldwell mentioned the award frequently throughout his life; although he claimed a distinct disregard for high-brow critical opinions of his work, the Yale award seemed to signal a certain level of achievement to him (*Experience, *p. 149).*

To Frank Daniel:

[EMO.tls] Mount Vernon, Maine
March 8th 1934

Dear Frank:
You are a great fellow, Frank, and I don't see how come we never get together. It looked for a while as if I might accept your managing editor's bid to attend something or other to do with the Georgia Press Institute in Athens a couple of weeks ago; but when I replied that I was a Negro and would that make any difference? he never answered. And so I didn't get a chance to come back to Georgia and see you for sure this time. . . .

I've only been to Hollywood on business once (last summer; some MGM tripe). I was there a previous year, but that was on foolishness, and doesn't count. I hope I may never have to go again. But if the bread-box gets empty again, and so on, what can a fellow do? Maybe next time I'll get a chance on a good script.

If you are going to New York this spring -- hurry! hurry! I'd like a lot to have you see the play and hear what you think of it. There are no culid folks in it, or wouldn't you feel at home?

Bet you can't guess the kind of weather we're having Down East -- a little slush, a little frostbite, a little sleet. Will you get the [Atlanta] Constitution to make it hot for me if I come back to Georgia?

Best wishes --
Sincerely, Erskine

To Frank Daniel:

[EMO.tls] Mount Vernon, Maine
March 30th 1934

Dear Frank:
It makes me homesick to hear from you. If you should keep it up, I'd probably desert Maine for Georgia.

There won't be a novel till January or February of next year. However, the play in book form is coming out in a week or two (Viking Press); and you might use that as a handle to twist somebody's tail. I've finished the novel, but it has been put aside in the ice box to cool for six months or so.

And I guess I'd better stay where I am for the time being. I've got a story coming in Scribner's in June or so that will make somebody's eyes smart. It's about a Negro who got done away with for his trouble.[215]

[215] *Caldwell is referring to "Kneel to the Rising Sun," one of his most acclaimed stories.* Scribner's *held it for the February 1935 issue.*

I'm getting a little tired of being America's banned writer. Sumner gave me a headache last Spring; a month ago Columbia University took a swing at my chin, and now Canada has blacklisted me.[216] But none of that compares to what I'm thought of in Georgia, probably. Or aren't you my only friend in the Empire-State-of-the-South?

I saw the Scottsboro play in New York about three weeks ago. It fills the bill for what it was cut out to be, and makes a pretty sight for Alabama eyes; but I don't think it's so good as a play. But I hope it runs its pants off just the same....[217]

Sincerely,
Erskine

To Alfred Morang:
[HAR.tls] Mount Vernon, Maine
April 13th 1934

Dear Alfred:

... The play fell down Holy Week, but I hear that it climbed back Easter Week. Anyway, I think the peak has been passed, and from now on it will taper off to June 1st. Even so, it's been a surprise to me. Maybe if I were one of these literary guys I could pound out a play and make a lot of money; somehow, though, I don't feel it in me. It takes me a month to get a short story done; a play would probably take the rest of my life.[218]

I hear that LIFE & LETTERS has become a monthly; maybe you'll get more than one story in it now. Anyway, I hope you do better in pounds than I did in marks. I got a check from Germany that amounted to $1.15. And why shouldn't I be Anti-Nazi now?...

Sincerely,
Erskine

---

[216] *In early March, Teacher's College of Columbia University removed* Tobacco Road *and* God's Little Acre *from the school's library, despite the fact that both novels appeared on required reading lists.* Publisher's Weekly *reported: "The books were withdrawn after several faculty members had complained that they were 'indecent and tending to corrupt'" ("Caldwell Novels Banned,"* MacDonald, Critical Essays, *p. 31).*

[217] *The infamous "Scottsboro Case" involved charges against nine black youths for raping two white women on a freight car passing through Alabama. All nine young men were convicted in 1931, but the case dragged on in appeals for years afterward. Caldwell refers here to John Wexley's new play,* They Shall Not Die, *which dramatized the trial's injustices.*

[218] *There is at least one piece of evidence that Caldwell did try his hand at writing for the stage: an unpublished (and undated) typescript of a play entitled "Pablo" in the University of Georgia's Erskine Caldwell Collection.*

In 1934, Granville Hicks was one of the strongest editorial voices of the *New Masses* and author, most recently, of *The Great Tradition* (1933).

To Granville Hicks:

[SU2.tls]   Mount Vernon, Maine
May 7th 1934

Dear Granville Hicks:

I'm making such a mess of being a reviewer that I've concluded it would be better to strike my name off the list for the present. For one thing, I'm not a literary guy; and perhaps for that reason I am unable to whip myself into reading a book when my mind won't stay in its stall long enough. This time I won't be able to read [T. S.] Stribling's new book[219] due to the fact that I plan to leave tomorrow on a two weeks' trip in behalf of The Daily Worker.[220] There is another engagement after that which I have also made plans to fill. And what else can I say? I'm sorry, of course; reviews for New Masses must be written, but I am sure there are others more capable of writing the pieces.

I did not read Stribling's earlier book, but I did read The Store. I thought it had a wonderful grasp of life but that it became mired in the sentimentality usually associated with the South. It sort of followed the groove, if you see what I mean. In a certain type of writer that would not be fatal; but being in Stribling, it tasted like lukewarm tea.

Best wishes --

                               Sincerely,
                               Erskine Caldwell

By mid June, Caldwell had completed the series for *The Daily Worker*, spent a week with Helen in Nova Scotia, visited New York to prepare James Barton to take over for Henry Hull in the role of Jeeter Lester, and—despite his thunderous departure the year before—accepted a new offer to write for M-G-M. The eight-week contract would earn him a total of $4800, a raise of $350 per week over what he had been paid for the same work the previous year. As he wrote Frank Daniel: "I'm sorry as hell to have to take back the invitation to visit us in Maine.

[219]Unfinished Cathedral *(Doubleday, 1934)*.
[220]*Caldwell was hired to report on working conditions in the Detroit auto industry. In a brief letter to Frank Daniel, he described the assignment a little differently: "My journalistic bent won't stay down, and so I'm going off to Detroit in a few days on an expense account to see if I can do five newspaper pieces for a New York editor who sees the world through Marxian eyes" (EC to Daniel, EMO 5-3-34).*

But you know how it is. These picture companies never think of personal obligations, or such. I held out against them two months this time, but what could I do in the face of gold?"[221]

[HAR.tls]

To Alfred Morang:
[MGM stationery, Culver City, California]
6/23/34

Dear Alfred:

I started in yesterday, and now I've got eight long weeks ahead of me. It should be better than it was last time, because I won't have to break in before I can do anything. I'm working on dialogue for a script that already has been written. The picture is "A Wicked Woman", the player is Mady Christians, and the director is Charles Brabin.[222] Brabin is an englishman, and is married to Theda Bara. I can't see that that is a help one way or the other; but I'll know more about that if I can fish a dinner invitation out of them.

The place is just about the same as it was last year, except that the faces have changed. Writers and players pass through like chips on a river. Some go up, some go down, and some hang on. Most of them are hacks on the way down. If a writer stays here two or three years, he either is top-notch or a hack.

If you can hold out, the best thing for a writer is to stay away until he has a name so big the producers are scared of his shaddow, and then he can write his own ticket. Otherwise you have to take orders, and either follow them or get out. That's my trouble; I'm neither a big nor a little fish, but just a medium sized one. I wish I could have held out against them a few years longer.

Most of the producers have already read advance proofs of the story that is to be in Cosmopolitan, but I don't think they will buy it.[223] They can't quite see "Tobacco Rd", they can't quite see me, and they don't think anything I write is movie material. Which does not make me cry.

This time I've got an office three times the size of last year's. It has six overstuffed chairs, a silk-covered divan, two desks, bookcases, fans and heaters, 1/2 inch pile carpet, two phones -- in fact everything Hollywood would have, except a typewriter. When I called up for one yesterday, I was told I could have either a secretary or a typewriter. In as much as the name of the picture is "Wicked Woman", I chose a typewriter. I'll probably be put in "the dog house" for not taking a secretary.

[221]*EC to Daniel, EMO 6-23-34.*
[222]*Caldwell had been assigned to this same project the previous year (See EC to Alfred Morang 7-17-33).*
[223]*Caldwell's only appearance in* Cosmopolitan *was in 1937, with "Snacker."*

Let me know what is happening. At the rate you are going, you'll be ace-high in Hollywood before long. Don't say I didn't warn you.
Best wishes --

                      Sincerely,
                      Erskine

To Alfred Morang:
[HAR.tls]   [MGM stationery, Culver City, California]
                                                    7/16/34

Dear Alfred:

My time is half up today, and I'd give 'most anything for it to be all up. Anyway, four weeks can't be as bad as eight weeks were to begin with. We'll be home in about five weeks from now.

Helen and Pixy are here now, and we are living on the beach. It is as far away from the picture mob as I could get. Even so, we have to keep the doors locked against screen writers and their bleached-headed females.

I've been on two stories so far, and tomorrow I'll be assigned to a third one. I was kicked off the first one -- A WICKED WOMAN -- when I refused to write a bunch of tripe the producer demanded. I never had a chance to write the second one -- A LADY COMES TO TOWN -- because I told the producer that even God himself couldn't write a screen play with any life in it when Joan Crawford was to play the lead. That cooked my goose on that opus. Tomorrow I suppose I'll be handed another story fished out of the grab-bag, and it will end with my saying what I think about it. They can't break me on the Hollywood water-wheel, no matter how hard they try. The can fire me, and black-list me, but I'll be damned if I let them break me as they try to do every writer that has ever come out. The ones that stay are the ones who allow themselves to be broken; the rest of us are fired and black-listed when we say the story is no good or the player can't act. In other words, if you write what they tell you to write, you stay and get your salary raised; if you refuse to write it, as I did on the first story they handed me, they do their best to get rid of you. And so when you come out, it would be just as well if you made up your mind beforehand what you were going to do: stay and be broken; or leave and remain what you are.

The San Francisco strike might spread to Los Angeles, and even if it does, it will undoubtedly mean that the picture lots will have to close up.[224] In that case, I'll come home, because it would be foolish to stay here waiting for them to open up. They might even never open again -- under capitalistic control.

The pictures have snatched Jim Barton, which means what it means.[225] It may have to close up or fail for that reason. He's coming out here August 15th, and it's hard to say what the play can do without him. That's one thing I've got against pictures: they've taken three of the best actors out of the play, but won't even bid a dime for it. They are even scared to talk about it. They are afraid to recognize poverty, or that there are people in America who don't have enough food to keep them alive.

Let me hear from you -- and best wishes --
Sincerely,
Erskine

To Frank Daniel:
[EMO.tls]   [MGM stationery, Culver City, California]
7/19/34

Dear Frank:

One thing I balk at, and that's dealing out a deck of photos. Surely you must be spoofing. However, MGM publicity department had me sweating an hour before a portrait camera, and so if you really wish something along that line you can ask them to pass one along.

You must be a member of Georgia's State Department out to bag us innocent guys who happen to land in Georgia for a visit. What are you trying to do? Get me down there and clamp me in the Tower for some two-fold lifetimes? The last time I was there they threatened to put me in jail and keep me there until I talked. When I said I was ready to talk, they threatened to put me in jail and keep me there until I stopped talking. Now, what is your game? I can't figure it out.

Yes, Helen and Pixy are here, and we are living on the beach, ten miles from the picture mob. More than that, we have a telephone without a number. And so you see how crazy I am about Hollywood.

It at last looks as if a few wise souls are coming around to seeing that the play is pretty good itself, rather than a show-off for a handful

---

[224] *Since the first of the month, the Los Angeles* Times *had been reporting on the violent protests and riots associated with a San Francisco dock workers strike. The Los Angeles harbor remained unaffected.*

[225] *Henry Hull's successor in the role of Jeeter Lester in* Tobacco Road.

of actors. At least, this month's Esquire sounds that note. However, I don't look for any stems from your friend Cora Harris.[226]

I've got only four more weeks here, and then once more I'll say never again. That's what I said last time.

Best wishes --

Sincerely,
Erskine

To Alfred Morang:

[HAR.tls] [MGM stationery, Culver City, California]
7/26/34

Dear Alfred:

It looks as if our letters have been getting crossed on the way, but since there is nothing of importance to chronicle from this end, nothing has been lost. . . .

MGM has been trying to close up the play so they could get Barton's services for two pictures. I sent Max [Lieber] a telegram telling him not to listen to them, but I haven't heard what happened. But don't think I didn't tell this studio what I thought of them for trying to close a play and throwing a dozen actors and another dozen or so stagehands out of work just because they had money on their side. They said they were going to star Barton in "Ah, Wilderness", but that didn't impress me any at all. Any studio that would try to close a play is a bunch of bastards, and those are the words I used. They've put me in the dog house because of what hell I raised about it, but it doesn't bother me in the least, because they can't stop my pay until August 13th.

Keep on working on the play and on a novel until you get them both in good shape. When you get them right to your own satisfaction, we'll make them bring in the bacon. Don't let a rejection stop you, because as long as you have a good piece of work in full length form, there is always a good chance for it.

I'll be seeing you in about a month from now. If in the meantime there is anything I can do, you know who to call on.

Best wishes --

Sincerely,
Erskine

---

[226] *A brief note in Esquire urged readers to see* Tobacco Road *"for Henry Hull's performance; for the presentation of Caldwell's extraordinary human beings; and because it is the most fought-over play of the year" (Gilbert Seldes,* Esquire *[July 1936], p. 134). As book review editor for the Charlotte* Observer, *Cora Harris had given Caldwell some much-needed freelance work during and just after his work for the Atlanta Journal.*

To Alfred Morang:
[HAR.tls]   [MGM stationery, Culver City, California]
August 10th 1934

Dear Alfred:

I got your letter yesterday, and I can't understand why Max [Lieber] did not take the stories. However, it does not mean anything, because I was up in the air myself for seven years before I got settled down.[227] The thing to do is to go your own way, and to hell with anybody else -- including me -- if he doesn't like what you are doing. Writing is still a lone-wolf job, in more ways than one, even though the American soviets say otherwise. A fellow still has to do his own writing -- no matter what his politics are. That's why I say to hell with anybody other than yourself, when you know what you are doing. There are plenty of agents in the sea, anyway. We'll talk it over soon.

It looks now as if it will be after September 1st before I get home, even though we are leaving here Wednesday. [C. A.] Hathaway wishes a series of pieces for the Daily Worker on the dried-up Middle West. If I write them, it will take me a week longer to get home, because we'll have to travel through Montana, the Dakotas, Wisconsin, Iowa, and elsewhere in the drouth area. I'll know by Tuesday if I'm going to write them.

Liam O'Flaherty is out here, and wishes he were somewhere else. He's not working in pictures, but is too broke to get back to Europe. He is coming on the lot today to have lunch with me.

Paramount made a hell of a big offer to stay, but to save my life I couldn't see it. I never thought I'd live to turn down a- thousand-a-week offers, but I'm so damn sick of this place I'd hitch-hike out of it if I didn't have car fare home. Metro offered to extend the contract another four weeks, at the same sum, but it would take all the money they've got in the bank to get me on this lot again. It's no job for a white man. That's why I'll be back in Mount Vernon around September 1st. . . .

Sincerely
Erskine

---

[227] *In* Call It Experience, *Caldwell says he received his first acceptance letter in early 1929, when Alfred Kreymborg notified him that "Midsummer Passion" would be included in* The New American Caravan. *This was, he recalls, "a little more than six years after I first began trying to write fiction at the University of Virginia" (p. 70).*

Back in Maine, Caldwell must have realized that 1934 had been a very unproductive time for fiction writing. Besides the excerpt from *God's Little Acre* in Van Doren's *Modern American Prose*, he published only four stories that year. Worse, on October 15, Harold Guinzburg at Viking had notified Max Lieber of their firm decision regarding the still unpublished *Journeyman*: "You and Erskine both know that we do not think that *Journeyman* is as good a novel as *Tobacco Road* or *God's Little Acre*, and it is our opinion that it will not advance his reputation or his position in the book field.... In addition, we feel that the book is definitely dangerous, particularly in view of the renewed activities of the censor." Guinzburg's proposal, which he admitted was not "an ideal solution from an author's point of view, was that they issue the novel "in a limited edition, preferably signed ... manufactur[ing] enough copies to give the book a respectable circulation" and giving Caldwell "the publication which he so much desires."[228]

To Alfred Morang:

[HAR.tls] Mount Vernon, Maine
October 17th 1934

Dear Alfred:

... I've seen only one paper so far that is running the cross-America series, and it is published in the South.[229] So far as I know no paper in Maine would stoop so low as to come down where we are. Maybe it is just as well, after all.

Nothing new, except that after two weeks I've finally got three stories done. One isn't so much, but the other two may be up to par for this course. That is to be seen, of course.

I don't know when I'll be able to get down, maybe after I finish some more work. Right how I'm haveing a headache about the novel. Viking is scared it is a dirty book, and they are trying to get our consent to publish it in a limited edition, away from the hands of Sumner.[230] In other words, if I don't agree, they say they will not defend it at court. What the hell can I do? Yes or No. A publisher has got you, no matter which way you turn. The only alternative, as in presenting plays, is to get it out yourself, and how can a guy go into business when he thinks he is a writer? Some of these days one of these blows will be the one that killed father. He could spend his time better selling hot dogs, with mustard.

Write when you can,
Erskine

---

[228] *Guinzburg to EC, DAR 10-15-34.*

[229] *In writing this new series for the* Daily Worker *as he drove back to Maine from California, Caldwell was gathering materials for the book of nonfiction vignettes he would call* Some American People *(McBride, 1935).*

[230] *Sumner was still acting as monitor for the New York Society for the Suppression of Vice.*

To Alfred Morang:

[HAR.tls] Mount Vernon, Maine
October 24th 1934

Dear Alfred:
   ... Still trouble with The Viking Press. They say they will either publish in a limited edition, or else the book will have to be censored for a trade edition. That's the way they put up the proposition, and you have to take it or leave it. I told them to go to hell before I'd change it, and I don't know what is going to be done. They'll have to get a hump on if they are going to get it out within the time set by the contract, or the book will revert back to me and I can take it somewhere else.
   I haven't done much lately since finishing two or three stories. It's hard to do anything when these publishing bastards keep you up in the air all the time.
   We might get a chance to come down some Sunday afternoon and if you are going to be away or busy during the next two or three, we cane come again. I don't know when it will be; I've got to do some more work before I can leave. ...
                                    Sincerely,
                                    Erskine

To Alfred Morang:

[HAR.tls] Mount Vernon, Maine
November 18th 1934

Dear Alfred:
   ... I have a copy of Basshe's script for the play, but have not read it yet.[231] Max [Lieber] is boiling with an idea about the new book for a play, and he says he is coming up next week to argue me into doing the script myself. I don't know. Bein[232] is anxious to try his hand at it, and I'm inclined to let him have it. I'll wait and listen to Max before I do anything one way or another.
   Barton is stepping out December 1st, and everybody from L[ionel]. Barrymore to J[ohn]. Gilbert has been mentioned for the part. Still nothing is settled, but it will have to be in another week in

---

[231] *J. Basshe had at last finished his adaptation of* God's Little Acre.
[232] *Here Caldwell misspells the name of his old friend Harry Behn, with whom he had worked on several unsuccessful scripts during his 1933 stint in Hollywood.*

order to get in some rehearsals. Or maybe Tobacco Rd Inc will call it a day and go out of business. But people keep on going to see it, and I don't know what about that.

I looked the new book over and shipped it back to The Viking Press Inc. If they still insist on being cussed about it, it'll mean that it will be out in February in a Ltd.Ed. There is nothing I can do about it, because the contract merely calls for publication, and not the kind of publication. But what the hell! Maybe it's as rotten as that after all.

A couple of anthologists (not E.J. O'B[rien]) asked to reprint stories, but we turned one of them down because he wouldn't pay. That's a pretty good racket: get up a book of stories, not pay royalty, and collect everything for yourself. It's a wonder more of them aren't done.

If the casting of the play bothers me, I might take a trip down to New York December 1st to see what the hell it's all about. First there was talk of taking it to England intact, and then everybody changed his mind and decided to stay in NY. Now anything might happen, from closing it up to making it into a Sunday School prologue. These bastards on the money end are as jumpy as a barrelful of frogs. . . .

                Sincerely,
                Erskine

In January 1935, Viking published *Journeyman* in the limited edition Guinzburg had required, and Caldwell began making selections for his next book of stories, *Kneel to the Rising Sun*, which Viking brought out in June. Also in January, with his father, Caldwell undertook a driving tour of Georgia in order to make notes for a four-part New York *Post* exposé on tenant farming in Georgia—a return to the kind of journalistic writing which, he later reflected, "never failed to renew my spirits."[233]

To Alfred Morang:

[HAR.tls]   Mount Vernon, Maine
                                                  February 6th 1935

Dear Alfred:

    I got your letter today, and I'm glad you sent me Snow's.[234] that's what you call criticism with a shine one it. Letters like that are a great help, because they keep a writer on his toes. For one thing, I think if it were my case I would accept it in all seriousness and show the bastard

---

[233] Experience, *p. 127.*
[234] *This letter—likely from* Anvil *guest co-editor Walter Snow, to whom Morang had been unsuccessfully submitting stories—was not saved.*

that I could take it. By that I mean I would not answer him, but work even harder to produce work that would prove how wrong he was. There is nothing to be gained by answering him. I have got letters and reviews to almost equal it, and I think they were a great help, after I had worked off my steam in several stories. Anyway, you know (I think I said it before) that the higher you go, the harder the whacks on the head. It's true in every case. We'll talk it over when I get down again.

The contract for the new play has not been signed yet, but the producers are anxious to get their hands on it. As soon as their financial standing is investigated, we are ready to talk turkey. It is not a Broadway item, but an experimental bunch uptown.

I've just finished a series of pieces for the NY Evening Post about a trip to the South. If I can get hold of next week's copies, I'll send them to you. The only trouble is they may not come out then. That's what you have to put up with by living away from town. . . .

                        Sincerely,
                        Erskine

When the *Post* series appeared in late February, it instigated an uproar of discussion concerning Caldwell's motives and the truth of his reporting.

To Alfred Morang:

[HAR.tls]   Mount Vernon, Maine
                                                        March 12th 1935

Dear Alfred:

. . . Three counties in Georgia claim to be investigating in this new flare-up, but to date all I have seen have been statements from "prominent citizens". It looks as if the people involved still have no chance to say a word; "the prominent citizens" always take care of that. I guess it will be played out as soon as they can hush it up.[235]

See you Sunday afternoon --
                        Sincerely,
                        Erskine

---

[235] *In May 1935, Phalanx Press reissued the* Post *series as a pamphlet entitled* Tenant Farmer. *In* Critical Essays, *MacDonald reprints the* Post *articles and a sampling of the colorful responses they elicited. For example, "prominent citizen" James Barlow, Jr., wrote: "Erskine Caldwell has not been to Georgia recently or he writes on hearsay or he treats veracity too lightly. Never have I seen any one in Georgia eating cow dung, but perhaps Mr. Caldwell is referring to his own experience.... Please inform Caldwell that Georgians would prefer that he cease referring to Georgia as his birthplace" ("Letter to the Editor of the New York* Post: Share Cropper Conditions Denied," *p. 111).*

To Alfred Morang:

[HAR.tls] Mount Vernon, Maine
June 13th 1935

Dear Alfred:

There isn't much happening here, and so Helen and I are going to Manitoba and Saskatchewan -- and possibly British Columbia -- for a few weeks. If I don't fall off the Canadian Rockies and break my neck, I'll be back by the middle of next month.

I've got to finish up some work first, and it will probably be Wednesday before we can leave.

The reviews of the book[236] have been of the expected variety. Half plus, half minus. At this late date I have no expectations of settling down to writing standard, solid, and society books -- and consequently I never expect to see a surplus of favorable reviews. When I can't keep them on their ears any longer, I'll back out of the picture....

Sincerely,
Erskine

In late September, Caldwell received word that one of the traveling companies of *Tobacco Road* had run into trouble with censors in Chicago. The city's mayor, Edward J. Kelly, had declared the production "filth" and ordered it closed. An exasperated Caldwell was summoned to help defend the play.

To Helen Caldwell:

[DAR.als] [Hotel Sherman stationery, Chicago]
Saturday [October 19, 1935]

Dear Helen:

I got your night letter this morning. I don't know how much longer this is going to last, but it should be over Monday afternoon, possibly Tuesday. It looks pretty bad for us because one of the three appeal judges has already committed himself against the play. If we lose Monday, there is only one more stop -- the U.S. Supreme Court, & Sam[237] says he won't give up.

I am afraid we will lose Monday on a point of law, or rather because of some error in the first trial before Judge Holly.[238]

---

[236] Journeyman.

[237] Two possibilities: Sam Grisman, the play's producer, or Sam Gerson, western representative for the Shuberts, who booked the play in Chicago.

[238] Judge William H. Holley had intervened by granting a stay of the order to close the play, which the city immediately countered.

I saw [?] yesterday, & gave him a copy of the new book & the Nov. 6 issue of the New Republic.[239] He is going to talk in our favor at his church Sunday, & he is influential. I have not been able to get to see [Rev. Preston] Bradley[240] yet, but I am in hope he will take it up also. His talks are broadcast at 11 o'clock Sunday.

I believe I'll come straight home instead of stopping in N.Y. It would save a lot of time & money. If that suits you, I'll probably do that. I may be able to get away Monday night, or Tuesday, I'll be home as soon as I can.

Love,
Skinny

In December 1935, the Caldwells left Maine for an extended family vacation in California. Perhaps exhausted by the events of the preceding year—particularly the controversies surrounding the *Post* series and the play in Chicago—Caldwell devoted himself almost wholly to his family. He wrote little, except to maintain a few personal contacts and to attend to business.

To Frank Daniel:

[EMO.tls] Burbank, California
January 5th 1936

Dear Frank:

I thought surely I would be able to come to Atlanta to se you in December, but for some unaccountable reason it did not work out that way. Anyway, Helen stopped over, and I wish to thank you for the splendid interview you wrote and sent copies of. It made me want to go back to the Journal and beg for my old $20 a week job.[241]

---

[239] An item in the "Week's News" called "[t]he exclusion of 'Tobacco Road' from Chicago by virtue of the action of Mayor Kelly in withdrawing the license of the Selwyn Theatre is one of the most outrageous cases of current censorship in the arts.... Once more Chicago ... is the victim of the provincialism of its officials.... The characters in 'Tobacco Road' are forgotten people. Mr. Caldwell deserves the gratitude of all who honestly care for decency in American life by bringing them so powerfully to mind." The item went on to indict Mayor Kelly for his hypocrisy, since he himself had "stained" the city's reputation by permitting the use of city monies "to pay for the pleasures" of city officials (New Republic [6 Nov. 1935], p. 348).

[240] Pastor of the People's Church of Chicago.

[241] Traveling with Janet to join Erskine and their two sons in California, Helen stopped in Atlanta before a brief trip over to Wrens to visit Caldwell's parents. Daniel asked Helen to comment on the controversy surrounding the dramatization of Tobacco Road and the possibility that it would be produced in Atlanta the following spring: "'I believe southern people will understand it,' she said, 'and realize that Erskine wrote out of compassion and understanding and brotherliness about a man whose fine qualities survive even the lowest bitterest depriva-

There is no doubt about "Tobacco Road" wanting to come to Atlanta. If a theatre manager could get the city to promise to keep its hands off, he would have no trouble booking it for a week's run, besides grossing $15,000. Anyway, that's the story from Cleveland, St Louis, Cincinnati, Milwaukee, and Minneapolis. A fourth road company is getting ready to start out, and Atlanta should be played if any city is. I believe I would make a special trip just to be there for the fun. After all, I was born only forty miles from Atlanta, and it is a sort of home town to me.

I heard that you had a touch of State of Maine weather not long ago. Maybe now you know why I would rather come to California than stay in Maine. There is quite a difference between 70 degrees, and -20 degrees, especially when the difference lasts for about five months.

Your friend, Louis Joseph Haloff, is no mean critic. The piece in which he reviewed me is one of the best of the kind I have seen. There ought to be a yearly prize for the boys who know what they don't like. I'll be glad to donate a box car full of gophers, if you'll agree to unload them in his front yard. . . .[242]

Sincerely,
Erskine

Formerly an assistant professor of English, William Stanley Hoole was serving as librarian at Birmingham Southern College in Alabama when he solicited Caldwell's input for a series of articles he was planning to write on contemporary Southern letters.

---

tions.... *Erskine is a Georgian and knows best the soul of Georgia people. Therefore I like best the stories he writes about Georgia. I believe every line he has written about his state is inspired by affection'" ("Wife of Author of 'Tobacco Road' Pauses Here and Discusses Play," Atlanta* Constitution, *Erskine Caldwell Scrapbooks, DAR 12-?-35).*

[242]*In a review for the Atlanta* Constitution, *Haloff had reproved Caldwell for the recently published* Some American People *(McBride, 1935): "The author of that blasphemous, 'God's Little Acre,' and that no less disgusting volume, 'Tobacco Road,' has again tried his hand at insulting the intelligence of our great nation, in his first book of so-called non-fiction, in which he attempts to throw a veil over our eyes and tell us about 'Some American People.' ... The motives for the writing of this book are clear: a hatred of the capitalistic state and the propagation of a ridiculous socialism.... And as for you, Erskine Caldwell—you, not the American people, should hang your head in shame. What a pity! What a pity that you don't use your splendid vocabulary and your talent in producing clean, decent works, something of which you and we could really be proud, not ashamed" ("Genius Misapplied," Erskine Caldwell Scrapbooks, DAR 12-?-35).*

To William Stanley Hoole:

[CBY.tls]
Burbank, California
February 22nd 1936

Dear Mr Hoole:

I certainly do not mind your asking the questions, but the trouble is that I do not know anything worth saying. I am just another writer, and I don't think that gives anyone out-of-the-ordinary understanding. But I'll try --

At present I have nothing for immediate future publication. There are two books I'd like to finish before the year is out, however. One a story about some characters in Maine, which is my home at present; the other is a book about the South, fiction I suppose, although it has no classification at present. I am deeply interested in dramatizations of two earlier stories, although I am not actually writing the stage pieces. And, incidently, I am not working in pictures, as I am here merely for a short visit.

I do not consider the recent activity among Southern writers anything more than a normal crest of productivity. There have always been Southern novels, and there will continue to be many written and published. I think that one reason for the attention paid to Southern writing during the past five years was because American writers in general had gone completely over-board in search of "form". When the tide turned, the Southern writer who had been geographically isolated from the schools in Paris and New York, was able to present his work as "content". His novels and stories were loaded with reality, people, and story. As long as he remains in his home-country, I don't think there is much danger of his ever losing sight of the fact that "content" is the imperishable element of fiction. But all this is abstraction --

I believe sometime in the future Southern writers will find that all the material they can use is to be found in their everyday lives. This is not to say the novel and story should be a retelling of folk-tales, and such; but that the character of the Southern people provides the richest fiction-mine in America. The rest of the country is such a boiling-pot of races that it is almost impossible to define native characteristics; in the South they stick out like sore thumbs. And that is why I believe the Southern writer is the more fortunate. . . .

Sincerely,
Erskine Caldwell

By April of 1936, after much consideration, Caldwell had made a definite decision about his next major project: a work that would "vindicate my writings about the South." It would be a photo-text documentary, "a factual study of people in cotton states living in economic stress," created with the specific "intention to show that my fiction was as realistic as life itself in the contemporary South." He had a title in mind from the start: *You Have Seen Their Faces*.[243]

Though Caldwell expressed doubts about her "ability" to do the job, Max Lieber eventually persuaded him to accept *Life* photographer Margaret Bourke-White as his collaborator. Bourke-White was not immediately available, however, and several times the trip was delayed because of her demanding schedule and miscommunication about when she could join Caldwell on the project. Caldwell grew so frustrated that he finally told Bourke-White that he thought they should simply give up on the prospect of working together.[244] But by late July, their differences had been resolved, and firm plans had been made: Caldwell, Bourke-White, and Ruth Carnall, Caldwell's secretary, left from Wrens, Georgia, on a driving tour across the South to gather material for the book. Despite the portrait Caldwell painted in his letters home to Helen, early into the trip he and Bourke-White had begun an affair.

To Helen Caldwell:
[DAR.als]   [Albert Pike Hotel stationery, Little Rock, Arkansas]
                                Saturday a.m. [July 26, 1936]
Dear Helen --

I have all your letters since July 24th. We will be here until the 27th, & will start back. I will not have another address until I get to Wrens in about 10 days --

This is the worst trip I have taken so far -- It must be the heat. But the trouble is, I suppose, we get on each other's nerves.

I told B-W not to come when she called on the phone -- But she came anyway the next day -- We started off on even terms & that lasted for 2 days.

We had a scrap in Montgomery that could be heard for miles around -- Naturally she cried -- But promised to follow my suggestions.

She had another spasm the next afternoon in Meridian, Miss. & then we had a second big scrap that night in Jackson, Miss. Yesterday Ruth had one with her, & I don't know what will happen. If I get so I

---

[243] *Might, p. 145.*

[244] See William Howard, "Dear Kit, Dear Skinny," *Syracuse University Library Associates Courier*, 23 (Fall 1988), pp. 23–44; also, "'I Want to Do This Job': More Margaret Bourke-White Letters to Erskine Caldwell," *Syracuse University Library Associates Courier*, 25 (Spring 1990), pp. 37–52. Howard admirably unravels the beginnings of the Caldwell/Bourke-White association. Also see Robert L. McDonald, "The Moment of 'Three Women Eating': Completing the Story of You Have Seen Their Faces," *Syracuse University Library Associates Courier*, 29 (Spring 1994), pp. 61–74.

can get along with her, I may have to let Ruth go home -- She asked this morning if she could leave.[245]

I don't know what would happen if I were left alone. The trouble is B-W is in the habit of getting her own way -- & so am I -- What happens when we fall out is all that can be imagined. The whole thing is on a day-to-day basis now -- & it may be called off at any minute during the next week.

I don't know how I can answer all your questions now, because I don't ever have time to write, since we have traveled from 6 a.m. to 8 p.m. every day so far. . . .

I will try to write again tomorrow if we get back early enough.

I wish you had notified the Dept. of Justice in Boston about the phone call, as they instructed -- to call them collect if you received any more calls without names being given, or if of a suspicious nature.[246]

If B-W & I could get along together there might be a book -- But as things are going I'll be doing well to get back with a sane mind.

Try not to get down -- Because it is a lot worse for me than it is for you --

Love,
Erskine

By the middle of August, Caldwell was back in Maine and desperately lonely for Bourke-White, whom he had affectionately nicknamed "Kit." Caldwell did not immediately confront Helen with his feelings for Bourke-White, but Helen certainly knew about the affair and, probably as well, that her marriage was in trouble.[247] Caldwell's attentions and interests were elsewhere.

To Margaret Bourke-White:
[SU1.tls]　　　　　　　　　　　　　　　　　　[Mount Vernon, Maine]
　　　　　　　　　　　　　　　　　　　　　　　　　[n.d., 1936]
Dear Kit:

As you may have guessed, I am pretty well down these days. One thing on top of another brings these things about. I have an

---

[245] *Carnall had been Caldwell's secretary at M-G-M. Accounts (e.g., the Howard essays listed in the previous note) suggest that she was jealous of Bourke-White. Carnall did in fact quit and leave Caldwell and Bourke-White to finish the trip alone.*

[246] *Caldwell's fame had begun to affect his cherished privacy: there had been "threatening phone calls placed to Helen and the children" (Klevar,* Biography, *p. 163).*

[247] *Helen later recalled that Bourke-White "was a very vital human being," and "was the sort of person who, if she were to go on a trip with you—and you might have your wife and both children, that wouldn't matter—she would get into your bed before the night was out.... Ruth [Carnall] wrote me a blow-by-blow account of the affair before she left" (Klevar, "Interview," p. 95).*

awful feeling that I will not see you again; I have a terrified feeling of our drifting apart. Then when I do think I may see you again, the feeling is that I'll be merely another customer coming into your house on a schedule that may or may not conflict with the previous customer on the schedule, the following customer on the schedule. The whole thing amounts to this: I think of you as part of us, never as you alone. It is a sort of need for you to make us one, and you have said in no uncertain terms that you are not interested. And so, I am at the point where I can't go down much further.

You know how I love you, and how so very much I want you, and how so completely I need you. There is nothing much I can say on top of that. If I don't suit you, if you do not care for me to that extent, if you are determined to keep me from crossing the line, I bow to your wishes. That last thing I would ever do would be to try to force you into something you have no desire for.

I am going up into Quebec for a while. This will be my only address. If you would a letter send, it will be forwarded, and I'll be the most delighted person in the world when it reaches me. I have no idea when I am coming back. Though, as a matter of truth, if you should send for me, I'd come as fast as I could even if I had to make a couple of trips around the world to reach you. I still have that extraordinary feeling I had when I first came to know you: that I was waiting for you to say, come into my arms and stay as long as you wish to, and stay forever if you want to. And even now I still believe you will say it, either this time, or the next, or the next. It is that hope that makes me look forward to seeing you so eagerly the next time, the time after.

I have your pictures, your touch still resting on me, your kisses: I have all these things with me day and night, and they seem to be a sort of promise. If they were not that, I would not even be able to write letters to you, much less look forward to your asking me to come to see you, to come in a hurry.

But it is precisely that which I do look forward to. I have a feeling that this time you may feel differently, that you may let me come inside of you, that you may let me stay this time. What else is there to live for, if a person has an animal-like instinct to love someone as I do you? I am not in love with your knowledge, your style, your this and that -- I am in love with you, your heart and your soul. Everything else about you, your skill, your dress, your education, is something I take delight in merely because you possess them.

This could go on and on. I would much rather talk to you about such things than to try to write to you about them. But you seem always so anxious to change the subject, that I never am able to tell you how and why I love you. As if you cared, I guess.

Anyway, it will take the heart out of me if you don't write and say you wish me to come down to see you. I can't come on any other basis, because I've got so now that I feel as if I am an intruder. If you do want me, you can think of some strictly businesslike matter that wants attention without delay. I am afraid if you said, simply, come and sleep with me, I would be at a loss to explain what-s-this-all-about-and-what-s-it-leading-to. And no wonder, if it should lead to what I want most in the world.

I love you.

           Skinny

As Caldwell's obsession with Bourke-White increased, his attention to writing dwindled proportionally. He spent the remaining months of 1936 traveling to New York ostensibly, and sometimes in fact, to work on assembling *You Have Seen Their Faces*, matching Bourke-White's photographs with his prose. That year his only publications were a limited-edition printing of *The Sacrilege of Alan Kent*, which had appeared originally as the final section of *American Earth*, and seven stories, most of which were not very impressively placed.[248]

By early 1937, both Caldwell and Bourke-White had become increasingly uncomfortable with the possibility that their affair might be exposed, and after much pleading on his part, Caldwell convinced a hesitant Bourke-White to share an apartment with him in New York's Beekman Towers. Eventually with Helen's permission—since she wanted Erskine to decide for himself the quality of his interest in Bourke-White—Caldwell would split time between Mount Vernon and New York, and Bourke-White began posing as "Mrs. Caldwell." The arrangement was complex and particularly difficult for Caldwell, who often found himself alone or out of direct touch while Bourke-White continued her *Life* assignments.[249]

         To Margaret Bourke-White:

[SU1.als]   [Mount Vernon, Maine]
                     [February 8, 1937]

My sweetest love --

I am at the dentist's -- who says I do have a slight trace of trench mouth. I am taking treatment, & he assures me he will cure it before I come back to you. This means that you probably have it, too. If you have not done so, you should see your dentist right away. I shall get

---

[248] *Besides one story in the* New Yorker *("A Small Day"), there were four in* Mid-Week Pictorial *("Carnival," "The Fly in the Coffin," "The Man Under the Mountain," and "A Short Sleep in Louisiana") and one each in* College Humor *("New Cabin") and* Parade *("The Sunfield").*

[249] *Miller's biography of Caldwell (pp. 241–249) and Klevar's interview with Helen Caldwell (pp. 96–97) are helpful in understanding the circumstances and chronology of the affair.*

well before coming back to you.

I have dreamed of you every night since I left. They were the nicest dreams anyone could have, because I love you like nobody's business, sleep or awake.

Sweetheart, I can't stay away from you much longer. If I did not have the end of next week to look forward to, I could not stand it. Let me know as soon as you can what your plans are. I hope it will work out that next week will be the last one away from you.

I have not heard from you since I got back, but maybe I'll get a letter today or tomorrow. Write to Gen. Del. Augusta & also Mt. Vernon.

I don't know why I love you as I do -- is there a good reason why I should? All I know is that you are woman enough to make me love you, & I just can't help it. -- I want you as long as we live, because I can't be happy unless you are letting me try to make you happy. If you don't want that, then there is no excuse for me being here. I wish you would just for once show me in some way that you do need me. That is, if it is true that you do need me. But whatever you do, don't tell me a lie -- that would hurt worse than any thing else. -- All the trouble I'm having is because nobody seems to think that I love you, or you me. Only Helen thinks so, & she thinks you love me more than I am willing to admit. But she does not know how much I love you. All the others say we are having nothing but a sex holiday. -- For my part, I have to laugh at them, knowing how deep my love for you is. -- I've turned in the typescript of the book. All I'm doing now is waiting for you -- and you won't make me wait an unnecessary minute, will you? Please don't. . . .

S.[250]

To Margaret Bourke-White:

[SU1.telegram]   [Mount Vernon, Maine]
                                                    1937 FEB 15 PM 4 35

NBA812 42 DL=U BOSTON MASS 15 406P
MARGARET BOURKE WHITE=
    320 EAST 42 ST
WHAT WE HAVE MEANS EVERYTHING IN THE WORLD TO ME

[250] *Two possibilities, as Bourke-White notes in her autobiography. Caldwell called her "Kit, because he said I had the contented expression of a kitten that has just swallowed a bowl of cream." In trying to find a nickname for him, however, she was frustrated: "Nothing can be made out of 'Erskine' but Skinny, and even though he was anything but skinny, he had been called that by everyone most of his life. I disliked the name and searched for another. We tried 'Skeats' for a while, but it never seemed to belong to him"* (Portrait of Myself *[New York: Simon and Shuster, 1963], p. 130, emphasis added). Hereafter cited as* Bourke-White, Portrait.

IF ANYTHING SHOULD GO WRONG ILL NEVER RECOVER I FEEL AS THOUGH IT IS EVEN NOW ONLY THE BEGINNING ALL MY LOVE AS YOU WELL KNOW AND SOME YOU DONT KNOW YET=
  SKEETS.

To Margaret Bourke-White:
[SU1.als]   [Mount Vernon, Maine]
Sunday [February 20, 1937]

Dearest Sweetest Girl --

    I don't see how I can stay away from you any longer -- When I left, two weeks did not seem long, but now it seems impossible. What I fear now is that you will go away, & be gone the first week in March. I had counted on coming down the end of this week -- Now I don't know what to think. Staying here after Thursday or Friday will be more than I can do.

    What? When? Where? I miss you so much it hurts going to bed, trying to sleep, & getting up is a 24-hour nightmare.

    There may be a reason, but I must be too dumb to understand -- I can't see why I should have to stay away from you a day when all I want in the world is to live with you. Can you explain?

    And if you want the same thing, why do we live apart a day more than necessary?

    You are my love, Kit -- I've got to come so I can brush your hair & buy you flowers and squeeze you to sleep at night & tell you I love you & undress you & God only knows all the other things I crave to do to you & for you.

    One more trench-mouth treatment promises to cure me so I can kiss you germ-free. Tuesday is the final day of treatment, the dentist says.

    I've got to have you sweetheart, & once I get you again you will have a hard time making me leave you. I think about 40 years will be the length of the stay next time. But don't let that scare you -- Nobody will be loved so much in that time as you will be --

    Please write a lot -- & tell me when I can come -- from Thursday on -- & I can't wait much longer --

    All my love --
                        Skeets

Caldwell's second venture in the theater was a thin dramatization of *Journeyman* starring Will Geer which opened at the Fulton Theatre in New York on January 29, 1938. As Caldwell recalled, "The reviews ... were so unfavorable that it did not appear to be rational to open the doors for a second performance. The playwrights themselves [Alfred Hayes and Leon Alexander] walked out on their own dramatization and never returned."[251] The play had a three-week run, nevertheless, and Caldwell defended it against its harshest critics, like Brooks Atkinson, who quipped in the New York *Times*: "After one glimpse of 'Journeyman' ... this department expects to think kindly of every play from now until doomsday. From this time forward every play will seem gentle, witty, innocent, original and brilliant."[252] He dispatched the following response to Atkinson's office at the *Times*.

To Brooks Atkinson:

[SU1.tl(cc)] [Mayflower Hotel, New York]
[February 2, 1938]

When "Tobacco Road" opened on December 4th, 1933, the entire press pounced upon it as a piece of bawdiness and indecency. It was criticized as being false. At that time such an attitude, while not to be condoned, was understandable in the light of the fact that people knew very little of that section of the South depicted in "Tobacco Road."

Since then, as a result of the play, many controversies have been started and much has been written about the South. The final culmination of all this was "You Have Seen Their Faces." (This project had always been very close to me, and Margaret Bourke-White's pictures perhaps convinced people where the written word did not.) One would think that the critical fraternity would have learned something in the past five years and come away from "Journeyman", even though with revulsion, with at least a sympathetic understanding. Instead of this we find the critics reviling the play instead of the condition out of which it stems.

After reading Mr. Brooks Atkinson's review of "Journeyman" in The Times it appears probable that the theme of the play is larger than Mr. Atkinson's ability to handle it.

Instead of calmly dismissing a play that it is his privilege to dislike, he screams like a man beset with devils. His indignation mounts to wrath when he visits a play that jolts him from the plush-lined lodgements of his contentment.

To judge by Mr. Atkinson's review, there is no doubt that his prejudices have been assaulted.

Life is larger than the world Mr. Atkinson lives in. Whether we

---

[251]Might, *p. 158.*
[252]"'*Journeyman,*' from Erskine Caldwell Novel, with Will Geer as a Traveling Preacher in Georgia," Erskine Caldwell Scrapbooks, DAR 1-31-38.

like it or not, a great number of men, women and children indulge in primitive forms of religious excitement.[253] Some are frank exhibitionists, others are devout believers. To dismiss them merely because we do not subscribe to their creed is a sign of ignorance and prejudice. The sect known as the Holy Rollers, for one, had been in existence long before either Mr. Atkinson or myself was born, and it will flourish long after both of us are dead.

I myself deplore many of the ends and means of this religious mania. I heartily despise a man like Semon Dye. But, on the other hand, I do not close my ears to what I hear. I know all too well that his presence in America is a disgrace to a nation that calls itself civilized. With or without Mr. Atkinson's permission, I refuse to close my eyes and mind to the hundreds of pseudo-ministers such as Semon Dye who are perched like vultures on fence posts in the South, waiting to claw and devour the flesh of ignorant people.

            Erskine Caldwell

[GU2.als]
To the Reverend and Mrs. Ira S. Caldwell:
[Mayflower Hotel stationery, New York]
Sunday [February 1938]

Dear Mother & Father:

I still dont know how we managed to do it, but we still have the new play running, & it will run through the coming week at least. One thing in particular has kept me from giving up, & that was the sentence in Father's letter in which he wrote "A man is never beaten until he admits it". We have a long way to go yet, but I'm going to stick at it until the last ditch.

To day is the first time in two weeks that I've had any time to rest. I've got to start again Monday, but I'm going at it with all my might.

I still have three more weeks of lecturing at the New School.[254] I

---

[253] *The plot of* Journeyman *concerns the duping of a small Southern community by a lustful traveling evangelist named Semon Dye.*

[254] *On February 2, 1938, Caldwell began offering a short course on "Southern Tenant Farmers" at the New School for Social Research in New York. Six weekly lectures explored "the present social and economic condition of tenant farmers, white and Negro, under the ruling system of cotton production in the South"—a topic Caldwell had already written about in* You Have Seen Their Faces *(1937) and the pamphlet* Tenant Farmer *(1935), as well as his fiction. In a brief letter to the New School's librarian, he provided "a suggested list of outside readings" for the course (in this order):* Economic and Social Problems and Conditions of the Southern Appalachians *(U.S. Department of Agriculture Report 205, 1935); Gerald W. Johnson's*

hope [?] I can get away by that [?] time & take a rest. If make a success of the play, I'll be able to feel I've earned it.

I'll write again as soon as I can.

Love,
Erskine

In March 1938, Caldwell and Bourke-White left for Europe to begin their second professional collaboration, *North of the Danube* (1939), a well-received documentary of life among the Czechoslovakian proletariat that would be Caldwell's last book with Viking. Acknowledging Caldwell's clear devotion to Bourke-White, and giving up on any hope of reconciliation, in April 1938 Helen had finally obtained a divorce. By October, Caldwell and Bourke-White had bought a house together in Darien, Connecticut, which they wryly named "Horseplay Hill." While his "Sweetest Girl" continued her photographic assignments, Caldwell wrote little and, in November, found himself again managing problems with touring companies of *Tobacco Road*. This time the trouble was in Atlanta. As he wrote to Morang, "The censors put the play on the fire, but they couldn't cook it, and a fine time was had by all.... All I need to say is that the play finished out the week."[255]

To Frank Daniel:

[EMO.tls]
Darien, Conn.
December 2nd 1938

Dear Frank:

I wouldn't take anything for the trip to Atlanta. That was one of the best vacations I've ever had -- if it can be called a vacation.

Margaret, Janet and I got back Saturday morning.[256] We came back by plane because Margaret had to be in early that morning. We found a lot of snow and cold weather, and it has been here ever since. I suppose it is the setting in of an old fashioned New England winter.

The Wasted Land *(1937)*; C. S. Johnson's Collapse of Cotton Tenancy *(1935)*; B. Y. Landes and G. E. Haynes's Cotton Growing Communities *(1935)*; H. H. Kroll's I Was a Sharecropper *(1937)*; Charles Spurgeon Johnson's Shadows of the Plantation *(1934)*; Elizabeth Madox Roberts's Time of Man *(1926)*; Arthur Franklin Raper's Preface to Peasantry *(1936)*; Rupert B. Vance's Human Geography of the South *(1932)*; Howard Kester's Revolt Among the Sharecroppers *(1936)*; Harris Dickson's The Story of the King of Cotton *(1937)*; and Caldwell's own Tobacco Road *(1932)* and You Have Seen Their Faces *(1937)* [EC to Liv Smith, SU1 12-29-37]. This letter, the course description quoted above, and a typed draft of what appear to be notes for Caldwell's first lecture in the series may be found in Syracuse's Caldwell Collection, Box 6.

[255] EC to Morang, HAR 12-2-38.

[256] According to Caldwell's 2 December 1938 letter to Morang, while he responded to protests against Tobacco Road and Janet spent time with her grandparents, Bourke-White photographed Franklin D. Roosevelt's visit to Georgia.

I don't know how we would have got through the Atlanta trouble if it hadn't been for you. I can never thank you enough for what you did. Now that it is all over, we can be glad the censors made things interesting. But most important of all, maybe it will keep the little Hitlers from causing so much trouble after this, not only in the South, but all over America as well. As long as we are able to tie tin cans to the little ones, there is not much danger of a big one getting a grip on America.

I am hoping I'll never be so long again in getting back to Atlanta. I guess I rather like the place, after all. . . .

            Sincerely,
            Erskine

To Alfred Morang:

[HAR.tls]   Darien, Conn.
                        January 19th 1939

Dear Alfred:

You'll probably be getting a copy of NORTH OF THE DANUBE in about a month from now, and I hope it's worth a year's work, after all.[257]

The Daily Worker is starting a Sunday magazine section, but I guess you've heard before this. I should think they will pay for stories and pieces, but I don't know.

I'm afraid I just don't have anything to send for the magazine. The book is the only thing I've got to show for a year's work, and that's that. Maybe I'll get around to some stories soon. . . .

Best wishes,

            Sincerely,
            Erskine

---

[257] *Though he was proud of* North of the Danube, *just after completing the manuscript Caldwell worried privately to his parents that its quality might not match that of* You Have Seen Their Faces: *"I am not sure it is as good as the other book. For one reason, we spent six months there [in Czechoslovakia], while I feel as though I spent a lifetime in the South" (EC to Rev. and Mrs. Ira S. Caldwell, GU2 12-28-38).*

After many appeals—including this telegram-proposal, sent while Bourke-White was on assignment in Cleveland—Bourke-White finally relented and agreed to marry Caldwell. About this moment in her life, Bourke-White rather casually reflected, "finally a time comes when it is just too troublesome to remain unmarried."[258] The two were married in Reno, Nevada, on February 28, 1939, followed by a much-publicized honeymoon in Hawaii.

To Margaret Bourke-White:

[SU1.telegram]　　　　　　　　　　　　　　　　　　[Darien, Connecticut]
　　　　　　　　　　　　　　　　　　　　　　　　　1939 FEB 8 PM 6 43

NA 904 53 DL=TDST DARIEN CONN 8 605P
HONEY-CHILE BOURKE-WHITE=
　　HOTEL CLEVELAND CLEVE=
HONOLULU CHAMBER OF COMMERCE IS PLACING ORDERS FOR MARCH SUNSETS AND WISH TO KNOW YOUR PREFERENCE. REQUEST FROM SS LURLINE FOR YOU TO LEND YOUR CHARM AND GRACE TO DECK A FOR 1ST MARCH SAILING. COUNTY CLERK OF RENO WISHES YOUR AUTOGRAPH. I DONT WANT MUCH MYSELF. JUST ONE PREPAID WORD SPELLED YES=
　　SKINNY.

While Bourke-White continued her work, at home and abroad, Caldwell remained largely in Darien, managing the house and Bourke-White's beloved gardens and taking care of their cats. In May he began drafting *Trouble in July*, but his concentration was clearly disturbed by his new wife's prolonged absences.

To Margaret Bourke-White:

[SU1.telegram]　　　　　　　　　　　　　　　　　　[Darien, Connecticut]
　　　　　　　　　　　　　　　　　　　　　　　　　1939 JUL 27 AM 11 41

NA36 98=TDSM DARIEN CONN 27 1111A
MISS KT BOURKE WHITE=
　　=NELSON HOUSE POUGHKEEPSIE NY=
=I LOVE YOU, I LOVE YOU I LOVE YOU. I LOVE YOU. I LOVE YOU. I LOVE YOU I LOVE YOU I LOVE YOU I LOVE YOU I LOVE YOU. I LOVE YOU. I LOVE YOU I LOVE YOU. YOU WILL GET THE DRIFT OF THIS BETTER IF YOU LOOK AT YOURSELF IN THE MIRROR WHILE YOU READ IT. I LOVE YOU. I LOVE YOU I LOVE YOU. I LOVE YOU. I LOVE YOU I LOVE YOU. I LOVE YOU. I LOVE YOU I LOVE YOU. I LOVE YOU I LOVE YOU. I LOVE YOU. I LOVE YOU=
　　=SKINNY.

---

[258]Portrait, *p. 169.*

On October 17, Bourke-White left the United States for a five-month trip to Europe, where *Life* editors had assigned her to cover the beginnings of World War II.

To Margaret Bourke-White:

[SU1.als] [Darien, Connecticut]
Thursday
10/19/39

Dearest Wife:

I got your [wishes?] today. It was just as if you had slammed a door or knocked over a lamp -- it made you that real to me. I hope you will want to send me many more....

Suzy came back this afternoon, after being away since Thursday. I set out 3 sizes of dishes: big, little & medium-sized, and all three sat down and ate without a growl.

Lottie has learned how to purr, and her purr is even louder than Fluffy's, which is very good itself. She likes to play a lot. And it looks as if she has made up her mind to sleep on the bed every night.

I have just finished reading, and writing a review of, a book for the Herald-Tribune Book Section. It is called "The Southern Poor-White: From Lubber-Land to Tobacco Road".[259] That's all very well, but I'll be a lot happier when I read reviews of "A Child's Garden of Insects", and "The Praying Mantis at Home", by M B-W. The world is waiting; don't let it become tired of waiting.[260]

I saw Charlie Duell in town yesterday. He is starting a publishing house with [Charles A.] Cap Pearce.[261] He said he was sorry he did not meet you before you left, and that he hopes the stories he's heard aren't true.

The gardener is coming tomorrow again. He still hasn't finished

---

[259] In The Southern Poor-White: From Lubberland to Tobacco Road *(U of Oklahoma P, 1939)*, Shields McIlwaine elevated Caldwell and William Faulkner as the two most important innovators of a modern literary prototype: "By virtue of their additions to the literary chronicle of the lowest Southerners, Faulkner and Caldwell have given these folk their most important literary existence. The creation of Jeeter [Lester, from Tobacco Road] would alone warrant such a verdict, for thereby the Southern poor-white became established in contemporary literature alongside of Babbitt and other American types. Jeeter Lester is to the poor-whites what Uncle Remus is to the Negroes—a name for his class" (p. 240). In his review, Caldwell heaped praise on the book as one "that has been needed for a long time. It reveals both the wealth and the poverty of the South, which has always had an abundance of both" (New York Herald Tribune Books *[29 Oct. 1939]*, p. 16).

[260] Caldwell had been urging Bourke-White to write a series of children's books based on her life-long fascination with insects. When they made their Southern trip to gather material for You Have Seen Their Faces, for example, Bourke-White had brought glass bottles containing praying-mantis cocoons so that she could photograph "the life cycle of this dramatic insect" for Life *(Bourke-White, Portrait, p. 128).*

[261] Duell, Sloan and Pearce.

the beds. That is the stoniest ground on the whole place, but when it's finished, the flowers will look fine there.

After I give that lecture at Columbia on the 25th, I'll probably go down to Georgia for a while. That probably won't be before Nov. 1st, though. I may take a trip out to Santa Fe to see Alfred Morang, too. However, every letter and telegram will be forwarded to me the same day it arrives, because I'll see to it that every word from you reaches me the quickest possible minute....

All my love to the dearest girl in the world -- from her
Husband

In late October Caldwell at last broke with Viking. The final point of contention seems to have been a disagreement over the amount of his advance for *Trouble in July*. Given recent poor sales figures, particularly for his past three books, Viking was reserved in its expectations for the new novel. They were also uncertain about a series of books on "American Folkways" that Caldwell had proposed editing. By the end of the first week in November, Max Lieber wrote to confirm the details of a very lucrative contract with the new publishing house of Duell, Sloan, and Pearce.[262]

	To Margaret Bourke-White:	
[SU1.als]		[Darien, Connecticut]
		#10[263]
		11/5/39

Dearest Wife:

The gardener was so pleased today with some of the things we've done that he said he hoped you would be here to see the things burst in the spring. He said "Mrs Caldwell will have the surprise of her life when she sees what we've done, won't she?" It certainly looks fine -- all the beds & plants as neat as an exhibition.

I think the Duell, Sloan & Pearce arrangement is going to be fine. I draw $2,500 a year for three years even if I don't write another line. Plus $1,500 in three years for the six books I'm going to edit. They said they would do the best jobs on our books next year that has ever been done. I've got to make final corrections in the galleys of "Trouble in July" soon. Will you send me further corrections & suggestions before it goes to press in about 6 weeks? They want more than anything for us to collaborate on a new book as soon as possible. Pearce

---

[262] *EC to Maxim Lieber, SU1 11-6-39.*
[263] *Caldwell began numbering his letters to Bourke-White, so that she could read them in order, but also, we may guess, as a reminder of how often she was on his mind.*

said they want to give the biggest cocktail party ever given in N.Y. on March 1st, the publication date. I told him I'd agree conditionally -- if my wife were home to share it with me. So there the matter stands. It would be pretty nice -- our first wedding anniversary and the party at the same time. It will be the first book of the company -- except for a new poem of A. MacLeish's which they are publishing for Christmas. . . .[264]

I can't hide it. Every where I go, I'm told I look lonely. I am. I'm very lonely. I don't think I could live without you. I wouldn't want to live -- Getting things to surprise you when you return keeps me alive now. It's like marking off days in prison -- every day is an achievement and the marking off is a ceremony -- a day's victory. I couldn't stand it if there were to be more than a day over six months of this. And every single day sooner than that will be like getting that much credit for good behavior. Well, you must know that I love you more than life itself --

Your husband

[SU1.als]
To Margaret Bourke-White:
[Hollywood Plaza Hotel stationery, California]
#22
Dec 4, 1939

Dearest Girl:

I'm finishing up here tomorrow, having interested Edwin Corle in doing one of the books for the series, and am going to Tucson & Phoenix, Arizona.[265] I'll probably be there about a week. Cap [Pearce] & Charlie [Duell] want me to go to the Northwest on this trip, but I've decided not to go now. I thought it would be nice to save that trip and take you with me. Don't you like the prospect of a trip like that?

I have the galley sheets of "Trouble in July" and I'll finish correcting them during the coming week. I still hope you will send me

---

[264] *Archibald MacLeish,* America Was Promises *(1939).*

[265] *Caldwell actively pursued writers for his American Folkways series, which he described to Stetson Kennedy as studies of "contemporary life in terms of its social and economic implications," written by expert natives about particular regions of the country (EC to Kennedy, GEO 8-25-40). When he invited Otto Ernest Rayburn to write* Ozark Country *(which he did), Caldwell urged Rayburn to "plan your book with the idea of presenting the Ozarks not as a tourist area, but as though you were seeing it as a historian of contemporary America" (EC to Rayburn, ARK 5-9-40). Edwin Corle's* Desert Country *(1941) was the first book in the series.*

some notes of changes to make because you must have thought of many things you think should be changed. I'm sorry you did not finish reading the manuscript. Naturally I consider you my best friend & severest critic, and I had looked forward to your help. It would be a much better novel with your advice.

I will be glad to get back and see Suzy, Fluffy & Lottie. Mrs. S[266] says Lottie has been a very bad kitten. I suppose she needs you to train her.

You have been gone almost two months now; don't you think you could send a word of hope and cheer to your lonely husband? You can't imagine how much it would help to have some little word like that to live on. Surely, you can see day light by now. Won't you tell me something like that to keep me from being so despondent, and give me a time to look forward to. If you only knew how much it would help, you would [consider?] it!

Your S.

Caldwell busied himself with several projects between 1940 and 1942. He continued recruitment for the American Folkways series and, in 1940, published two new books: *Trouble in July*, his first novel since *Journeyman;* and *Jackpot*, an omnibus of the seventy-five stories Caldwell considered his best to date. Reviews of the novel were mixed, drawing praise from tough critics like Margaret Marshall and Richard Wright, but also charges of unoriginality from Clifton Fadiman and even longtime admirer Harold Strauss.[267] *Jackpot* was a clear success, however. Reviewers loved it, and complimentary copies prompted warm, personal notes from Caldwell's contemporaries, including Sherwood Anderson, Theodore Dreiser, Edna Ferber, Ernest Hemingway, H. L. Mencken, Eleanor Roosevelt, and John Steinbeck, who responded generously, "Dear Caldwell: I don't know why I shouldn't like them. I've liked everything else you've done. . . ."[268]

Also in 1940, Caldwell and Bourke-White traveled the country making notes and photographs for what would become their third collaborative documentary work, *Say! Is This the U.S.A.?* By early May of 1941, the couple found themselves in Moscow, planning a book on contemporary Russian life and working independently, as well: Bourke-White on occasional *Life* assignments, Caldwell on drafting stories that would become *Georgia Boy*. When the Germans attacked the

[266] *Margaret Salter, Caldwell's personal secretary.*
[267] *Marshall reviewed the novel for the* Nation *([24 Feb. 1940], p. 283), Wright for the* New Republic *([11 March 1940], p. 351); Fadiman reviewed it for the* New Yorker *([24 Feb. 1940], p. 74), Strauss for the New York* Times Book Review *([25 Feb. 1940], p. 2). Writing for the* Library Journal, *L. M. Kinloch described* Trouble in July *as "Thoroughly unpleasant. Not recommended for conservative libraries" ([1 Feb. 1940], p. 117).*
[268] *Steinbeck to EC, DAR 8-12-40.*

city on June 22, despite an "anti-camera law" in effect, Bourke-White realized she was "facing the biggest scoop of her life: the biggest country enters the biggest war in the world and I was the only photographer on the spot, representing any publication and coming from any foreign country."[269] During the siege, Caldwell was drafted as a broadcaster for CBS Radio and as a reporter for the newspaper *PM* and *Life* magazine. In November, the couple returned to America, their celebrity mightily enhanced. Max Lieber, engaged in soliciting outlets for the material gathered overseas, wrote his client: "I've continued calling various other editors, and there's no getting away from it, but you must submit to being lionized. After all, not many people have been to the Soviet Union, in these recent months, and certainly none has yet come back, except the Caldwells."[270]

In 1942, DS&P published three books based on Caldwell and Bourke-White's experiences in Russia: *All Night Long: A Novel of Guerilla Warfare in Russia*, *All Out on the Road to Smolensk*, and *Russia at War*. In March, at her special request, Bourke-White left for Europe again on a war-related assignment for *Life*. Caldwell was back at home in Darien, lonely but working.

To Alfred Morang:

[HAR.tls]

Darien, Conn.
June 11th 1942

Dear Alfred:

I'm enclosing a pitifully small check which isn't much, but you might find it useful nevertheless.[271] I wish I could make it more at this time, but I'm pretty low, what with the second installment of income taxes falling due next Monday, since my income this year is smaller than my taxes for last year's income.

I'm finishing up the novel, which right now is called ALL NIGHT LONG: A Novel of Guerrilla Warfare in Russia. It will be done July 1st unless I drop dead before then. I don't know if it's any good or not, because I've been working on it ten and twelve hours a day since I saw you in Santa Fe, and just now my mind and feelings are so numb I couldn't tell you whether I'm coming or going.

If all goes well I'll leave here July 1st and head for Tucson.[272] I'm hoping to get my house here rented for six or nine months so I can

---

[269] Portrait, *p. 174.*

[270] *Lieber to EC, DAR 11-6-41.*

[271] *Morang seemed always in debt, and since the mid 1930s, when his own financial condition began to improve, Caldwell had routinely helped his friend with small gift-checks. He had also paid for the Morangs' move from Portland to Santa Fe in 1937, after Alfred, a life-long heavy smoker, had been diagnosed with tuberculosis and needed a dryer climate.*

[272] *Bourke-White loved Tucson, so Caldwell bought a house there, hoping to entice her to stay in the United States—with him—instead of going back overseas. A career-minded professional, Bourke-White resented the offer, considering the house "another set of golden chains"* (Portrait

stay in the West until next Spring. I'll be getting to Santa Fe sometime during the summer, I hope.

Let me hear how everything is.

    Best,
    Erskine

Caldwell submitted the following note as an introduction to "Country Full of Swedes," which, upon invitation, he had chosen for inclusion in Whit Burnett's new anthology, *This Is My Best*.[273]

To Whit Burnett:

[PR3.tls]   Darien, Conn.
June 11th 1942

Dear Whit:

I like to write about people. I put them into the traditional form of the short story or novel merely because they happen to be ideal means of expression for me. However, I do not write short stories and novels and people them with characters. I fit people into fiction, not fiction around people. At least, these are the things I try to do; sometimes I succeed to some extent, sometimes I fail.

There is nothing unusual about the fact that COUNTRY FULL OF SWEDES, for example, is a story of people in the State of Maine. I have written many stories about people in the South merely because it happened that I spent more time in Georgia than anywhere else. I have written a few stories about people in Northern New England because I lived there for a short time. If I had lived in Montana, Wyoming, or Utah, I would have written about people I lived among there.

There is more than one way of skinning a rabbit. I found that out early in life when one rabbit skinner told me to do it in such-and-such a manner, and another one told me to do it differently. I tried both, but either the rabbit's legs slipped off the knob on the barn door, or I could not get the jacket down over the shoulders. After that I did it my own way, and I've been doing it that way ever since.

Best wishes,

    Sincerely,
    Erskine

---

[273] *(Dial, 1942)*. Burnett describes Caldwell as "rank[ing] among the leading practitioners [of the short story] in America" (p. 1128).

In July, Caldwell returned for a third stint in the movie business when Warner Bros. contracted him to write the script for *Mission to Moscow*. He accepted the offer of $1250 per week, despite the fact that he felt he needed "a rest."[274] While Bourke-White was in England photographing Churchill, among others, and the American Air Force, Caldwell typed the following letter on Warner Bros. Inter-Office Communication stationery. Addressed to "Honeychile," from Skinny, its subject is identified as "Missing you." On the second page, Caldwell called his wife's attention to the reminder printed at the bottom of the form:
VERBAL MESSAGES CAUSE MISUNDERSTANDINGS AND DELAYS.
(Please Put Them In Writing)

To Margaret Bourke-White:
[SU1.tls]   [Warner Bros. stationery, Burbank, California]
August 15th 1942

Dearest Kit:

As I wrote you last time the furnishing of the house is pretty well in its last stages. The only trouble is that I can't very well put in the odds-and-ends, because those things have to have your touch. The Master Bedroom is going to be the most striking of all, not only because you planned it that way, but also because I was able to find a custom furniture-maker who went crazy about your decorating scheme. He is making an over-size bed, 6X7, in what here is called Provincial. This is a better style than 100% modern for the Tucson situation; the tables, chests, dressers, chairs, etc., which he is making to go with it will stun you. The furniture for the living-dining room and the library is also being made to order. The guest room and maid's room and porch furniture has been bought out of stock, partly from Sloan's-Beverley Hills and Barker Brothers L.A.

I think it would help things a lot if you ordered from some store in New York a few things like combs, brushes, mirrors, etc, for your dressing table. (It is very pale blue with off-white border designs -- the chair is tufted all over in deep-cushioned shocking pink). You might like Lucite to go with this. Will you order some things like this, and anything else you want and have them shipped to Tucson? . . .

Another thing I need to know is whether you wish sterling or life-time plated silver for the dining room. I'll have to get this soon because neither will be available much longer.

I'm still working on Mission. I've completed about 2/3 of the 1st draft treatment (adaption), which means that it will take me another two, three, or four weeks to finish. As you well know there is no picture story in the book itself, and I've had to write what amounts to an original story. The characters are the same, but in my adaption there

---

[274]*Experience, p. 214.*

is no other resemblance to Davies' little squib.[275] I've put everybody in it from Roosevelt to Stalin, and that includes Hitler, Hess, Goebbels, Trotsky, Molotov, Voroshilov, Tukhachevsky, von Ribbentrop, Shigemitsu, Matsoaka, Timoshenko, Rykov, Bukharin, Yagoda, Vyshinsky, and Henry Shapiro. Don't you think a picture with all that in it ought to hold the movie-going public at least through the last half of a double-feature for 27¢ before 1 p.m.? Of course, I don't know if the picture will eventually come out like that, because nobody has seen it except the producer, Bob Buckner, who likes the treatment I've done. Everybody in Hollywood said doing a treatment for Mission was the hardest job in pictures during the past ten years. I agree. I don't think I'll want to write on the screen play, because after ten weeks on the treatment, I'll have enough of Mission. There are two other Russian pictures that I've been asked to do; one, "Russians Don't Surrender", and the other, "All Night Long", sometimes known as "Vengeance of the Earth." The government has, in its casual way, give me to understand that it would be best for me to work on war pictures, Russian, English, Chinese, or American, than to do correspondence, bond selling, radio reporting, or other such things. I take that to mean that it's more of a command than a request.

They are already working on the screen play of our novel at Metro, and Red Book has bought the serial rights. They paid ten thousand for them, and it will run in three issues beginning October 1st. The book publication, therefore, will have to be set back to December 1st. . . .[276]

Tell me what and when to look forward to. You know I've got to look forward, or I don't amount to much in life. Is it to be December 15th?

All my love,
Skinny

---

[275] *Based on the memoirs of former U.S. ambassador to Russia Joseph E. Davies,* Mission to Moscow *(dir. Michael Curtiz) was a propaganda piece explicitly intended to generate support for Russia during World War II. Caldwell was not listed in the credits when the movie was released in 1943.*

[276] *Caldwell refers to* All Night Long, *based on his and Bourke-White's observations in Russia, but written entirely by Caldwell. In a review for the* Nation, *Margaret Marshall expressed common opinion pointedly, calling it "one of the worst novels I have ever read" ([26 Dec. 1942], p. 720).*

Two weeks later, using the same office stationery, Caldwell's subject in this intense, rambling letter had broadened to simply "You."

[SU1.tls]
To Margaret Bourke-White:
[Warner Bros. stationery, Burbank, California]
Aug 29th 1942

Dearest Kit: Looks as if I just don't hardly ever hear from you and as though the letters I write you have an arriving average of about one out of three. This is letter #10 that I've sent you since August 1st. What happens to things? I sent you a cable ten days ago asking if you were getting cables and letters, and I received an answer from you today. I'll keep on sending, but it's a lot more important that I get letters from you. You already know how much I love you, but unless you write me every few days I never know whether you love me just the same or more. . . .

There is a good review of "Shooting" in the Saturday Review.[277] I haven't seen any other good ones recently, and I still can't locate the clippings you received before you left. If you'll tell me where they are, I can get your clipping books finished right away.

I'm still up a tree about the whereabouts of the safe deposit box key I sent you. Please let me know so I can get into the box. The furniture will be ready to be shipped to Tucson Monday. It's pretty out-of-the-ordinary stuff. Be sure and send things to Mrs. E. Caldwell, %Peter Rooke-Ley, 45 West Jackson Street, Tucson, Arizona, because the place will be only a dump without some of your touches in it. Any doo-dads will do. The Master Bedroom is as you planned it, done in Provincial style, which is very simple and grayish and whitish and a little faint bluish. The guest room is Mexican, as you planned it. The Library is white leather chairs, doe skin desk, brownish-yellow sofa, etc. The living-dining room is strictly colorful -- bright red nine-foot sofa, bright blue chairs (2), soft gray chair-and-pouf, eight-foot gray table matching gray doors and ceiling, doe skin radio-phonograph automatic combination, black ebony topped dining table with straw-wood base (sideboard the same, and eight black ebony chairs upholstered with the black-and-yellow material you selected. And, last by not least, a sterling silver service for eight (70 pieces) in a wonderful design called Courtship and made by International Silver Company. It cost $235 but it's for you because I know how much you like nice things, and some day you can give it to our daughter. The only other thing I can think of is the porch furniture. There are seven or eight pieces in heavy rattan with palm leaf

---

[277] *Bourke-White's* Shooting the Russian War *was published by Simon & Schuster in 1942. The reviewer called the book "chatty, gay, witty, and, withal, informative" (Mark Gayn, "With Notebook and Camera in Russia,"* Saturday Review of Literature *[22 Aug. 1942], p. 10.)*

upholstery -- seven foot sofa, two end tables, five foot coffee table, four foot ottoman (round), two chairs and center table, and two rattan lamps. I think I've told you all I know. But now you'll have an idea of what things are like and you can send some odds and ends to put here and there.

Pix has been transferred. . . . He would be awfully pleased to hear from you. The last time he wrote he asked about you.[278]

You could write to me, too, you know. About twice a week would be just about right. I've received only two letters since you left, and only two cables.

All my love which is a lot and I don't know how I could love you any more than I do because I love you more than anything else in the world.

Skinny

[SU1.tls]
To Margaret Bourke-White:
[Warner Bros. stationery, Burbank, California]
September 9th 1942

Dearest Kit:
. . . I'm finishing up here on Sept 15th. I haven't decided whether I'll do another short picture job or not. I want to get to Tucson and start on the new book as soon as possible. The history of ALL NIGHT LONG to date is as follows: bought by Metro for $50,000 cash, plus $20,000 bonus if the book sales go over 130,000, which look more than probable now; serialized in Red Book magazine beginning November issue (out Oct 1st), and paid $9,000, plus $1,000 if it is run in more than three installments, which is also probable; selected by Book League of America for December, which will distribute 100,000 copies to its members; and to be published by DS&P on December 2nd, with plans calling for an advance sale of between 25,000 and 50,000 copies. That's about all there is so far (it still won't be published for two and a half months). I think you ought to take a lot of credit for the novel, because this time was nothing like the other time,[279] and I have the feeling you will be even better about it the next time. In other words, you helped me while I was doing it more than

---

[278] *Pvt. Erskine Caldwell, Jr., had been transferred recently to the Marine Corps Air Station at Quantico, Virginia.*

[279] *Bourke-White, traveling on assignment, had neglected to offer commentary on* Trouble in July *in manuscript. Caldwell had appealed to her in November 1939, "This is the last chance to make changes in 'Trouble in July'—your book! The first one I've done under your spell—& I want it to be perfect—" (EC to Bourke-White, SU1 undated 1939).*

you realized. I only wished you had had the time to see it through to the last page. You could have added a great deal to it. Please try next time to see it through from beginning to end. Promise?

Al Manuel says he wants to do something about the deal I told you about before you left.[280] He may write to you about the three-year contract. A studio told him today that they would sign you immediately for one of the pictures they are putting into production next week. So you see, it can be done. It's up to you to tell people that you will consider these not to be sneezed at offers. Ten thousand for a few weeks' work isn't bad, you know.

Why don't you write to me more often? Twice a week would be a lot better than the way it is now. How about it?

I guess you know I love you. But do you really realize how much I love you? It's more than you think. The reason is that you are the only person. There'll never be anyone else but you. Unless it is the second Kit, and I think I would love both of you enough to go around.

Skinny . . .

Back in Tucson, feeling he had done all he could to keep his marriage together, Caldwell sensed that Bourke-White "was unyielding in her decision not to live with me in California or Arizona," and "in time it became plainly evident that we would be able to live together again only on Kit's terms and that even then there would be no assurance that we could live in harmony for the remainder of our lives. And so, in effect, I had to accept the fact that our marriage could no longer exist and that my presence in Kit's life had come to be unwelcome."[281]

To Margaret Bourke-White:

[SU1.telegram] [Tucson, Arizona]
1942 NOV 10 AM 10 49

ML5 TUCSON ARIZ 63 9
NLT MARGARET BOURKE WHITE
    AMERICAN EMBASSY LDN=
=HAVE REACHED MOST DIFFICULT DECISION OF LIFETIME STOP DECIDED THAT PARTNERSHIP MUST DISSOLVE IMMEDIATELY SINCE PRESENT AND FUTURE CONTAIN NO PROMISE OF ULTIMATE MANIFEST STOP NO SINGLE FACTOR OR COMBINATION COULD RECTIFY UNTENABLE SITUATION STOP

---

[280] *Manuel acted as agent for all Caldwell's Hollywood concerns. At Caldwell's urging, Manuel had arranged a job for Bourke-White to photograph on-set stills at one of the major studios, an offer she firmly rejected* (Portrait, *pp. 196–197).*

[281] Might, *p. 201.*

BELIEVE ME WHEN EYE SAY AM TRULY SORRY AND UNCONSOLABLE STOP PLEASE NOTIFY WEISS[282] STEPS YOU WISH TAKEN=
=ERSKINE CALDWELL.

Except for a brief inquiry about whether another woman was involved, Bourke-White did not oppose Caldwell, and just before Christmas he was granted a divorce in Mexico. The day after he returned home, on December 21, 1942, Caldwell was married again, this time to June Johnson, a student he had met when he gave a presentation to his old friend Harry Behn's radio writing class at the University of Arizona. Their courtship had begun at least two months earlier.[283]
To Charles A. Pearce:

[DAR.tl(cc)] [Tucson, Arizona]
December 8 [1942]
Dear Cap:
By this time you have undoubtedly gotten the first letter I sent you about <u>Georgia Boy</u>, but probably you would still like a little more information about the content, so here goes.
As I said, the book will contain fifteen stories, three of them which have already been published in <u>Jackpot</u>, under the title of "My Old Man" and done in three parts. The book will be about 175 pages in length.
Part of it is centered around the trials and tribulations of a Georgia family and, and with, their colored houseboy, Handsome Brown, who has been with them since he was eleven years old and whose energies, such as they are, run mainly along the lines of getting out of work, this coupled with the jobs that the Stroup family can manufacture for him, presents a problem in itself, however "My Old Man" isn't far behind.
The Georgia family is made up, in kin, of three people. Morris Stroup, Martha Stroup, his wife, and their son William. William though, as the young narrator, takes very little active part in the happenings around him. Rather he is carried along by the incidents, swayed and molded by the lives of his immediate predecessors as they touch him each day. Morris Stroup is constantly getting into and

---

[282]*Longtime Caldwell attorney Julius Weiss. According to Virginia Caldwell, despite repeated requests to have her husband's correspondence with Weiss returned to her, Weiss's son confiscated and perhaps destroyed his father's papers after his death in the mid 1980s.*
[283]*For fuller accounts of the circumstances of the divorce, see Vicki Goldberg,* Margaret Bourke-White: A Biography *(New York: Harper and Row, 1986), pp. 254–256; Klevar,* Biography, *pp. 247–252; and Miller, pp. 315–317.*

having trouble wished upon him, only and always getting out by the skin of his teeth. Martha Stroup, working her way thru life confronted with a young son to raise, a somewhat itinerate husband, aggrivating goats, game cocks and a lazy houseboy bears the cultural load of her community as well as that of raising her family with the grace of any woman who has been supporting herself and household by washing and ironing for as long as she can remember.

While the complete measure of the book might be humorous in tone, it is balanced by sentiment, irony and enough of the ordinary in every day life to take it away from alongside Perelman, I think.

As ever,
[Skinny]

Following the April 1943 publication of *Georgia Boy*—the book he would often call his personal favorite—Caldwell was again working in Hollywood, this time for Twentieth Century–Fox. The two-year contract guaranteed him $1750 per week for the first year and $2000 per week the second. That kind of money was "something to think about," he confessed to his parents.[284] Caldwell worked nearly nine months before, he says, he "asked to be released from the agreement so that I could return to writing novels."[285] Already planning a new novel, *Tragic Ground*, he was also working with DS&P to issue a paperback reprint of *Jackpot*, and significantly, to arrange a new collection of his short stories to be selected and introduced by Henry Seidel Canby, a scholar carefully chosen for his reputation—and because he had already gone on record as one of Caldwell's admirers. In his introductory essay, Canby described Caldwell as "primarily and essentially a short-story writer" in the tradition of Irving, Hawthorne, and Poe, but distinguished as "the first [American short-story writer] who has consciously viewed the rich materials of his native experience as sociology, and then turned the[m] into successful art."[286]

---

[284] *EC to the Rev. and Mrs. Ira S. Caldwell, GU2 10-26-43.*

[285] *Experience*, p. 222. Klevar suggests that it was studio executives who decided to urge Caldwell toward an early settlement of his contract, since "everything he wrote was unusable and because none of the producers wanted to work with him" (Biography, p. 257).

[286] *Henry Seidel Canby, ed., Stories by Erskine Caldwell: Twenty-four Representative Stories*, (Duell, Sloan and Pearce, 1944), p. vii. Canby's introduction was one of the first concerted efforts to "package" Caldwell as a serious writer. Letters from this period in the Dartmouth collection indicate that other scholars considered to introduce the stories were Joseph Warren Beach and Carl Van Doren.

To Henry Seidel Canby:
[DAR.tl(cc)] [Twentieth Century–Fox stationery, Beverly Hills]
September 27th 1943

Dear Dr Canby:

Charlie Duell has told me that you have agreed to write the introduction for the volume of 'Selected Stories' which his firm plans to publish. Needless to say, I am highly pleased to hear of this.

I assume that you will want to have some biographical information to draw upon. If such is the case, I would be glad to supply what I can in the matter. I am perfectly willing to be pumped but, not being used to this sort of thing, I think we will get a better flow if you primed me with a few questions.

As for your critical method there is, of course, no possible suggestion I would offer. I do hope, however, that you will feel free to probe the spirit and purpose responsible for these culled and winnowed apples of my eye. I don't believe any writer has ever been satisfied with the work behind him; I know I am not. However, if one did not accept and cherish some of the products of his mind and body there would be a lot less literature and children in the world today. As a storyteller, I have produced an unforgivable number of black sheep, but black sheep we will probably have with us always, and I am willing to be responsible for my share.

I look forward to hearing from you and I hope I can be of some help to you.

With best wishes, I am

Sincerely,

Ever vigilant against censorship, perceived or real, Caldwell responded with biting sarcasm when asked to tone down some potentially offensive phrasing in a few stories for the mass-market paperback of *Jackpot*.

To Charles A. Pearce:
[DAR.tl(cc)] [Twentieth Century–Fox stationery, Beverly Hills]
October 13th 1943

Dear Charlie:

I am returning the list of "essential" changes, signed & approved, and I hope it will make a lot of folks at Avon [Books] happy. However, I am sure a lot of customers are going to feel cheated when they don't find a single "bastard", "prick", or "cunt" in the whole book. Don't you think we should print a leaf that can be tipped in, containing all the words, and supply it to those who feel the need of having a few household words that can be written into the text? For example, let us say one of the censored lines reads: "They went out on the lawn for a quickie and, when he laid her down, the cool wet grass tickled her behind". The reader then could refer to our list of words on the supplementary sheet, choose, say, the words "coke", "drank", "his", "liquid", "his", and "throat". The reader the would have something to snicker about. He would have: "They went out on the lawn for a coke and, when he drank his down, the cool wet liquid tickled his throat". I think that's pretty hot stuff to get for only two-bits.

If you decide you want a list of words for the supplement, let me know.

          Best as ever,

[attachment]

JACKPOT, SHORT STORIES, by Erskine Caldwell

Page 8-Line 11
 Omit "son of a bitch" insert "jackass".
Page 8-Line 21
 Omit "bastard" insert "mule".
Page 9-Line 16
 Omit "God".
Page 9-Line 19
 Omit "the son of a bitch" insert "that skunk".
Page 9-Line 21
 Omit "son of a bitch" insert "skunk".
Page 9-Line 28
 Omit "God".
Page 10-Line 17
 Omit "raped" insert "in trouble".
Page 10-Line 19
 Omit "rape" insert "get in trouble".
Page 11-Line 8
 Omit "God".
Page 28-Line 16
 Omit "breasts" insert "busom".
Page 138-Line 16
 Omit "and both her legs across my lap".
Page 139-Line 31
 Omit "and how she put her legs across my lap".
Page 656-Line 22
 Omit "he pushed her down again".
Page 656-Line 23 & 24
 Omit "he tried to kick her dress above her waist with his foot".

<u>JACKPOT (Avon Edition)</u>.

The manuscript of *Tragic Ground* was completed in March 1944 and was published the following October—the first novel in Caldwell's projected "Southern Cyclorama" since *Trouble in July* four years earlier. Reviews again were mixed, and Caldwell himself seems to have had doubts about the level of his writing.[287]

To Alfred Morang:

[HAR.tls] Tucson, Arizona
October 5, 1944

Dear Alfred:

I've just received copies of <u>Tragic Ground</u>, and I am sending one off to you in this mail via parcel post. It will be published at the end of this month.

I don't know if the novel is any good or not. Sometimes I think it is, other times I think it's not. Anyway, I know it could be a lot better. Maybe one of these days I'll do a book that satisfies me. The only trouble is that if I like it, maybe nobody else will. It's a dull circle to live in.

We have been here nearly three weeks now, and I've pretty well settled down. I don't know when I'll be able to get started on a new book, but I ought to do something about it. I am planning now to go to New York in January or February, and I still mean what I suggested about taking along a representative lot of your work to show to agents -- provided you still want me to by then. As I wrote you, I settled my contract at Fox, for a good year's living, and I hope I am free of Movietown for all time. Just before we left Hollywood, MGM made an offer, but I couldn't see it, and here we are. All I have to worry about now is doing another book, running the four weekly newspapers in South Carolina,[288] and such odds and ends. And, of course, making a living.

When and/if travel opens up, June and I will be up to Santa Fe to see you. Nobody knows when that will be, though, and right now we have only enough gasoline to get to town several times a week.

Write when you have time.

Best,
Erskine

---

[287] *In reviewing the novel, even a steady Caldwell supporter like Jonathan Daniels had to admit: "It seems to me that it is time for some decision as to whether Erskine Caldwell is a writer concerned with the socially significant lower depths of American life or whether he has found modern pay dirt in comedy at the expense of the half-wit and the deformed, which so delighted audiences long ago" (Saturday Review of Literature [14 Oct. 1944], p. 46).*

[288] *With his father and brother-in-law, Caldwell was the principal investor in purchasing the newspapers of Allendale, Hampton, Jasper, and Beaufort counties. For details, see Miller, pp. 319–320.*

To Alfred Morang:

[HAR.tls]   Tucson, Arizona
                                                                           October 16, 1944

Dear Alfred:

I suppose you have received the novel by now. I got your letter two days ago.

The new book isn't so much, at least it's not as much as I'd like for it to be. After you finish a book you're pretty well full of it, and it is difficult to read the thing with any sort of critical evaluation. Then six months later you go back to it and the thing is all thumbs; you see where you should have done this, that, or the other thing to it -- but of course it's too late. It would be ideal to put a book away for a year, then read it and rewrite it before publishing it. The only trouble about that is that you'd probably be so disgusted with it that you'd throw it in the waste basket, and then of course you wouldn't have anything to publish. Maybe, after all, the best than can be done is to plug along, doing the best you can, writing one book after another, and then, God willing, at the end of fifty years may be one book of the lot would be worthwhile. I hear there is a review of it in the Sunday Times Book Review (Oct 15), but I haven't seen it yet.[289]

Maybe after you read it you would be able to tell me what's wrong with it. I know something's wrong with it, but I can't quite put my finger on it. I wouldn't be at all surprised to see it get panned all over the map, but I'm used to that, and I wouldn't be surprised, anyway, I suppose.

Let me hear from you when you have time.
                                                  Best,
                                                  Erskine

To Alfred Morang:

[HAR.tls]   Tucson, Arizona
                                                                           October 23, 1944

Dear Alfred:

What you have to say about <u>Tragic Ground</u> is good, not because you praised it but because you grasped the meaning I wanted to put

---

[289] *Reviewer E. B. Burgum saw* Tragic Ground *as evidence of a certain artistic development: Caldwell's "latest version of Jeeter Lester may struggle ineffectually against outward circumstances and inner weakness, but he is not without allies and he is not altogether lost"(New York* Times Book Review *[16 Oct. 1944], p. 6).*

into the story. Most of the reviewers, and many of the readers, so far have expressed either confusion or repugnance. You, however, have gone beyond the mere limitations of words and sentences and found the meaning of the novel. I am enclosing some extra copies of reviews so you can see why I value your criticism so highly. The review closest to your way of thinking is from the [New York] Times Book Review: it is as if you two fellows got to gether and found your had the same mind about it. On the other hand, some readers think it is merely a dirty book. Maybe it is, to those who are incapable of reading any deeper than the mere wordage. Sure, it is dirty in the sense that the people are dirty -- but to me there is no such thing. People are what they are, and if you write about what they are, you are a fraud if you try to make them appear different. I think if you compare a story like this one with one of the serials in the Ladies Home Companion, for example, you will see what I mean. You may be writing about the same thing and the same people, but to my mind the author of the latter is a fraud because he gives you only the good things of life, and highly polished at that; but real people do not live that way. They grunt and they groan in an effort to win existance, and it is not always pleasant to watch or hear about. You could say I tried to make it dirty, because I did try to make it real, and I don't see how you can be real and a fraud at the same time. I make no pretense of thinking that this is a great book -- the greatest ever written -- because I know it's not; but I do know it is not dirt for dirt's sake any more than it is art for art's sake. I am merely trying, in this book and in others, to reveal life. . . . Don't bother to return the clippings; I have other copies.

        Best,
        Erskine

In *With All My Might*, Caldwell recalls the 1940s—and in particular, the years of his marriage to June—as a time when "I was continually finding myself coming to terms with so many irresistible causes and appealing choices that it was not easy for me to be able to allot six months or more to my cherished preference for writing a novel or series of short stories in undisturbed isolation."[290] Indeed, by 1946 he seemed more occupied with the business of being Erskine Caldwell than he was with his writing: undertaking promotional tours, negotiating reprint and foreign publications of his works, investing in a local radio station, and even supporting a miserably unsuccessful attempt to bring *Georgia Boy* to the stage.[291] That

---

[290] *p. 205.*
[291] *A great professional (and financial) disappointment for Caldwell,* Georgia Boy *closed*

year he did, however, manage to get out a very poorly received new novel, *A House in the Uplands*. And at the urging of Cap Pearce, he consented to yet another compendium of previously published work, *The Caldwell Caravan*—conceived as a "sampler" to display for readers, new and old, the best of America's Most Popular Writer.[292]

To Alfred Morang:

[HAR.tls] Tucson, Arizona
April 13, 1947

Dear Alfred:

... Things have been so-so with me. There hasn't been anything seriously wrong, but there have been ups & downs. One or two things have kept me in a stew, and I can't see daylight yet, but I'll let you know when I get them worked out. Some day I hope I can take things easy and not have to spend half my time in worry and such. You know how it can get you down, because you've had your share of it, too.

I started a novel January 1st and I'm trying to get it finished by June 1st.[293] If nothing goes wrong, I'll get it done by then, but I wouldn't know whether it'll be any good or not. I work at it from 9 to 5, and after three and a half months so far it's all a big blur. After another month and a half I'll probably be so sick of it that I can't even read it. It's a hell of a life to be a writer and be so dumb you can't do anything else.

I finally got KCNA [Tucson] open last week. I have 1/3 interest in it, and the two local newspapers have 1/3 each. It's a good set-up from that angle, and they will look after the management. I've sunk $20,000 in it, and that really made me scrape the bottom of the barrel. I'm really broke now. ... I've worked at it for a solid year now and I think I must know close to all there is about getting a station started and on the air. It's a headache, but I'm glad I got into it.

I'm planning on begging & borrowing the money somewhere and making a trip to Paris and London in August. It will be a four-week trip via air, and June and I will spend two weeks in Paris and two weeks in London. ...

Penguin 25¢ Books has sold 2,000,000 copies of <u>God's Little Acre</u>,

---

in Boston after losing at least $40,000. Jack Kirkland, who had made theater history with Tobacco Road, *had written the script, but as he explained to Caldwell:* "Chiefly, I think, the reason for the failure was that I simply didn't write a good enough play.... my script read well, but it simply did not play. It was not very funny and it was dull.... In reading one supplied [dramatic conflict and characterization]; in playing, they were simply not there, and a great void descended—the stage was just plain empty.... I'm very sorry" (Kirkland to EC, DAR 1-17-46).

[292] Pearce to EC, DAR 9-19-45.
[293] The Sure Hand of God.

and they may sell another million by the end of this year. They say they will sell at least one million of <u>Tobacco Rd</u>, which they published last month, also for 25¢. They have one more to do, <u>Journeyman</u>, but I doubt if they'll sell anything like a million of it. They sold about 500,000 <u>Trouble in July</u>, and that's about finished. Pocket Books is publishing [Canby's] <u>Stories [by Erskine Caldwell]</u>, but I haven't heard what they are doing with it.

That's about all I know to the present. If I can ever get this novel finished, I'll feel a lot better about life in general.

Let me hear from you.

                                                 Best,
                                                 Erskine

Caldwell delighted in receiving letters from his readers, and he often wrote back if the writer seemed genuinely interested in his work. The Dartmouth Collection in particular contains literally reams of letters, both positive and negative, he received over the years, many of them bearing his scrawl, "ANSWERED." It is rare, however, to find one of his responses, such as this one to an unidentified teacher.

                            To Mr. [?] Sumner:

[GU1.tls]   Tucson, Arizona
                                                                      April 26, 1947

Dear Mr. Sumner:

Thank you for your letter. I am not surprised to hear there has been some discussion in your class about "Daughter".[294] Many readers have asked the same question.

If the story is vague, it is purposely so, as that was my conception of a situation where such things could happen to anybody, so to speak. In my mind, a man, black or white, could find himself in such a jam regardless of class or color, and become the innocent victim of mass feeling. In this particular case, I would say he was a white man and that he was freed. It could be otherwise, depending upon an individual's own mental attitude towards society.

I hope this will help explain the idea behind the story to some extent.

                                               Sincerely,
                                               Erskine Caldwell

---

[294] *Once a frequently anthologized story, "Daughter" appeared first in the November-December 1933 issue of Jack Conroy's little magazine,* Anvil.

While Cap Pearce told Caldwell he thought *The Sure Hand of God* (1947) was "a honey" of a book and that from it they were "all expecting great things, obviously," his opinion did not coincide with those of reviewers, who roundly panned the novel.[295] Similarly, when Caldwell sent DS&P the manuscript of *This Very Earth* in March of 1948, Pearce responded that he found it "a super, super job," that "some of [the] characters are hard to love but each is real as can be." "Having read *This Very Earth* twice quite carefully," he maintained, "I can only repeat that there is only one Caldwell and that he seems to get better all the time, an achievement which combines several small miracles in this day and age."[296] But there were few kind words from other quarters for Caldwell's latest. An anonymous reviewer for *Time*, for instance, called the book "as scrawny a literary turkey as has been hatched in 1948," and characterized its author as "a once-talented dancer who still remembers all the steps and postures but has forgotten how to dance."[297] Faced with such criticism, Caldwell took special care to acknowledge any support he received.

To James Gray:

[MHS.tls] Tucson, Arizona
September 11, 1948

Dear James Gray:

I am writing this letter in appreciation of your review of "This Very Earth" in the St. Paul Pioneer Press two weeks ago. I am glad, of course, that since the days of "American Earth" your reviews have been favorable, but even more than that it is gratifying to know that you, alone among American critics, have been consistently understanding of my work. Please accept my sincere thanks for your most recent review, and all others during the past almost twenty years.[298]

---

[295] *Pearce to EC, DAR 11-1-47, 6-16-47. The unsigned review from* Time *is typical of the critical response to this novel: "The godless little acre of squalor and lechery staked out by Novelist Erskine Caldwell has been tilled to exhaustion.... But Caldwell still goes on. His latest harvest is an unappetizing literary turnip called* The Sure Hand of God.*" If the novel "is gamy enough to attract the censors," the review concluded, "[i]t has little to merit anyone else's attention" ("Turnip,"* Time *[3 Nov. 1947], pp. 108, 100).*

[296] *Pearce to EC, DAR 3-11-48.*

[297] *"Caldwell's Collapse,"* Time *(30 Aug. 1948), p. 84. An anonymous reviewer for the* Courant, *of Hartford, Connecticut, lampooned the novel's publication with a poem-review:*
  Hail to Caldwell, the Knight of the Muckraking Pen!
  Hooray for these zombies he's exhumed again!
  Here he bows with one more of his hot-boiling novels
  About the 'Po' White Trash' fast rotting in hovels....
Originally published on 29 August 1948, the poem is reprinted in McDonald, Critical Response *(pp. 146–147).*

[298] *Gray had nearly always found something good to say about Caldwell's books. His review of* This Very Earth *portrayed Caldwell as "an enormously important writer, an artist of sober intent who—no matter how foolishly and grievously his values have been misinterpreted, even by his admirers—has kept on saying what he thought America ought to know about itself." He excused Caldwell's apparent repetitiousness as merely evidence of the artist's belief that it is "his*

The series of novels I have been writing about the South is, I think, drawing to a close. It is possible there will be one more, perhaps two or three more, before I am satisfied with my attempt to depict what I consider the most important phases of community life in a particular region. I am attempting to explain these various phases of life in individual introductions to these novels which, beginning this fall with "Tobacco Road" and "Tragic Ground", will be issued in a uniform edition. I have never felt that a story so complex could be told in one novel and that is why the complete story will require eight or ten volumes. Of course, I had no such plan in mind in the beginning, but after finishing "Tobacco Road" and "God's Little Acre" I was dissatisfied with the result, and from that dissatisfaction grew the desire to write the complete story of a particular region in the South, as I knew it, in as many volumes as the story demanded. I believe that it is my insistence on a common background for these novels that has to some extent prompted some critics to say the stories are repetitious. I hope that by the time I have completed the series that it will become clear that the over-all story would have been unsuccessful without this unified background.

With all good wishes, I am

Sincerely,
Erskine Caldwell

To Alfred Morang:

[HAR.tls] Tucson, Arizona
February 5, 1949

Dear Alfred:

I finished up the novel yesterday, which I've been working on since last August, almost since the day after I saw you, and I'm just about out on my feet.[299] June and I are planning to go to New York in a week or ten days, mostly to wrangle with Charlie Duell over a new contract. This new novel might be pretty good. Anyway, I like it better than any I've done in five or six years. But we'll see. . . .

It's been cold down here for a month now, and it even snowed

---

job to keep on repeating himself until a reasonably large and responsible number of citizens have waked up to the fact that he means it and that what he says is dismally true" ("Caldwell Repeats Theme in New Book," St. Paul Pioneer Press, *Erskine Caldwell Scrapbooks, DAR 8-29-48).* Gray's reviews of Tobacco Road, Kneel to the Rising Sun, *and* Tragic Ground *are reprinted in McDonald,* Critical Response.

[299] *He had finished drafting* Place Called Estherville.

one night. I woke up the next morning, thinking I was back in Maine, and probably would have done away with myself if I hadn't seen the palm trees in time.

Let me hear how things are with you.

Sincerely,
Erskine

Caldwell came to know Manuel Komroff in the 1930s when they shared the attention of editors of such publications as *Pagany*, *Scribner's*, *Story*, and *Esquire*. Now, soliciting the input of his friends for a textbook on fiction-writing, Komroff asked Caldwell to address a series of specific topics, including "My writing habits," "How the idea of writing *Tobacco Road* came to me," and his opinion of "a theory that Justice holds the story and characters together and determines the direction."[300]

To Manuel Komroff:

[CU3.tls]　　　　　　　　　　　　　　　　　　　　　Tucson, Arizona
July 19, 1949

Dear Manuel:

It's been a long time since you wrote me your letter of April 21st, but I've been abroad for several months and have just got home.[301]

I don't know the answers to most of your questions, and you'll have to forgive me for not trying to answer them. About all I can say is that I have writing habits, and perhaps peculiar ones at that. I can't read my own handwriting, and so use a typewriter, a habit I formed when I was a cub reporter many years ago in Atlanta. I like to work all day, from nine or ten to four or five or six. I take Sundays off. I take two or three months a year off, too, usually summer. It is difficult for me to write anything that satisfies me, and I find myself rewriting a story five, ten, fifteen times. As I get to the tenth or fifteenth version, I don't want to quit working on it and I generally hold on to it until I convince myself that I am doing it more harm than good. That usually happens about the ninth or tenth month, and then I am through with it forever. I wouldn't want to revise a story once it's in print, because by that time I'm too much interested in the one I'm working on. That's me, and I hope other writers have a much easier time of it than I do. Maybe that's why I don't read much, too. I can't get interested in anything once it's in print, my work or another fellow's, because I get completely tied up in trying to make words do

[300] *Komroff to EC, DAR 4-21-49.*
[301] *He and June had been vacationing in Europe.*

what I want them to do -- that is, tied up in the actual process of making words perform. Once they are in print I have the feeling that I have no part in them -- that they are dead and cold and inactive. That's about all I can say on the subject, and I hope you can find some use for what I've said.

All good luck to you.

Sincerely
Erskine

In rapid succession—too rapid, many have said—Caldwell had published a novel a year between 1946 (*A House in the Uplands*) and 1950 (*Episode in Palmetto*). With each new title, it seemed, reviewers' patience dwindled, and so did sales. Soon after the publication of 1949's *Place Called Estherville*, for example, Cap Pearce notified Caldwell that they were experiencing "difficulties" with the book: "As you know the reactions have been pretty uneven. Hengerers Department Store in Buffalo, for instance, reports not a single copy sold."[302] Understandably, Caldwell's interest in keeping his older titles in print developed as a real priority. He was wholly unamenable to Pearce's suggestion that, given the country's current political climate, they not make too loud a flourish in reprinting *All Night Long*, the novel based on Caldwell's experiences in Russia. Pearce suggested that they wait "a year or two, until we can see how the picture has changed," and then perhaps bring it out "routinely," as "one more Caldwell title" in the Uniform Edition of his work that DS&P had been reprinting at intervals.[303]

To Charles A. Pearce:

[DAR.tl(cc)]   Tucson, Arizona
                                           December 17th 1950

Dear Charlie:

I have taken counsel of myself in regard to <u>All Night Long</u>, and have slept on it as well, and I have come to conclusions. I perhaps came to these particular conclusion because I feel it is wrong for a book to be brought out or reissued on the principle of having it appear as quietly and secretly as possible. I can appreciate having a book published quietly for the purpose of securing copyright or some such reason, but I am unable to appreciate a scheme for publishing a book with the announced purpose of selling as few copies as possible. It sounds ridiculous to me. It sounds like something out of "Believe It Or Not."

I can only say now that, in view of your pronouncements, the

---

[302] *Pearce to EC, DAR 10-25-49.*
[303] *Pearce to EC, DAR 12-14-40.*

only two courses open are: 1) reissuing <u>All Night Long</u> in the Uniform Edition, and 2) having the rights revert to me. Since my previous suggestions have been rejected, the decision now rests with you. And because you are the authorized publisher, it is only right that you make the decision.

For my part, I would like to say once more that I do not share your feelings about <u>All Night Long</u>. I am not ashamed of the novel, and am not sorry it was written. I believe it serves the purpose, now as then, of enlightening non-Russians as to the psychology of the Russian mind. War or peace, I hold that this is a good thing for Americans to know. I believe this novel furnishes, to some degree, information of a useful character; at this period in our national life I think it is wise for us to know our friends, and enemies, to the fullest possible extent. . . .

        Sincerely,

Stirred by the brisk sales of the Pocket Books edition of Canby's *Stories*, the urge to reprint continued with Caldwell's apparently playful but very real insistence on publishing a "new" volume of his already often-recycled short stories.[304]

To Max Lieber:

[DAR.tl]   Tucson, Arizona
                             3/25/51

Dear Max:

I feel as a spurned bridegroom must feel on the unconsummated night of his honeymoon who must squirm and toss in the shadows of his sorrow with only repetitious masturbation to console him. During all these bright years of anticipation -- since the year 1947 with DS&P; since December 1949 with BAL[305] -- I have suggested, intimated, requested, urged, and begged that I be invited into the nuptial chamber for the solemn purpose of propagating a book of short stories. But, alas, many have been the books propagated by others during those long years of travail while I paced the dark and chilly corridor

---

[304]The Humorous Side of Erskine Caldwell, *a collection of previously published stories and novel excerpts, was published by DS&P in 1951. Robert Cantwell was selected from among Mark Van Doren, Horace Gregory, Lionel Trilling, and Bernard De Voto to write the introduction, which laid the foundation for a revisionary look at Caldwell's fiction: "In light of this background, the humor of Erskine Caldwell's fiction becomes a far more impressive creation, much more truly the work of a great humorous imagination, than it seems when it is considered the product of a semi-sociological observation of a backward people" (p. xvi).*

[305]*Actually NAL, or the New American Library, Caldwell's reprint publishers.*

hopefully waiting for a beckoning invitation to the solacing pleasures of the marriage bed.

My years are numbered now. My shoulders are slightly stooped. I am no longer shockheaded and pristine in appearance. Philosophical and seasoned by adversity, I am nevertheless able to lift my voice in a final cry of desperate supplication. Surely, somebody, somewhere, will hear my plea, and tenderly helping me carry the seven short stories, lead me to sanctuary. In the end, may there I be found, perhaps in the voluptuous arms of a whore but, nevertheless, content and consummated.

So be it.

Sincerely,

A more assertive Caldwell, mastering the intricacies of his publishing interests, revised his approach the next day.

To Max Lieber:

[DAR.tl(cc)] Tucson, Arizona
March 26th 1951

Dear Max:

I believe it would be a good thing for me to attempt to clarify matters by placing my books on the table. My reasons for doing so are:

(a) I wish, selfishly perhaps, to have my work published while I am alive, and don't care particularly about it when I'm dead; and

(b) there seems to be misunderstanding on the part of DS&P and NAL in regard to my interest at this time in regard to publishing certain short stories.

You will find enclosed a sheet listing the short stories involved in the present discussion.[306] A study of this sheet will show that, all told, seventeen short stories are involved. Total words: approximately 45,000. The present discussion has evidently come about because an outside publisher has offered to bring out the stories in Category III. It would be foolish of me not to consider any reasonable offer directed toward the publication of my work. I live to write, and writing is my living.

As you know, there has been, since about 1947, some discussion between DS&P and myself regarding the publication of these stories

[306] *Missing.*

in a separate volume. Nothing, to date, has come of this. In mid-year of 1949, NAL came into the discussion, but nothing in the nature of a concrete proposal resulted. Consequently, I have waited these many years to no end. I feel now that if neither DS&P nor NAL care to propose publication, I should interest myself in any reasonable offers from any other quarters. . . .

. . . It seems to me that if all parties who now make known an interest in what has come about, were to apply thought to the matter that something related to our mutual interests would be brought about. Charges and countercharges are not apt to give birth to a worthwhile creation. Legal and moral matters are certainly involved, and beyond that is something of greater concern, as far as it touches me, and that is the economic and literary value of what we are talking about.

In any continued discussion of the matter it should be remembered that I would not be interested in a stop-gap policy. I do not wish anybody to publish a book of mine merely because I wish it published. At this point in my life I should not be expected to endorse any proposal which was not a satisfactory union of economic and literary values.

In sum, all I have to go by at this time is the fact that I have stories to publish in a book, outside publishers have offered to publish, and I have no offers from DS&P and/or NAL to issue the seven, ten, or seventeen short stories in question, either in part or in whole. And in addition to the matter of these seventeen stories, it will be important to consider the physical composition and future composition of Jackpot and A Woman in the House[307] in relation to them.

I trust this will clearly present my position to all concerned in such a manner that a speedy, and satisfactory, conclusion may be arrived at. Comments from all will be appreciated.

Sincerely,
Erskine Caldwell

Caldwell's vast success in the reprint market—*God's Little Acre* alone had sold over 6,000,000 copies by 1951—also meant exposure to a larger readership for whom his books might seem objectionable, particularly given the sexy cover art used to sell them.[308] When the paperback industry was subjected to an investigation by

[307] *NAL had issued this paperback edition of previously published stories in 1949.*
[308] *Bill Crider has argued that Caldwell's paperback presence spawned a whole new genre, the "backwoods novel" ("Sons of Tobacco Road: 'Backwoods Novels,'"* Journal of Popular Culture *16.3 [1982], pp. 47–59).*

the House of Representatives Select Committee on Current Pornographic Materials, Caldwell's books were among those cited as violating certain standards of "taste."[309] Caldwell received enough letters from readers objecting to his books that NAL chairman Victor Weybright urged him to compose a stock response that they could send out directly from their New York offices. Weybright called the final product "a masterpiece."[310]

To Mary Ann Whitlow [et al.]:
[DAR.tl(cc)] [Tucson, Arizona]
June 4th 1951

Dear Miss Whitlow:

I have received your letter in which you express concern about inexpensive pocket-size books and the moral effect of such books upon young persons of teen-age. Since I am the author of a number of novels and volumes of short stories, which are published by The New American Library of World Literature, I take it that you would like for me to reply to your letter. I am very glad to do so.

I am sure that the majority of us, both young and old, realize that we are fortunate to have the privilege of living, in this day and age, in the United States of America. One of the things that has made the United States the envy of other nations of the world is the fact that Americans have the privilege of selecting their reading matter without fear of disapproval and punishment by a dictator in power. This privilege, however, is also a responsibility. It is our responsibility to learn how to discriminate and select, and this implies that each individual should educate himself so that he will be capable of selecting

---

[309] *The investigation had ended by 10 December 1952, when Victor Weybright, who had not been invited to testify before the committee, issued a reply to the range of complaints that had been raised against the paperback industry. Acknowledging certain apparent "abuses" of the freedoms of the publishing industry, he was nevertheless vehement in his defense of modern literature's turn toward "realistic detail," which includes "sex and sin":* "Of course our writers are more outspoken today than they were forty years ago. Whether this is an evil depends on one's view of the function of literature as a whole. The courts, the critics and the public have swung increasingly toward the view that the truth cannot hurt us" *(The Complete and Unabridged Statement to the Gathings Committee by the New American Library of World Literature, Inc., CU1 1952).*

[310] *Weybright to EC, DAR 6-6-51. Around the same time as this letter, another disgusted reader, a teacher, had finished* God's Little Acre *by shredding it and mailed Caldwell a few of the pages with furious annotations scrawled in the margins:* "After reading this book I started tearing it up piece by piece & throwing it into the stove in my school room. On second thought I felt it my Christian duty to cry out against evil!! If the whole book isn't rotten, ok? Yet we treat our bodies better than our minds & souls. If the carcas of the beef isn't all rotten we can eat it all (tumors & all) & not be hurt! Oh, this wicked sinful world. Oh for Christian lawyers, judges, authors!..." *(Anonymous to EC, DAR undated 1951). As noted earlier, the Dartmouth collection is rich with letters, both "fan" and "pan," from Caldwell's readers.*

the best and rejecting the bad. The only way this is possible, as I see it, is to be able to judge for one's self what is good and what is bad; if this were not the case, then Americans would find that they, too, had to have a dictator to tell them what they could or could not do.

As to the moral, or immoral, values of books, I feel that students such as you and your friends are capable of learning to judge for yourselves what book you can read to advantage. The fully educated person is one who has read some portion of the literature of the world and is able to select those books which he believes will enlighten his mind and thereby enable him to understand and evaluate life around him.

The purpose of my books is to reveal and explain the lives of human beings in contemporary America. I believe that if you read my books, or the books of other authors with similar purpose, and read them in this light, you will find that you are acquiring the ability to choose the kind of books which contribute to your understanding of people everywhere. In this way you will acquire the ability to select and judge not only reading matter, but also to discriminate between good and evil in any phase of life. The good political leaders of our country are elected by thoughtful and discriminating people; the bad political leaders gain office by taking advantage of unthinking and undiscriminating people.

Coming of age in America now is a wonderful experience for anyone fortunate enough to be a citizen of the United States. I hope you and your friends will think about this privilege and strive to keep the freedom to select and reject reading matter and to select and reject political leaders. Without this freedom, there would be no United States of America as we know it; we would live in a nation ruled by the selfishness and prejudice of one man or a small group of men.

I hope you will wish to go back and read one of my books in the light of what I have said, weighing the moral values carefully and observing the evil that comes to people who unfortunately have not gained the ability to discriminate between good and evil. When you find this in any book, I believe you can assure yourself that you are well on the way to becoming a fully educated person and a useful citizen of the United States.

I should very much like to hear from you again.

                        Sincerely,
                        Erskine Caldwell

When Caldwell moved his family to Santa Barbara for the summer, he maintained his correspondence about NAL's continued reluctance either to reprint *All Night Long* or to reject it so that he could place it elsewhere. In January, Weybright had warned Caldwell that because the book "is undeniably pro–Russian," Lieber's pressing the reissue "would undoubtedly unleash an attack on you and all your other books as reflecting a pro–Russian, or pro–Communist, viewpoint."[311] In July, Weybright and NAL president Kurt Enoch pointed out that if Lieber attempted to place the novel elsewhere, its "partisan thesis" could easily be exploited by an unscrupulous reprint publisher. This would not only "have an adverse effect upon the sales of your [other] books," but might mean "catastrophe" for Caldwell's reputation.[312]

To Kurt Enoch and Victor Weybright:

[DAR.tl(cc)] Santa Barbara, Calif.
July 21st 1951

Dear Kurt and Victor:

I have received your letter of the 18th and, after a thoughtful twenty-four hours, I remain disturbed by some of the implications to be found in it. Perhaps I am being overly sensitive; however, the fact is that I am necessarily so.

Re: ". . . the book and its time and place of origin." The publishing history of <u>All Night Long</u> is a matter of public record and available to any interested party. The story originated within me and I was prompted to write it by the events of the time. It would seem that I should be more familiar with this circumstance than anyone else you could inquire of.

Re: " . . . to assure certain critics that we know nothing of your politics." This infers, to me at least, that I am suspected of being subversive or disloyal in thought or action. No one has ever asked me anything concerning my politics (I lean toward Single Tax more than anything else); if anyone should ever ask me, I shall be glad to explain myself to the best of my ability.

Re: ". . . or of Maxim Lieber's politics. . ." I have never questioned Max concerning his politics; for that matter I have never questioned anyone connected with my publishing affairs as to his politics or religion. If I should ever be presented with proof that anyone I was connected with businesswise were disloyal or dishonest, I would not wish to continue such association. . . .

---

[311] He continued: "It is bad enough to have some of our competitors constantly reminding the Government, censors, and some elements of the trade that you are a favorite author in Russia and the Iron Curtain countries, but it would be hopeless to argue against this criticism if Maxim Lieber, who has been identified as close to inner Communist circles, should place this book with any publisher for fresh current publication, promotion, and a new audience in today's divided world" (Weybright to EC, DAR 1-8-51).

[312] Webyright and Enoch to EC, DAR 7-18-51.

I cannot take issue with you regarding sales prospects of <u>All Night Long</u>; unhappily, it probably does have limited sales appeal. More than that, I do not feel that I am capable of changing the book and its story to another setting.[313] This is a task I would hesitate to undertake.

Has it ever occurred to you that opposition to <u>All Night Long</u> may come about, not by reason of its subject matter, but instead, because of the intensity of feeling or sympathetic treatment brought to the story by the author? For many years I have felt that opposition to <u>God's Little Acre</u>, as one example, and to <u>Trouble in July</u>, as another example, was caused by the author's sympathetic treatment of his characters and not by his choice of subject matter. I do not believe I would have the desire to write any story if this element were to be denied me.

As to publication, or consideration, of the book, I suggest that we agree to postpone decision until December 31, 1951, or until we can discuss the matter in person, which ever time comes about first. Please let me know if this is agreeable to you. I am writing to Maxim Lieber in this mail and informing him of my suggestion.

Sincerely,

On July 25, Weybright and Enoch thanked Caldwell for "the gracious delay," and reassured him: "We do not question your politics, or your integrity; but, frankly, we do sometimes have an apprehensive feeling about Maxim Lieber's political effect upon your literary fortunes if he continues to campaign actively to revive *All Night Long*.... We would greatly deplore it if, through your misguided friends, no matter how well-meaning they may be, you and your work were to be smeared by some of your critics and some of our competitors as pro–Communist. We know better, but all the publicity we could muster could never overtake such an attack if it should commence in the United States."[314] NAL did not reprint *All Night Long*.

By November of 1951, Max Lieber had fled the country for Mexico, presumably because of the pro–Communist leanings Weybright and Enoch had said were so widely perceived.[315] After a search guided by attorney Julius Weiss, James Oliver Brown became Caldwell's new agent. From the moment of his association with Brown, Caldwell's attentions seemed ever more absorbed by business mat-

---

[313] *In the July 18 letter, Weybright and Enoch had suggested that "[a] transposition of ALL NIGHT LONG's setting and characters to Korea with Southern Korea guerrillas as the protagonists" might be a way to reinvigorate the novel's "universal thesis against tyranny and aggression."*

[314] *Weybright and Enoch to EC, DAR 7-25-51.*

[315] *Caldwell describes Lieber's unannounced flight in* Might, *although he mistakenly cites the year as 1949 (pp. 220-221). See also Miller, pp. 350-351; and Klevar,* Biography, *pp. 298-299.*

ters. At least in part, this must have been necessitated by the total absence of Lieber's records, which held the details of all negotiations and rights concerning Caldwell's work since their association began in 1931. Caldwell was also increasingly dissatisfied with the way DS&P were managing his affairs.[316]

To Charles Duell:

[CU1.tl(cc)] [Tucson, Arizona]
November 26, 1951

Dear Charlie:

I am writing this letter in the interest of harmony and perspicacity.

Since each of us apparently has his own ideas about how the matter of Tob.Rd: Play should be handled, and since there seems to be controversy as to how to proceed at this juncture, I would like to suggest that each of us satisfy the craving of his native-born acquisitive instinct by agreeing to: (1) you selling the plates of the book at a price to be determined, and (2) my buying the plates at a price to be determined. Should I think you are charging too much for the plates and the rights that go with them, and should you think I am offering too little, don't you think we could somehow arrive at a figure that would give both of us the feeling of having been successfully acquisitive in our time here below (or above)?

It seems to me that this is a sensible method of arriving at a state of well-being; and, more, it is at the same time true to the traditions of American publishing & authoring, seeped in the spirit of public welfare & convenience, and plump & rosy with cosmic materialism. All I would have in the end would be some heavy metal plates I couldn't carry around with me but I could try hard to get a well-made, endearing, nice-to-hold-in-the-hands, trade edition and then, after a decent interval, a reprint. What you would have & to hold at once would be money in the pocket that you could carry around with you wherever you went, and also the satisfaction of knowing that you had made a good bargain with a fuzzy-visioned writer who likes books more than money.

May I hear from you? Please reply to the address below.[317]

Sincerely,

---

[316] *Caldwell was particularly upset about how reprint rights and profits were being managed and with how his most recent book, the autobiography* Call It Experience *(1951), had been produced and promoted. Among other things, it was to have had an index and photographs. He wrote to Brown: "I am dissatisfied with the new publishing methods of DS&P.... I can't write under present conditions with the knowledge that any book I turn over to DS&P will be damaged in the way Call It Experience was damaged. I want to get out from under the current DS&P contract" (EC to Brown, CU1 11-16-51). He told Brown he felt as if he had been subjected to a "blood-letting" (EC to Brown, CU1 11-18-51).*

[317] *Caldwell supplied Brown's address.*

To James Oliver Brown:

[CU1.tls] Tucson, Arizona
December 5th 1951

Dear Jim:
    I think the whole trouble is that I am unhappy about the turn of affairs at DS&P -- not knowing whether they are publishers, high-priced middlemen, or something in the twilight zone -- and I don't see how I can continue writing books, under such a cloud, to be handed over to them. I have leaned over so far backward during the past ten years that at last I've fallen out of the chair. I've cooperated with them to the best of my ability and done more than I would have for any other publisher, all because of loyalty and friendship. Now, for some reason, contact has been broken. I don't know the cause of this, but I do know that I no longer have access to DS&P. A coolness is in the air. Editorially and businesswise both of us suffer because of this, due to the fact that the friendly spirit formerlly existing has evaporated. Perhaps I no longer fit into their scheme of things and they are taking these means to get rid of me. It would have been much better if they had spoken frankly of their dissatisfaction and said what they wanted or did not want out of me. I suspect, for one thing, that they are peeved because I expressed such dissatisfaction as I did in the presence of you and Julius [Weiss]. This could have been avoided if they had asked me to sit down with them and discuss the whole matter we are involved with; however, they did not choose to do this and, so, I did it my way. So be it.
    It is possible that if DS&P want to call it quits now that we could do so on a friendly basis and in an atmosphere of cooperation so that they could continue selling the list they have and be relieved of me. You might tell them, if they think we are trying to hurry & get another publisher, that I have no book for publication, I am writing no book, and I have no plans for writing one at this time. . . .
    I am prepared, after offering the above suggestions, to follow your advice concerning the over-all DS&P situation. . . . All I want out of it is a happy & livable life. . . .
    With best wishes, I am

                            Sincerely,
                            Skinny

In July 1951, in a move aimed at cutting costs, DS&P joined forces with the publishing house of Little, Brown. Under the terms of an extended contract, Little, Brown would manufacture and market all DS&P titles, which would carry the dual imprint of DS&P/LB. Although Caldwell's new agent, Jim Brown, was initially apprehensive about the arrangement—he expressed specific concerns about "the ability" of Little, Brown's president, Stanley Salmen—both agent and client were soon convinced that the new association would be a good one. Caldwell himself welcomed the change. As he said to Brown near the end of their negotiations: "After disastrous association with Charlie Duell, I have come to feel like a country cousin; now perhaps I can get to feel like a professional writer who is associated with a businesslike publisher. I sure hope to God so."[318]

Meanwhile, Caldwell had indeed begun writing again—albeit, producing work considerably less interesting, and less salable, than ever before in his career. In addition to resurrecting the old "Autumn Hill" manuscript and publishing it as *A Lamp for Nightfall* (1952), over the next few years Caldwell wrote several new, but very thin, short stories. After many attempts each, Brown could only place them in slick men's magazines, which paid well but whose editors were too eager to capitalize on Caldwell's well-established reputation for "know[ing] life in certain of its less discussable phases."[319] When "A Gift for Sue" appeared in *Cavalier*, for instance, without Caldwell's permission the editors changed the title to "Just a Quick One"; and when *Manhunt* published "Kathy," the story that accompanied the following note, its title had become "The Motive."

To James Oliver Brown:

[CU1.tl] [Tucson, Arizona]
4/7/52

Jim:

Here is the third and final story of the current series. It makes me feel sad, because I wish I could be doing more and more right away. Maybe some kind soul will come along with a scheme before too long and make it possible for me to get back to doing what I would rather do than anything else (I wonder if I'll ever get fed up with writing?).

EC

---

[318] *Brown to EC, CU1 12-11-51; EC to Brown, CU1 4-16-52. There was no relationship between Jim Brown and the publishing house of Little, Brown.*
[319] *Anonymous review of God's Little Acre, North American Review (May 1933), p. 478.*

Caldwell dashed off the following response to Brown's notification that a new story, "To the Chaparral," had been rejected by *Today's Woman*.

To James Oliver Brown:
[CU1.tls]
Tucson, Arizona
May 11th 1952

Dear Jim:

Be not mistaken; I'm always willing to lend an ear, as well as an eye, to Eleanor Stierhem.[320]

I think the trouble here is that we are talking about two different stories. The story that Eleanor wants to hear is a good one, and one that the female element in the twenty-thirty bracket never tires of. I can't deny that I enjoy the experience of telling it to them, married or unmarried, because it is a thrilling sensation to sit in a cozy corner of a dimly lighted room and feel the quickening pulse and racing heartthrob of a young woman in the thros of yearning. But, this is a workaday world peopled with workaday creatures and the chores of life, in a harsh dawn, call most of us from the downy bed of dalliance. The story I wanted to tell, which is admittedly unglamorous in the cruel morning light of the chaparrel, is, nevertheless, a good one, too. Why not let me go ahead and tell the story I want to tell, and then perhaps we can tell Eleanor, at some opportune time, the story she wants to hear?

Best wishes,

Skinny

A year after publication, *Call It Experience* was reviewed by Walter Harding for the University of Virginia's *Alumni News*. Harding, who was then teaching at the school, praised the autobiography as well as Caldwell's abilities as a storyteller, but he went on to explain his feeling that while Caldwell had probably "started out with the best of intentions … he was corrupted by success and has never progressed beyond his first novel or two." Harding concluded that Caldwell's classmates at the university must "join with many of us in the field of American literature in regretting that he so soon fell into a formula pattern and has never grown into the major author we thought he promised to be." Caldwell responded to the editor of the *Alumni News*.[321]

---

[320] *Fiction editor at* Today's Woman, *later at* Collier's. *"To the Chaparral" was eventually published in* Esquire.

[321] "Erskine Caldwell: His Place in American Literature Today," *University of Virginia Alumni News* (June 1952), pp. 23–24. Caldwell attended Virginia from 1923 to 1925 and then again in the fall of 1926; he did not graduate.

To Robert K. Turner:

[VR2.tls]

Tucson, Arizona
September 13th 1952

Dear Sir:

I was pleased to read in the June, 1952, issue of <u>Alumni News</u> (page 23) a notice by Mr. Walter Harding of a recent book of mine, <u>Call It Experience</u>. Like most writers, I am always pleased when any notice is taken of something I have written. I was especially pleased because Mr. Harding had so many favorable and perceptive comments to make about my work.

It grieved me, however, to see that Mr. Harding made statements as a matter of fact which I feel should have fuller explanation. I would appreciate the opportunity to make mention of some of these.

The comment was made that ". . . Mr. Caldwell has failed miserably at drama." The fact is that I have never written a play, not even a dramatization of one of my own novels. Further, I have at this time no intention of ever attempting to write a play.

Mr. Harding says ". . . <u>Journeyman</u> was one of the coldest turkeys to hit Broadway." That is certainly true, but the dramatization was not mine. It can be said also that the dramatization of <u>Georgia Boy</u> was a distinct flop at its try-out in Boston, but the dramatization was likewise done by someone other than me.

Mr. Harding says "Mr. Caldwell has no one but himself to blame for this." He refers here to the current practice among publishers of having jackets and covers of books designed in a manner of "letting the necklines on their cover-girls drop lower and lower and their skirts rise higher and higher." Perhaps Mr. Harding is in a position to tell his publishers how his books are to be designed, the covers drawn, the weight of paper to be used, the typography to be used, an so on. If so, Mr. Harding is perhaps the most fortunate author in America today.

Mr. Harding says ". . . we can assume that he has forgotten the Lawn." This statement was made in connection with the comment that I had given some of my books, manuscripts, and papers to Dartmouth.[322] I have given many such things to Baker Library at Dartmouth, but I did not give anything to that library before first writing to the University of Virginia Library and asking if anything of this nature would be acceptable. Unfortunately, my offer was not acted upon. No, I have not forgotten the Lawn. I have visited the Lawn and walked upon it and taken delight in it five times during the past ten

---

[322] *"The Lawn" is the familiar name for the oldest section of the University of Virginia campus. Caldwell had begun giving materials to Dartmouth in 1940 (see Henry Terrie, "Caldwell at Dartmouth,"* Erskine Caldwell Reconsidered, *ed. Edwin T. Arnold [Jackson: UP of Mississippi, 1990], pp. 36–41).*

years, and I hope I can continue to visit the Lawn and the University no less as often during the next ten years. I consider that I was fortunate to be able to spend three years at the University of Virginia, I read the <u>Alumni News</u> with avid interest, and I take pride in the fact that I carry membership #1467 of The Alumni Association of the University of Virginia.

Perhaps it can be arranged so that Mr. Harding and I may smoke a pipe of peace the next time I come to Charlottesville.

Sincerely,
Erskine Caldwell

To Alfred Morang:

[HAR.tls]

Tucson, Arizona
October 3rd 1952

Dear Alfred:

It was good to get your letter and to hear from you. I hope things are going to work out a lot better from now on. I'm glad I was able to arrange it so your former rent was cut in half, and I think that will be a big help to you from now on.[323] I think the way it is set up now is about the best that could have been done, because for one thing you will always know you can buy back the house. As you know, I didn't do this to try to make money, but only to make it come out as even as to taxes, repairs, insurance, etc. You can be sure that no matter what happens not a dime will ever find its way to my pocket.

I've been back about a month now. It may be that I'll take a quick trip to New York in a couple of weeks. An off-brand publisher[324] says he has rights to <u>The Bastard</u> and <u>Poor Fool</u> and says he is going to publish them in quarter editions. I don't think we want it done, but even my lawyer and agent are afraid we can't stop them. We'll have to decide whether to let him go ahead, or else figure out if we could win if we brought suit against him. Just one more headache.

I hope I can get settled down to work by the first of November.

---

[323] *In March, after repeated requests from Morang for financial help, Caldwell had instructed his attorney to draw up papers for him to purchase Morang's property; he would then rent the house to Morang for $25 per month for three years, with an option to renew the arrangement if the rent had been paid in full each month. As a "personal favor," Caldwell would contribute $1000 per year to cover the taxes and interest on the mortgage (EC to Julius Weiss, DAR 3-18-52). His health deteriorating due to a heart attack and other serious physical ailments caused by lifelong heavy smoking, Morang was in dire straits: "... Kept going into comas that lasted for hours, and the doctor is giving me a new drug that wakes me up enough so I can work. School is bad, one student at the moment. I'm been peddling water colors for $2.00 each every where from museums to bars to get enough to eat...." (Morang to EC, DAR 10-1-52).*

[324] *Alex L. Hillman.*

I'm pretty far behind, and I want to give myself plenty of time on the next book I write....

> Best wishes,
> Erskine

As he began drafting his next novel, *Love and Money*, Caldwell was also planning a "complete" edition of his short stories.[325]

To Stanley Salmen:

[CU1.tl(cc)]

Tucson, Arizona
November 29th 1952

Dear Stanley:

As a matter of course in my dealings with you, I have devoted my prime thinking during the past several days to your suggestion that I myself arrange the order of stories in <u>The Complete Stories of Erskine Caldwell</u>. It is my understanding that Little Brown plans to publish this book in December 1953 and that an outstanding critic or essayist will be obtained to write an Introduction for it.[326] Further, it is my understanding that you desire to have an arrangement of the stories made prior to turning the manuscript over to the introduction writer....

First of all I shall say that I will attempt to furnish you with the manuscript by the earliest date above, and certainly no later than the latter one.[327] The manuscript will be at least 95% complete; the remaining 5% of material will be furnished as soon as it is possible to locate several stories previously published in magazines now out of print and of which I have no copies. We are now engaged in searching for these stories.

Next it should be noted that several unpublished stories may or may not be withheld for the present, although I feel it is desirable to use them in the book if possible in order to make it a complete volume of short stories by me. The only reason any stories may be withheld is that Jim Brown and I would like to find magazine publication for them prior to book publication.

Now as to the matter of my making the arrangement of stories in the book. I am not qualified for this task, and ill-fitted to attempt it. As you know, I prefer that your own editorial staff undertake it. You

---

[325] *Scott MacDonald explains that in fact several stories are omitted from the collection, which was published in 1953. See his "Check-List," p. 355.*

[326] *Caldwell recommended Harvey Curtis Webster of the University of Louisville, but Salmen decided against any introduction at all (EC to Brown, CU1 10-6-54).*

[327] *Respectively, 15 and 31 December 1952.*

have people under your roof who by training and experience would do an outstanding, professional job of it, whereas I would be a mere amateur in the big league. One of my reasons for having this attitude is that I feel that this is to be the final and complete collection of my short stories (unless later there should be revised editions of the same book), and I would like it to be the best of all possible ones.

If I still fail to warm your heart about this, I can say that what I'll have to do is to take Jackpot without disarranging the present order and, after inserting the newer stories here & there in it, prepare a manuscript of it. (The manuscript you will receive will be made for the most part by pasting printed pages on manuscript paper.)

I would like to have you tell me what your better judgment tells you to do about this. It is my practice to bow to superior judgment in all things.

Best wishes,

Caldwell was offended by Salmen's observation that the sheer size of the *Complete Stories*, some 296,000 words, would increase its price, which might then limit sales, Caldwell's royalties, and the publisher's ability to keep it in hardback print in the future. He also noted that the volume would have limited appeal, since all the stories had been published before, some of them many times. Finally Brown felt compelled to agree that, given "Stanley's rather pessimistic views from every point of view," perhaps "we haven't a good idea here."[328]

To James Oliver Brown:
[CU1.tls] Phoenix, Arizona[329]
June 24th 1953

Dear Jim:

I have given what I consider decisive thought to your letter of the 22nd and to Stanley's letter of the 18th.

All in all, I feel that it would unwise and unsound, from my point of view, to let the book we call Complete Stories go unpublished in 1953.

---

[328] *Brown quoted Salmen's comment verbatim in relaying the news to Caldwell: "This collection of Erskine's stories cannot be described as new in any way. What we are doing is putting the result of twenty-five years of short story writing in one collection for those who will enjoy Erskine's work in that form" (Brown to EC, CU1 6-22-53).*

[329] *In late 1952 or early 1953, Caldwell announced to June that he was buying a house in Phoenix and asked her to move there with him. When she refused, he bought the house anyway, forcing a de facto separation, although they continued to uphold the appearance of marriage (See Klevar, Biography, pp. 309–310). Caldwell liked the fact that there was a "guest house on the property that provided an ideally secluded place for writing" (Might, p. 231).*

My reasoning is this: 1) The collection is a continuation of Jackpot -- bigger & better -- and Jackpot was not a poor book. 2) I cannot subscribe to the policy of abandoning the publication of the collection until some time in the indefinite future. Even if I were to write a novel now, it would not be finished until January 1954; that means the collection might not be published until 1955 or later. I can't presume to live long enough to see this through. 3) Stanley should consider giving up the idea of a chronological arrangement of the contents.[330] In that way the objections as to a lapse from 1944 to 1953 would be done away with. (I think I did a pretty good arrangement of Jackpot, and I'm sure the L/B staff can improve on what I did.)

This is one man's opinion.

Best wishes,
Skinny

To James Oliver Brown:

[CU1.tls]

Phoenix, Arizona
August 15th 1953

Dear Jim:

Re: Promotion of Complete Stories

Naturally, the best way to get a break-even of 15,700 copies, it seems to me, is to take a complete full page ad in the N.Y. Times. This probably costs about $1,250 plus. I think when you consider the fact that what you are doing with a full page ad in the Times (I assume we are talking about the Sunday section) is not only promoting the immediate sale of the book itself but also allowing for an increased return on anthology rights and other reprint rights. The latter two items, as you know, will provide income to L/B (and to us) for the next fifty years. It has been my experience in the past that each time a book of this kind is issued, and promoted, a healthy spurt in anthology and reprint sales takes place. Due to the fact that we've got a goodly number of stories in this book that are appearing in volume form for the first time,[331] the anthology sales should certainly be better

---

[330] *In the same correspondence with Brown quoted above (6-22-53), Salmen wondered about the impression that would form when readers noticed the voids in Caldwell's publishing history—the stretch of years when he published no new short fiction—if they were to follow through with the chronological arrangement Caldwell had recommended. The compromise was to include information about the place but not the date of each story's original publication.*

[331] *Caldwell was mistaken; all the stories had appeared previously in collections.*

for the next few years than they have at any time in the past twenty-five years.

As you can see, I am among those who have a strong belief in intelligent promotion during this phase of American civilization. When you've got something that you don't believe is a weak sister, you've got to bring it to the attention of the people, etc, etc.

Therefore, I'd like to see a way worked out with L/B whereby the book can be given full statue. It is probably the last time we will have such an opportunity as this, and I believe in the book to the extent of suggesting that as much as necessary be used of the 6% Fund[332] to augment L/B's $1000 and provide a complete full page in the Sunday *Times*. I don't know how much this would amount to, but probably five or six hundred dollars. The reason I suggest doing this is that I feel now is the time to put The Fund to the use it was intended. Besides, for the first time in many years I feel that we are dealing with intelligent, knowing people, and I have complete confidence in their ability to bring this book up close to the top of the heap.

I look forward to your comments.

Best wishes,
Skinny

When Brown received the typescript for *Love and Money* on December 1, he praised it as "a very warm book and a very funny book." With a writer as its protagonist, however, he warned, "People usually assume that books about writers are autobiographical so be prepared for some snide comments on wrong assumptions."[333]

To James Oliver Brown:

[CU1.tls] Phoenix, Arizona
December 3rd 1953

Dear Jim:

I was very pleased with your reaction to the book as you expressed it in your letter of the 1st. The only fault I could find would be that maybe you've given me a higher rating than I deserve. Just the same, I can't help liking what you said.

As you know, I was fully aware of the deep-seated prejudice in the deep seats of publishers that is directed toward novels in which a writer plays the lead. Yet, regardless of that, or maybe even because

---

[332] *A provision of Caldwell's initial contract with Little, Brown, whereby this percentage of reprint royalties would be devoted to promoting the Caldwell list.*

[333] *Brown to EC, CU1 12-1-53.*

of it, I set out to show myself, and publishers, too, that a novel about a writer can be as interesting as one about a what-have-you. I may not have proved this to the satisfaction of deep-seated publishers, but perhaps the time will come when other writers will take courage and successfully prove the argument. In the meantime this's what we've got. The next step will be to see what readers think about it.

Of course I hope Stanley [Salmen] will like the book and that L/B will want to publish it with vim & vigor. Nothing would please me more than to see L/B take hold of it with all the enthusiasm they are known in the trade to be able to generate.

Should L/B wish to publish the book, I think you are very right in asking for a nominal advance of $5,000.[334] My own reasoning is that I want L/B to have every opportunity to do one of their usual fine jobs, and I want to leave them free to do it in their own way and fashion without our having to make all kind of demands to do this and that in order to protect ourselves. At the same time I would like to have this book work out our present contract (the one that was the outgrowth of the DS&P contract), with no more options, and then we can start again with the next book. I've been tied up with contracts and options since 1940, and I'd like to be shed of such things for a breathing spell. As soon as the present contract is taken care of, then we'll have a short vacation before signing more options and things. . . .

Best wishes,
Skinny . . .

Though he was hardly poor, Caldwell's financial situation increasingly dominated his concerns, particularly since he and June were moving closer and closer to formal divorce. One immediate cause of tighter cash flow, he thought, was a negligence on the part of NAL to ensure adequate sales of his paperback titles. Victor Weybright and Kurt Enoch routinely responded that the paperback market was in a general decline and that they were doing all they possibly could to market Caldwell's books. Would he be willing to engage in additional promotional activities to boost sales, they asked?[335]

---

[334] *According to Brown, LB did not feel they should have to be one of those publishers who had to offer "big advances to assure proper promotion" (Brown to EC, CU1 12-1-53).*

[335] *In August, writing to Arthur Thornhill at Little, Brown, Weybright was more blunt about the Caldwell situation. When Caldwell insisted on a larger advance for reprinting Love and Money, Weybright observed that not only was the paperback business in general bad, but Caldwell's sales especially were lagging: "We repeated [to Caldwell and Jim Brown] ... our observation that the Caldwell audience was not currently an expanding one, and that there was a*

To James Oliver Brown:

[CU1.tls]

Phoenix, Arizona
March 28th 1954

Dear Jim:

After thinking about the (my) financial situation brought about recently by NAL's statement to the effect that they are not selling enough copies of our books to keep up future payments, I'm still looking for some way out. Right now I have no ideas, but I'm keeping after them.

However, I don't think Victor's advice to us to go out and peddle our papers is in keeping with his august station in life. I should think he would, under the circumstances, be more helpful. Being in the business he's in, I should think he would make an effort to find a way to sell more of our books than he is doing. As to our making a picture sale, naturally we would like that, and perhaps Victor would want to lend a hand.

At the moment, I have no ideas about magazines; I suppose, year in and year out, my greatest interest in magazines comes from the fact that I like to have a place to publish short stories. When I have no stories to publish (like now), the next step would be to find a magazine that wanted me to write shories that it would publish. As for non-fiction, that is a matter that might become interesting to me, all things being favorable.

Right now I want to keep at this novel I'm trying to get going.[336] If I can keep at it for another couple of months, I'll have enough of it down on paper to let me take a couple of months off (July and August), and then get back to it in September with what I hope will be renewed gusto, or some such word.

If any ideas come to your mind, do let me know about them, because I know they will be good ones.

Best wishes,
Skinny

---

feeling among wholesalers that Caldwell's appeal was diminishing, largely because of the warming up of so many short story collections" (Weybright to Thornhill, DAR 8-19-54).
    [336]Gretta.

To James Oliver Brown:

[CU1.tls] Phoenix, Arizona
April 17th 1954

Dear Jim:

Re: Love & Money

Perhaps I over-stressed my thinking about this. What I had in mind was the fact that this is the first truly <u>new</u> book we've had in several years, and I thought perhaps it might be a good idea to bring that to the attention of those agents and publishers who have been going along with us all this time. . . . If anything is to be said that will underscore the idea <u>new</u>, it can certainly be done in your customary letter when you mail copies of the book. Anyway, I don't want you to think I'm presuming to tell you how to conduct your business; probably what I was doing was sitting here wondering how I could be of some help to you.

Best wishes,
Skinny

To James Oliver Brown:

[CU1.tls] [Phoenix, Arizona]
April 18th 1954

Dear Jim:

I've been thinking about the matter that I had "told a friend I thought I should have two reprint publishers." I don't know who the "friend" is, but I have probably said it a number of times during the past two years.

Two of the persons to whom I said it were Kurt [Enoch] and Victor [Weybright]. That was a year or two ago when I called to their attention the fact that they were going to have twenty-some books of mine on their list, and that at least half of them were going to suffer unless some method was worked out whereby each title was given a periodic new lease on life, either by regular re-issue or new promotion. As I told Kurt and Victor, unless they had other and better ideas, the only satisfactory way to handle it was to let us place the books with another reprinter when they were unable to keep them on sale in their regular outlets. I think you will find that both Kurt and Victor will recall this talk of mine if they will search back into their memories.

As for me, I would much prefer that Signet[337] continued selling the titles if they have plans for doing so. If they have no such plans, it

---

[337] *An imprint of NAL.*

is going to be distressing to us. For example: My corner druggist tells me the following story. -- In late January or early February he received about fifteen copies of <u>A Lamp for Nightfall</u>. The copies were sold over the week end. He asked the local wholesaler to bring more. When the wholesaler came around next, he said he was out of stock, and if he received more he would deliver. The druggist asked again in March. He received the same reply. Once more he asked in April (a week ago), and he was told that there were no copies, and would not be any unless the national salesmen shipped them in.

I think perhaps you can see why I continue to try to figure out how Signet can do this job as all of us -- you, me, and Signet -- want it done unless some sort of plan for keeping twenty-some titles of an author on sale is worked out. As it is now, it's pretty discouraging.

Please do not take this to mean that I am criticizing Signet. I am not. I like the job they have done. What I am saying is that times have changed, that we have twenty-some titles, and now some brain-work is called for.[338]

Best,
Skinny

Once the figures were in, Brown wrote to Caldwell with the unfortunate news that sales of *Love and Money* were "pretty bad," with only 3273 copies sold (compared to nearly 6000 in the same period after the publication of *A Lamp for Nightfall*).[339] On September 23, Salmen wrote to Caldwell directly: "*Love and Money* is not doing well and the reviewers' reception will not alter the bookstore reluctance to push it. The reviewers seem to recognize that you have done something different but, with only a few exceptions, they don't seem to realize what it is." Salmen, who had long urged Caldwell to undertake "a big book," added that the most common complaint was that *Love and Money* did not contain "enough involvement in the plot" and recommended, a bit sardonically, that Caldwell "twist around for a long time in the next one so that they will be more aware of your breadth."[340] Caldwell, again, blamed the problem on careless promotions.

---

[338] *Caldwell remained with NAL many more years after deciding that, for the moment at least, he was not willing to enter into "expensive, time-consuming, distasteful legal actions ... because I've got a book I want to finish as soon as possible ... and a book I want to start as soon as possible. I can't explain this in any other way than to say I like to write and I resent all things that keep me from it" (EC to Brown, CUI 9-22-52).*

[339] *Brown to EC, CUI 9-15-54.*

[340] *Salmen to EC, CUI 9-23-54.*

To James Oliver Brown:

[CU1.tls] Phoenix, Arizona
September 28th 1954

Dear Jim:

I have received from Stanley Salmen a letter dated 9/23/54. . . . What he says, in effect, is that things are terrible.

I don't know yet how I am going to reply to Stanley, but I'll try to find a way in a few days. The trouble is that it is almost impossible for me to talk about what I have written, what I am writing, and what I shall write. I can only do what I do. I'm like an old cow in the pasture who doesn't know and doesn't care where the milk comes from or where it goes as long as she gets some green grass and a bellyful of water all day long.

In my private opinion, and not for release, I don't think L/B handled <u>L&M</u> the way it should have been. It seems to me that it was done in the matter that Harold G[uinzburg][341] would call 'an item'. I think it would have been successful if it had been handled with forethought. Be that as it may, it was unsuccessful.

My trouble at present is that I am writing a book which I like and which I want to do.[342] It is not the big new package job that Stanley is talking about. It is a tight little story that I want to tell and is not what a publisher's conference would declare is what the public (and booksellers) want. If you want L/B to see it when it is finished at the end of October, well and good. If you don't want them to, then let's show it elsewhere. The idea I have for another book, which I plan to begin the first of November, may or not appeal to L/B. I cannot promise anything other than a book I'm going to like a great deal and it may take some time to do. It may be 200 pages, it may be 400 pages. I won't know about that until it is finished. And so there it is.

I hope the other writers on your list are nowhere as difficult as I am. I don't see how you put up with me.

Best wishes,
Skinny

---

[341]*An editor from Caldwell's days at The Viking Press.*
[342]Gretta.

To Stanley Salmen:

[CU1.tl(cc)]

Phoenix, Arizona
September 30, 1954

Dear Stanley:

I have been trying to think what to say in reply to your letter of a week ago. Regardless of what I do say, I am able to appreciate your comment and suggestions, and I am glad of that.

It is disappointing that <u>Love and Money</u> is not being successful. From my own point of view it is not a failure as writing, but of course that does not help the cause one whit here and how. It would be easy to blame Little Brown's production of it for the turn it took, saying perhaps that I myself would have made a different kind of presentation of it, but even so I feel no certainty that I am right and you are wrong.

The thing is now that I expect to finish a new book at the end of October, not that I am rushing what I'm doing but that I am anxious to clear the way to begin another book the first of November. The present novel is in a sense similar to <u>L&M</u>: it is a briefly worded book with an uninvolved theme; it is single-minded in purpose; and its sense perception is no more universal than mink petticoats. But there it is, anyway.

I don't know anything to say about the next book, and I won't know for a long time, except that it is something I want to do very much and perhaps it is going to fall into the field you speak of in your letter. Maybe I've been getting ready for it by getting these two other books written.

If you feel you can't be enthusiastic about the present book, after my discouraging note about it above, and don't want to wait a year or so to see the next one, I wouldn't blame you a bit for telling Jim Brown you didn't want to see it. . . .[343]

Best wishes,

---

[343] *Caldwell delivered the manuscript of Gretta on 27 October 1954, as promised. Salmen was unreserved in his praise and in his hopes for the kind of reception the novel would receive: "We are very much impressed with the new book. It deserves the best of critical appraisal and I hope that it will get it.... We shall not send the book out widely to reviewers but we shall send [it] to all literary reviewers and commentators who have given evidence of appreciation of true literature. We shall send the book only to those bookstore buyers and clerks who have genuine literary taste. This may seem like underselling but we believe that such treatment will be more effective in the long run in bringing the book to the notice of the right people." He concluded, "I don't believe we shall ever see much improvement over Gretta in craftsmanship from yours or from any other pen" (Salmen to EC, CU1 11-24-54).*

When Caldwell tried to renew his passport in December of 1953, as McCarthyite anti–Communism was sweeping the nation, he was asked "'to furnish the [State] Department with an affidavit setting forth whether you are now or ever have been a member of the Communist Party.'" Irritated, he informed Brown, "I wrote a letter saying 'I am not now nor have I ever been a member of the Communist Party.'... Now we shall see what we shall see." He did not push the issue and his renewal application was "held up."[344]

In early November 1954, however, Caldwell was invited to attend the Congress of Soviet Writers in Moscow later that month, and he again requested renewal of his passport. Mrs. R. B. Shipley, Director of the Passport Office, replied: "It is noted that you stated in your affidavit of December 4, 1953 that you are not and have never been a member of the Communist Party. However, information from other sources indicates that your name appears on a pamphlet entitled 'CULTURE and the CRISIS' issued by the League of Professional Groups for Foster and Ford as a supporter of those persons for President and Vice President, respectively in the 1932 campaign. Reports also indicate your connection with several front organizations during the late 30's and early 40's. I would appreciate receiving your comments regarding this matter."[345]

To Mrs. R. B. Shipley:

[DAR.tls] Phoenix, Arizona
November 14, 1954

Re: 130-Caldwell, Erskine

Dear Mrs. Shipley:

This letter is being written in reply to your communication dated November 12, 1954. I would like to make the following statements in regard to the questions raised therein:

1) If desired, I would be glad to re-affirm, in person or otherwise, my affidavit of December 4, 1953, to the effect that I am not now and never have been a member of the Communist Party.

2) I have no copy of the pamphlet entitled "Culture and the Crisis" issued by the League of Professional Groups for Foster and Ford in regard to the 1932 presidential campaign and have no knowledge of the circumstances that caused my name to be used in this connection.[346] However, it is possible that my name was used and did appear on this document, without my knowledge and consent, as I was in the habit during those early years of my writing career of endorsing almost anything that came along in order to find publication of my short stories and novels. Nevertheless, it has never been, and is not now, my policy to endorse any political party, and I especially reject

---

[344] *EC to James Oliver Brown, CUI 12-5-53.*
[345] *Mrs. R. B. Shipley to EC, DAR 11-12-54.*
[346] *Caldwell had, however, told Morang that he attended a Foster and Ford rally while in New York in 1932 (EC to Morang, HAR 9-26-32).*

the idea of supporting in any manner the Communist Party in the United States or any part of the world. In later years I have endorsed, for a fee, such commercial items as tobacco, whisky, and typewriters.

3) The reports that I was connected with several so-called front organizations in the late 30's and early 40's could be true only to the extent that I was a "joiner" of almost anything that came along in those days solely for the purpose of advancing my writing career.[347] However, when I became aware that any organization was being used as a so-called front organization, I at once resigned from such organizations. Two of the most recent incidents involved my resignation from The League of American Writers and The Nation Associates. To the best of my knowledge I am not now a member of any group that could be classified as a front organization.

4) During recent years I have devoted my time wholly to travel and the writing of fiction. However, I would like to call your attention to the fact that I received two citations from the United States Treasury Department, dated February 1, 1945, and March 6, 1945, with the wording "for patriotic cooperation", and also a citation from the Secretary of State, State of Arizona, dated January 14, 1953, "for esteemed citizenship".

5) I enclose herewith a translated copy of the invitation from the Congress of Soviet Writers. This is the only communication I have received in regard to this matter. I know of no reason why I should have been invited to attend this meeting other than the fact that I was a correspondent for North American Newspaper Alliance, Columbia Broadcasting System, and several London newspapers for six months in 1941, and perhaps I was remembered for my newspaper reports and radio broadcasts during that period. As a result of my stay in Moscow in 1941, I wrote a book of my experiences which was published under the title of "All-Out On The Road To Smolensk."

6) For several years I have wished to re-visit the Soviet Union for the purpose of gathering material that would enable me to write magazine articles and perhaps a book comparing Russia today with Russia as I saw it in 1941. In 1951 I attempted to get Russian permission to visit that country for such a purpose, but my request was not answered.

7) I would like to take advantage of the present invitation to visit the Soviet Union for the purpose of gathering such material. I have

---

[347] *In one of his most publicized gestures in support of the political left, Caldwell signed the "Call for an American Writers Congress," which in 1935 had resulted in the creation of the League of American Writers. The League sought to unite anti-imperialist, anti-capitalist writers who were fundamentally "revolutionary" in spirit. The "Call" appeared in the 22 January 1935* New Masses; *it is reprinted in North, pp. 313–315.*

no interest whatsoever in advancing the Communist cause; on the contrary I would do anything I could to hinder it. I believe the information I would obtain in the Soviet Union at this time would be beneficial to the United States.

8) In view of my statements above, I ask that I be given permission to travel to and from the Soviet Union and that my passport be validated for such travel.

Sincerely,
Erskine Caldwell

To James Oliver Brown:

[CU1.tls] Phoenix, Arizona
November 15th 1954

Dear Jim:

. . . In reply to your note about finding out the names of others who might have been invited to Moscow, I can only say that I don't think I would get any information if I asked.[348] In fact, I have heard nothing further from Moscow since their first letter.

Stanley Salmen's forthright reaction has led me to feel that it would not be wise for me to go to Moscow.[349] He has an understanding of the nature of the matter and he convinces me that it is a pretty sure thing that it would turn out to be a headache of perhaps long duration. I've got plenty of domestic headaches and that's enough without adding foreign ones. Let's say that I'm going to drop the idea, here and now, of going to Moscow at this time. Please know that I am grateful to you for gathering these reactions, and I hope I have not caused you too much trouble. If and when I hear again from the Soviet Writers' Union, I'll tell them that I will not be able to accept their invitation.

Perhaps tomorrow I'll be posting to you copies of letters from and to the State Department. Mrs. [R. B.] Shipley wrote me that I

---

[348]*Apparently, Caldwell was the only American invited. See Klevar,* Biography, *pp. 326–327.*

[349]*In a letter forwarded to Caldwell, Salmen told Brown that he could not "see any possible professional good" coming from the trip, and especially not since Caldwell would be "taking time away from producing the big book which will re-establish him in the market." More obviously, they worried, the invitation had undoubtedly come because "Erskine ... draws pictures of trouble spots in American society," something acceptable in America but "not the kind of activity which can do Erskine or this country any good abroad and particularly in the Soviet Union" (Salmen to Brown, DAR 11-10-54).*

would have to be re-examined before a validation of my passport would be given and invited me to defend myself. This is not surprising under the circumstances, and I guess it is a good thing to have it come up now rather than at some future time when I just wanted to go to Paris to see the sights. If I do not succeed in winning her approval, it means that I will have to appear in person, with Julius Weiss, and argue it out in Washington.[350]

Right now all I have to do is decide whether I'm going to write the screenplay for G[od's] L[ittle] A[cre] or write another novel. As of this moment I don't feel like deciding anything except whether I want a double dry manhattan or two single ones, with twists.

Best,
Skinny

Despite Salmen's and Brown's enthusiastic (and hopeful) responses to *Gretta* in manuscript, reviewers of the published book were far less generous. On June 23, Brown wrote with an interpretive account of the bad news: "The trouble with Caldwell is, as I analyze it, that he has been labeled as a champion of the poor and the oppressed. The people who interpret you in this way, don't understand you at all, and when they see you write about the kind of people you write about in *Love and Money* and *Gretta*, they think that you have abandoned a good cause, and have gone over to the other side. The reviewers on the left, therefore, think that your books are not as good. This is also true abroad. How we are going to overcome this misconception of your work is beyond me, but we will, give it time." Anticipating his client's tendency to blame a book's problems on promotions, Brown reminded Caldwell that they had all agreed "to give [*Gretta*] special treatment," avoiding regular news releases and such, but relying instead on "individual, personal letters being sent to key people . . . which would indicate that the publishers consider it a very special work by you."[351]

---

[350]*Caldwell did not have to write Mrs. Shipley. The next day he received a telegram from her:* "DEPT NOT WILLING TO VALIDATE YOUR PPT FOR TRAVEL TO SOVIET UNION TO ATTEND CONGRESS OF SOVIET WRITERS AS IT FEELS THAT MERE PRESENCE OF AMERICAN WRITERS OF YOUR REPUTATION AT SUCH CONGRESS WOULD BE SUED FOR COMMUNISTS PROPAGANDA PURPOSES" (*Shipley to EC, CUI 11-16-54*).

[351]*Brown to EC, CUI 6-23-55. Reviews were even harsher than Brown's synopsis indicated: in the New York* Times, *for example, James Kelly quipped,* "The same dead aim on s-e-x.... Readable it is; art it is not" *([5 June 1955], p. 37); and* Kirkus *observed,* "For all its investigation of the roots of nymphomania, [Gretta] does little to win reader sympathy or even interest" *([1 Apr. 1955], p. 258).*

To James Oliver Brown:

[CU1.tls]   Phoenix, Arizona
                                                                  6/26/55

Dear Jim:

I appreciate your realistic report on the current condition of Gretta and I am glad you are the kind of person who states facts as they are. With all due respect to our many and illustrious publishers, it is my feeling that if they had had less internal troubles and turnovers during the past couple of years that they would have had time to do more and better public relations for us. I have had my troubles, too, and I can appreciate theirs. Just the same, the old saw & saying keeps coming to mind: It's not so much what you've got, it's what you do with what you've got that counts, etc. Maybe that's why I can't get myself worked up to a frenzy about a "big book."[352]

Don't forget that even though I am not happy about the current state of affairs, I am most happy about the way you present them to me. And, so, many thanks.

                                                          Best wishes,
                                                          Skinny

---

With the disappointing receptions of his past two novels behind him, Caldwell returned to the short story, the form that had provided his earliest and most consistent successes.

To James Oliver Brown:

[CU1.tls]   Phoenix, Arizona
                                                            September 30th 1955

Dear Jim:

In this same mail I have sent you the twentieth short story I have written in 1953, 1954, and 1955. There may or may not be one more. Anyway, since there will be twenty or twenty-one new stories which did not appear in Complete Stories, I am going ahead, if you do not object, and put them into MS for book publication. I believe that you have either carbons or magazine copies of all of them.

The first thing I'm going to do is to arrange them in the order in

---

[352] *Repeatedly, for over a year, Stanley Salmen had used this phrase to express his hopes for the kind of book he hoped Caldwell write next. In objecting to the trip to participate in the Soviet Writers Conference in Moscow the previous year, for example, Salmen had written to Jim Brown: "As an author he will be taking time away from producing what we hope will be a big book* which will re-establish him in the market" (Salmen to Brown, DAR 11-10-54).

which I think they might read best. However, I do want your suggestions about this, and they can be shifted around later. In other words, if you think there is a particular story that should be first or last, we can do.

The title I want to put on the book is <u>Erskine Caldwell's Gulf Coast Stories</u>. What do you think? My reason for putting it that way is to make the book distinct from <u>Complete Stories</u> in much the same way that the stories in <u>Georgia Boy</u> are not identified with the collected stories. And I put my name first because I think it is a better idea than using "by". Of course, I am not hard-headed about any of these things, and will be more than glad to listen to what you have to say about it.

I guess I have reached a point in life where I have become, or will become, short-tempered with publishers who say "books of short stories don't sell". I think these are superior stories, and I hope we will be fortunate enough to find a publisher who will think so too and will be willing to treat the book as he would a beloved novel. As you know, all the stories in this collection have a background in the states bordering on the Gulf of Mexico, and are not a mere collection of stories written helter-skelter for magazines....[353]

I am writing all this now well in advance so that you can have some time to think about it and come up with your usual sage advice later. It will take about a month to get the MS ready, because Virginia[354] has all of her other work to keep up while typing this work. I judge that the MS will be ready about November 1st, which is the time I hope to be able to come to New York....

Best wishes,
Skinny

---

[353] *Even with their common background, the stories do in fact seem to have been written "helter-skelter" and, owing to their relatively poor quality, were difficult to place reputably. In rejecting "Letters in the Mail," for instance, Erd Brandt at the* Saturday Evening Post *noted, "Confidentially, I think this is a very weak effort for Erskine Caldwell" (Brandt to Brown, CUI 10-6-55). And after Bruce D. Cohen of* Esquire *read "Girl on the Road," he returned it with a six-word note: "A name but not a story" (Cohen to Brown, CUI undated 1955). Both stories were published for the first time in the collection.*

[354] *Virginia Moffett Fletcher, who worked as Caldwell's editorial assistant from 1955 until they were married on January 1, 1957.*

INDEX

Abernethy, Milton A. 90, 118; letters to 72, 81–87, 89–90, 96–98, 99, 103–04, 145, 148
Adams, Donald 82, 84
Aiken, Conrad 71
Alexander, Leon 185
All Night Long 194, 197, 213–14, 219–20
All Out on the Road to Smolensk 194, 238
Allen, Hervey 103
American Earth 6, 36, 46–53, 55–60, 62–64, 66, 71, 79, 86, 182
American Scene 149
Anderson, Maxwell 120
Anderson, Paul 92
Anderson, Sherwood 28, 56, 58, 93, 94, 103–04, 193
Anthiel, George 150
Anvil 140, 152, 173, 209
Arnold, Edwin T. 8
"The Artists" 47–48
Asch, Nathan 39
Atkinson, Brooks 161; letters to 185–86
Atlanta *Constitution* 163, 177
Atlanta *Journal* 21, 116, 120, 159, 169, 176
"August Afternoon" 82, 83, 124, 138
Augusta *Chronicle* (Georgia) 56
"Autobiographical Sketch" 8
"The Automobile That Wouldn't Run" 45
"An Autumn Courtship" 48–49
Autumn Hill (published as *A Lamp for Nightfall*) 68–69 72–75, 77, 81, 85–86, 97, 150, 223, 233–34
Avon Books 203
Awards 11

Babb, Sanora 139
Babbitt, Irving 43
Babson, Roger Ward 23
"Back on the Road" 132
Bandler, Bernard 42–44
Bara, Theda 166
Barr, Stringfellow 86–87
Barrymore, John 109, 122
Barrymore, Lionel 172
Barton, James 165, 168–69, 172
Barzun, Jacques 88
Basshe, E. J. 150, 159, 172
The Bastard 24, 26, 29–30, 45, 59, 70, 72, 79–80, 96, 226
Baum, Vicki 118
Beach, Joseph Warren 202
Beery, Wallace 122
Behn, Harry 124, 126, 128, 130, 132, 140, 172, 201
Benton, Thomas Hart 98
Bessie, Alvah 145, 150–51
Best Short Shorts annual (Anderson and White, eds.) 92
Best Short Stories annual (O'Brien, ed.) 28, 74–75, 115, 122, 124, 132, 138, 139, 150–51
Best, Marshall A. 90, 103, 110, 116–17, 120, 122–23, 126, 132–34, 138, 151, 153–54
Blues 24–25, 27, 33, 79
The Bogus Ones 24, 32–33, 35, 38–41
Book League of America 199
Bookman 36, 44–45
Bourke-White, Margaret (second wife) 179, 185, 187; letters to 180–84, 189–193, 196–201

Boyd, Albert Truman 138
Boyle, Kay 42, 71
Brabin, Charles 166
Bradford, Joe 77, 83
Bradford, Roark 111
Bradley, Preston 176
Brandt, Erd 242
Bride of the Bayou [*Lazy River*] (screenplay) 104–15, 118
Bromfield, Louis 42, 148
Broun, Heywood 140
Brown, Anthony 153
Brown, Clarence 130
Brown, James Oliver 220, 227, 236; letters from 223, 228, 230–31, 234, 240; letters to 221–24, 227–36, 239–42
Brown, Tony 158
Browning, Tod 106, 108, 111–12, 120
Burgum, E. B. 206–07
Burnett, Whit 42, 85, 90, 93, 108, 150; letters to 195
Burt, Struthers 65–66
Butcher, Fanny 84

Cabell, James Branch 103
Caldwell, Dabney [Dee] (son) 32, 57, 74, 111–12, 114–15, 121, 127, 133, 155, 176
Caldwell, Erskine: advice on writing 91, 93–94, 100, 119, 121–22, 142, 146–47, 149–50, 160–61, 170, 173–74, 206, 223; ambitions as a writer 21–22, 26–27, 32, 34–35, 73, 87, 206, 223, 229–30, 233–42; the "American Folkways" series 191–92; artistic integrity 114, 116, 118, 120, 123, 128–30, 166, 172; artistic intentions 24, 31, 36–37, 47–48, 50–54, 63–65, 67–68, 76, 82, 95–100, 102, 139–41, 195, 201–02, 207, 209, 213–20, 224, 235–36; censorship 29–31, 82, 102–104, 109–10, 115, 117–18, 164, 171–72, 175–76, 187–88, 203–04, 210–11, 213–14; Communism 59, 77, 100–02, 149, 219–20, 236–40; financial issues 23, 38–41, 60, 73–76, 78, 80–81, 110, 112–13, 117, 123, 126, 131–32, 140, 142–43, 146, 148, 157, 163, 165–66, 205, 215–16, 230–32, 233–35; foreign publication 27, 159–160, 164; lecture engagements 186–87, 191, 194; little magazines 28–29, 33–34, 43–46, 66–69, 71–72, 74, 77–79, 82–85, 87–90, 93–94, 108, 137–38, 145, 152; at Metro-Goldwyn-Mayer Studios 104–45, 163, 165–70, 179–80; modern poetry 88–89; newspaper ownership 205; non-fiction assignments 158, 165, 173–74, 193–95; radio station ownership 208; race relations 156–57, 163–64; regionalism 24, 36, 63–65, 156–57, 178, 195; relationships with publishers 33, 35–36, 38–42, 47–53, 55–56, 59–63, 69, 72–78, 80–83, 85, 87, 109–10, 116–18, 120, 127, 131–35, 138, 150–55, 171–73, 202–04, 213–16, 218–23, 226–36; reviews 56–58, 61, 70, 90, 95–98, 100, 118, 161–62, 175, 177, 185–86, 190–93, 205–07, 210–11, 234, 240–41; "Southern cyclorama" 205, 211; Southern literature 63–66, 71, 84–87, 90, 103–04, 148, 165, 178; strikes 143–44, 167–68; at Twentieth Century–Fox Studios 202–04; at Warner Brothers Studios 196–200; a writer's obligations 170; writing habits 212–13
Caldwell, Erskine, Jr. [Pix] (son) 32, 57, 75, 111–12, 114–15, 121, 127, 133, 155, 167–68, 176, 199
Caldwell, Helen (first wife) 21, 24, 32, 50, 57, 95, 113, 151–52, 157, 167–68, 175, 182–83; letters to 10, 73–75, 105–17, 119–21, 123–44, 153–55, 179–80
Caldwell, Ira S. and Caroline P. B. (parents) 23, 54, 74, 105, 126; letters by 22; letters to 10, 22–24, 32, 56–57, 186–88, 202
Caldwell, Janet (daughter) 52, 105, 113, 121, 141, 176, 187
Caldwell, June Johnson (second wife) 201, 212, 228
Caldwell [Hibbs], Virginia Moffett (fourth wife) 8, 10, 159, 201, 242
The Caldwell Caravan 208
Call It Experience 7, 11–12, 221, 224–26
Callaghan, Morley 31, 56
Canby, Henry Seidel 214; letter to: 202–03
Cantwell, Robert 31, 76, 101, 103–04, 138, 214
Capone, Al 73
Carnall, Ruth 179–80
"Carnival" 182
Cavalier 223
Century Company 23
Century 27
Cerf, Bennett 96, 118, 127, 151–52, 154

Chapman, William 74, 76
Charlotte *Observer* 169
Christians, Mady 166
Clay 68, 70, 79, 108, 145
Cohen, Bruce D. 242
Coindreau, Maurice 160
College Humor 182
The Complete Stories of Erskine Caldwell 227–30, 242
Congress of Soviet Writers (1954) 237–41
Conroy, Jack 140, 145, 148, 151–52, 209
Contact 70, 74, 77–80, 83–85, 91, 93, 108
Contempo 66–67, 71–72, 79–83, 90, 91, 103, 118, 127, 132, 140, 145, 148
Cook, Sylvia Jenkins 9
"The Corduroy Pants" 38, 42, 49, 54, 75
Corle, Edwin 192
Cosmopolitan 166
"Country Full of Swedes" 61, 80–81, 115, 124, 130, 162, 195
Covici-Friede 81–82, 154–55
Cowley, Malcolm 9, 61
Crane, Hart 148
Crawford, Joan 167
"Crown Fire" 78–79, 127
cummings, e. e. 71
Curtiss Brown 69

Dahlberg, Edward 76, 82, 92
Daily Worker 151, 165, 188
Daniel, Frank: letters to 159–60, 163–66
Daniels, Jonathan 148, 205
Dartmouth College 225
"Daughter" 209
Davidson, Donald 84
Davies, Joseph E. 197
De Voto, Bernard 214
Dimnet, Abbe 90
"Dorothy" 38, 42, 50
Dos Passos, John 10, 67
"The Dream" 51–52
Dreiser, Theodore 28, 112, 161, 193
Duell, Charles 190, 192, 203, 223; letter to 221
Duell, Sloan, and Pearce 190–92, 194, 199, 202–03, 214–16, 221–23, 231

Eastman, Max 67
Emerson, Ralph Waldo 45
"The Empty Room" 75

Enoch, Kurt 231, 233–24; letters from 219–221; letter to 219–20
Episode in Palmetto 213
Erskine Caldwell's Gulf Coast Stories 242
Esquire 83, 138, 169, 212, 242
Eugenics 22
Everitt, Raymond 69
The Express Train Robbery (screenplay) 144

Fadiman, Clifton 193
Farrell, James T. 71, 138
Faulkner, William 6, 9–10, 42, 71, 74, 87, 98, 104–05, 190
Ferber, Edna 193
"The First Autumn" 124, 127, 138
Fitzgerald, F. Scott 9, 30–31, 42
Flannagan, Roy 71–72, 90
Fletcher, John Gould 156–57
"The Fly in the Coffin" 182
Foley, Martha 42, 85, 93
Folk-Say 79
Ford, Charles Henri: letters to 24–26

Gallimard 160
Garbo, Greta 122
Geer, Will 185
Georgia Boy (adaptation) 120, 207–08
Georgia Boy (stories) 9, 193, 201–02, 242
Gerson, Sam 175
"A Gift for Sue" (also called "Just a Quick One") 223
Gilbert, John 172
"Girl on the Road" 242
Glasgow, Ellen 90, 103
God's Little Acre (adaptations) 125–27, 139, 150, 159, 172, 174, 240
God's Little Acre (novel) 5, 63–65, 72–73, 81–85, 90, 92, 95–100, 102, 109–110, 117, 123, 138, 151–52, 160–161, 164, 171, 177, 208–09, 211, 216–17, 220, 223
Gold, Mike 56, 59, 90; letter to 101–02
Gordon, Caroline 84, 148
Gordon, Donald 98
"The Grass Fire" 54
Gray, James: letter to 210–11
Green, Paul 67, 136, 137
Greenspan, Benjamin E. 109–10, 115, 117
Gregory, Horace 56, 95, 214
Gretta 232, 235–36, 240–41
Grisman, Sam H. 158, 175

Guggenheim Fellowship 29, 32, 60, 63–65, 148
Guinzburg, Harold 173, 235; letters from 171

Hale, William Harland 123
Haloff, Louis Joseph 177
Halper, Albert 101–02
Hansen, Harry 101–02, 115, 130
Harcourt Brace 23, 32, 38, 62–63, 69, 77, 86, 132
Harding, Walter 224–26
Harlow, Jean 131
Harper's 28, 116
Harris, Cora 169
Harris, Jed 120, 159
Hart, Henry 71–73, 90
Harte, Bret 58
Hartwick, Harry 6
Hathaway, C. A. 170
Hawks, Howard 124–25, 128–30
Hayes, Alfred 185
Hemingway, Ernest 10, 31, 58, 193
Hench, Atcheson T. 63
Henry Holt 23
Hepburn, Katharine 159
Herbst, Josephine 42, 65
Heron Press 38, 42, 43, 69
Heyward, DuBose 84, 103
Hicks, Granville 7, 101, 140; letter to 165
Hillman, Alex L. 226
Hoag, Ronald Wesley 20
Holley, William H. 175
Hoole, William Stanley; letter to 177–78
Hopkins, Miriam 137
"Horse Thief" 123, 129, 132, 138–39
Houghton Mifflin 115
Hound & Horn 27, 33–34, 36, 39, 42, 45–46, 79
"Hours Before Eternity" (also called "Falling Leaves") 35–37, 43, 75
A House in the Uplands 8, 208, 213
Hull, Henry 159, 161, 165, 168–69
The Humorous Side of Erskine Caldwell 214
Hurst, Fannie 37

I'll Take My Stand 86
"In Defense of Myself" 30
"Indian Summer" 75, 115
"Inspiration for Greatness" 34, 36, 43
Israel, Boris J. 46
"It Happened Like This" 49

Jackpot 193, 201–04, 228–29
Jagger, Dean 159
"Joe Craddock's Old Woman" 24, 27
Joffe, Eugene 107–08, 138, 145
"John the Indian and George Hopkins" 37, 50
Johns, Richard 69, 74, 93; letters to 6, 10, 26–29, 33–34, 36–37, 42–43, 45–46, 48–49, 61–62, 67–68, 76–77, 92–93
Johnston, Mary 84
Jolas, Eugene 24, 39
Josephson, Matthew 87, 104
Journeyman (adaptation) 185–86, 225
Journeyman (novel) 6, 104, 107, 110, 140–41, 146, 150–55, 161–62, 171–76, 196, 209
Joyce, James 28, 71

"Kathy" (also called "The Motive") 223
Kearney, Patrick 112, 152
Kelly, Edward J. 175–76
Kelly, James 240
Kennedy, Stetson 192
Kirkland, Jack 112, 143–144, 150, 152, 156, 158; letter from 208
Kirsten, Lincoln 42–44
Klevar, Harvey L. 11–12
Kneel to the Rising Sun 5, 173, 211
"Kneel to the Rising Sun" 163
Komroff, Manuel 28; letter to 212–13
Kreymborg, Alfred 22, 39, 170
Kronenberger, Louis 95

Ladies' Home Companion 207
Ladies' Home Journal 28
A Lady Comes to Town (screenplay) 167
Lambertson, Louise 138
Latimer, Margery 28
Lawrence, D. H. 98
Lawson, John Howard 118
League of American Writers 238
Leippert, James; letters to 78–79, 83, 88–89, 94–95
Let the Hurricane Roar! (screenplay) 137
"Letters in the Mail" 242
Lewin, Albert 131, 137
Lewis, Gordon 86; letters to 80–81, 95–96, 98–99, 109
Lewis, Janet 28
Lewis, Sinclair 67
Lieber, Maxim 76–78, 80–82, 85, 95, 101, 112, 123, 126, 128, 131–33, 150–51,

153–55, 162, 169–72, 179, 191, 219–221; letters to 8, 156–57, 214–16; letters from: 194
Life 179, 182, 190, 193
Life & Letters 164
Lion and Crown 78–79, 83, 88–89, 94
Literature of the American South (Andrews et al., eds.) 11
Little, Brown 222–23, 227–31, 235–36
Longfellow Square Bookshop (Portland, Maine) 21, 80, 143
Loos, Anita 118
Lost Laughter (screenplay) 131, 137
Love and Money 227, 230–31, 233–36, 240
"A Lover of Horses" 127, 132

Macaulay Company 76–77, 101, 116
MacLeish, Archibald 79, 192
Macleod, Norman 28, 61–62, 66, 76
Macmillan 22
"Mama's Little Girl" 77, 83–84, 90, 127
"The Man Under the Mountain" 182
"The Man Who Looked Like Himself" 116, 138
Manhunt 223
Manuel, Al 200
Marshall, Margaret 193, 197
Marx, Sam 112, 116, 123, 130, 132
"Masses of Men" 116, 124
"The Mating of Marjory" 30, 34
Mayer, Louis 120
McAlmon, Robert 74, 93
McIlwaine, Sheilds 6, 190
"Meddlesome Jack" 92, 161–162
"Memorandum" 31
Mencken, H. L. 193
Mercury 27, 38, 123, 138
"A Message for Genevieve" 61, 67–68, 77
"Midsummer Passion" (also called "July") 24–25, 27, 170
Mid-Week Pictorial 182
Miller, Dan B. 11–12
Mission to Moscow (screenplay) 196–97
"Mr. Caldwell Protests" 8
Mixon, Wayne 11–12
"Molly Cotton Tail" 49
Montgomery, Robert 114
Morang, Alfred 67, 94, 100, 108; letter from 226; letters to 10, 58–59, 68–70, 75–78, 85–86, 90–94, 113, 121–23, 128–29, 137–39, 142–43, 146–47, 149–53, 158–61, 164–68, 170–75, 187–88, 191, 194–95, 206–09, 226–27, 237
Morrow, Ann 24
Morse, Marjory 24, 59, 73
Moxley, F. Wright 90
Mühlen, Hermynia Zur 27
Mumford, Lewis 63, 67, 101; letter to 30

Nation 156–57, 197
Nativity 46, 79
New American Caravan (Mumford, Rosenfeld, and Kreymborg, eds.) 22, 24–25, 26, 29–30, 32–34, 36, 39, 79, 100, 116
New American Library 214–20, 231–34
"New Cabin" 182
New English Weekly 79–80
New Masses 56, 61–62, 93, 101, 138, 156–59, 165, 237–38
New Masses Book Service 66
New Republic 11, 61, 176
New Review 93
New School for Social Research (New York) 186–87
New York *Evening Post* 56, 98
New York *Herald-Tribune* 56, 95, 115, 190
New York *Post* 173–74, 176
New York Society for the Suppression of Vice 5, 82, 102, 171
New York *Times* 56–57, 95, 115, 121, 161, 185, 206–07, 229, 240
New York *World-Telegram* 101, 115, 120
New Yorker 182
Norris, Kathleen 37
North of the Danube 187–88

O. Henry Memorial Prize Stories annual (Hansen, ed.) 115, 130
O'Brien, Edward J. 28, 39, 42, 63, 74, 79, 115, 122, 124, 128, 138, 151, 173
O'Keefe, Georgia 101
"An Old Man's Tale" 48
Oppen, George 79
Oppenheimer, George 90, 123
Outlander 108
Oxford University Press 23

Pagany 26–29, 33, 39, 43, 46, 48–50, 61, 67, 68, 70, 74, 76, 79, 92–93, 100, 108, 124, 158, 212
Parade 182

Parker, Dorothy 42
Partisan Review 28
Patterson, Joseph M. 157
Paul, Elliot 24
Pearce, Charles A. (Cap) 190, 192; letters from 208, 210, 213; letters to 201–04
"The People's Choice" 75
Perelman, S. J. 131–132, 140, 143, 145, 202
Perkins, Maxwell 74; letters from 31, 35, 40–41, 54–55, 57, 59–63, 67, 69, 72, 85–86; letters to 6, 31, 33, 35–42, 43–45, 47, 53–55, 57–58, 60–63, 65, 69, 72
Peterkin, Julia 84
"Picking Cotton" 71–72
Pinckney, Josephine 84
Place Called Estherville 211, 213
Poor Fool 42, 44, 79, 96, 226
Porter, Katherine Anne 148
Portland *Express* (Maine) 59, 70
Posselt, Erich 38
Pound, Ezra 76
Pulitzer Prize 32, 161
Putnam, Samuel 92–93

"Rachel" 75, 145
Random House 151–52
Ravenel, Beatrice 84
Rayburn, Otto Ernest 192
Redbook 197, 199
Riggs, Lynn 132
Roosevelt, Eleanor 193
Roosevelt, Franklin D. 110, 187
Russia at War 194

The Sacrilege of Alan Kent 35, 39, 41–43, 45, 182
St. Paul *Pioneer Press* (Minnesota) 210–11
Salmen, Stanley 223, 229, 231, 235; letters from 234, 236, 239–41; letters to 227–28, 236
Salomon, I. L.: letters to 97, 99–100, 117–18, 146, 155–56
"Saturday Afternoon" 46
Saturday Evening Post 98, 242
Say, Is This the U.S.A.? 193
Scottsboro Case 156–57, 164
Scribner's Magazine 27, 30–34, 42, 45, 65, 67, 79, 163, 212
Scribner's 30–31, 35–36, 38–41, 46, 57, 59–60, 62–63, 74, 76–77, 79–83, 87, 97, 116, 150, 154
Seaver, Edwin 29, 140

Secker, Martin 150
Shipley, Mrs. R. B.: letters from 237, 239; letter to 237–38
Shooting the Russian War (Bourke-White) 198
"A Short Sleep in Louisiana" 182
Shubert, Lee and Jacob 112, 175
Signet 233–34
Skolfield, Raymond White 91
"Slow Death" 138
"A Small Day" 182
Smith, Charlie 126
Smith, Harrison 8
"Snacker" 166
Snow, Walter 173
Some American People 171, 177
Soskin, William 98, 100
Southern Writers Conference (1932) 84, 86
Sprague, Chandler 106, 108, 111
Stallings, Laurence 84, 118, 120
Stanwyck, Barbara 109
Stein, Gertrude 28, 79
Steinbeck, John 193
Sten, Anna 132
Stevens, Wallace 71
Stierhem, Eleanor 224
Stong, Phil 118–19
Stories by Erskine Caldwell 202–03, 209, 214
Story 68, 70, 79–80, 85, 90, 93, 108, 115, 118, 124, 138, 212
Strauss, Harold 193
"The Strawberry Season" 28
Stribling, T. S. 165
"Summer Accident" 127
Sumner, John S. 82, 102–03, 109, 171
"The Sunfield" 182
The Sure Hand of God 208–10
"A Swell-Looking Girl" 33, 36
Sykes, Gerald 31

Tate, Allen 84
"Ten Thousand Blueberry Crates" 51–53
Tenant Farmer 174, 186
Thalberg, Irving 107, 120
This Quarter 48, 79
This Very Earth 210–11
Thomas, Norman 67
Thornhill, Arthur 231
Timber (screenplay) 115–16, 124–25, 129–31
Time 149, 210

Titus, Edward W. 48
"To the Chaparral" 224
Tobacco Road (adaptations) 112, 139, 143, 150, 152–66, 168–69, 172–73, 175–77, 185, 187–88, 208, 221
Tobacco Road (novel) 5, 6, 10, 47, 49, 54, 56–64, 68–71, 74, 76, 79, 81, 83, 86, 87, 90, 92, 96–97, 101, 132, 150, 153, 160, 164, 171, 209, 211–12
Today's Woman 224
"Tracing Life with a Finger" 27, 34, 36, 42
Tragic Ground 202, 205–07, 211
transition (Paris) 24, 27, 33, 43, 70, 79
Trilling, Lionel 214
Trouble in July 191–93, 199–200, 205, 220
Turner, Robert K.: letter to 225–26
Twain, Mark 58

Uzzell, Thomas H. 115

Van Doren, Carl 150, 161, 171, 202; letter to 161–62
Van Doren, Irita 84
Van Doren, Mark 214
Vanity Fair 27, 123, 128, 132–33, 138–39
Variety 121
"Var-Monters" 47–48
"A Very Late Spring" 30, 34
Vidor, King 137
Viking Press 77–78, 80–83, 85, 90, 93, 95, 102, 109–10, 117–18, 122, 128, 131–32, 140, 151, 154–55, 162–63, 171–73, 187, 191
Villa, José Garcia 108, 138, 145–46, 148, 150
Virginia Quarterly 86–87
Virginia, University of 63, 80, 170, 225–26
"The Visitor" 44
Vogue 138

Wagenknecht, Edward 8
"Warm River" 54, 75
"We Are Looking At You, Agnes" 75, 127, 145
We Are the Living 92, 110, 116–18, 127–28, 132–35, 138, 142, 145–46, 149–50, 160
Webster, Harvey Curtis 227
Weiss, Julius 201, 220, 222, 239; letter to 226
Wertenbaker, Charles Christian 80, 99
West, Mae 101
West, Nathanael 71, 132, 139–40, 142–45
Wexley, John 164
Weybright, Victor 217, 231–34; letters from 217, 219–21, 231–32; letters to 219–20
Wheelock, John Hall: letters from 46, 47, 50–52, 56; letters to 10, 49–53, 55–56, 65–67
Whipple, T. K. 6, 61
Whitlow, Mary Ann: letter to 217–18
A Wicked Woman (screenplay) 142, 166–67
Williams, William Carlos 24, 28, 37, 43, 45, 70, 74, 77–79, 83, 90–91, 93
Wilson, Edmund 101
Wilson, James Southall 84, 87
Windsor Quarterly 108
With All My Might 7, 11–12
Wolfe, Thomas 9, 10, 148
A Woman in the House 216
Woodman, Lawrence C. 149
Wright, Richard 193

Yale Review 61, 78–82, 124, 162
"Yellow Girl" 124, 138
You Have Seen Their Faces 179–80, 182, 185–86, 188, 190
Young, Kathleen Tankersley 24, 103, 135
Young, Stark 67

www.ingramcontent.com/pod-product-compliance
Ingram Content Group UK Ltd.
Pitfield, Milton Keynes, MK11 3LW, UK
UKHW041936140426
5217IPUK00014B/505